Pelican Book A73

The Unattached

Mary Morse was born in 1936, in Lydney,
Gloucestershire. She took a B.A. degree at Birmingham
University and a social science diploma at the London
School of Economics. In 1958 she was awarded
a Fulbright Scholarship to study and practise social work
in Philadelphia, and in 1960 she won a Commonwealth
Fellowship to McGill University, Montreal, where
she received a Master of Social Work degree.
In 1961 she returned to England to work for the
National Association of Youth Clubs on its research
project with the unattached. She was also concerned with
the Association's training programmes for club
members, youth leaders, and youth organizers.
Miss Morse's special interests are in the fields of group
dynamics and juvenile delinquency. She is married
and now living in New York.

The Unattached

MARY MORSE

A report of the three-year project carried
out by the National Association of Youth Clubs
with an introduction by Robert Beloe

PENGUIN BOOKS

Penguin Books Ltd, Harmondsworth,
Middlesex, England
Penguin Books Inc., 7110 Ambassador Court,
Baltimore, Maryland 21207, U.S.A.
Penguin Books Australia Ltd, Ringwood,
Victoria, Australia

Published in Pelican Books 1965
Reprinted 1965, 1966, 1968

Copyright © Mary Morse, 1965

Made and printed in Great Britain by
Hazell Watson & Viney Ltd, Aylesbury
Set in Linotype Plantin

*All names of persons and places of assembly in this
book have been disguised and any resemblance to
living persons or to real places of assembly is
entirely coincidental.*

Contents

Foreword

I am very happy to commend this book and hope it may be widely read and that its recommendations will receive careful consideration and practical support. Our society, which faces young people with so many problems, must take active steps in helping towards their solution.

The National Association of Youth Clubs is deeply grateful to Mr Beloe and his colleagues who have sponsored and guided this scheme and also to the Department of Education and Science who made it financially possible.

A. OGILVY

Chairman of Council National Association of Youth Clubs

Introduction

The origin of this book lies in the recommendations of the Albemarle Committee to set up the Youth Service Development Council. One of the first acts of this Council was to announce its readiness to consider grants for experimental work and special development. Young people unattached to any kind of youth organization had already been the concern of the National Association of Youth Clubs, who decided to seize this new opportunity to make contact with them. As the Albemarle Committee had stated, it seemed to the Association 'that many who are not now attached either officially or unofficially could, if properly approached, be attached and benefit from the attachment'.

Application was therefore made in April 1960 for a grant to appoint research workers in four key areas, and a sum of £6,000 per annum for three years was offered and accepted. It was agreed that the terms of reference should be:

to make contact with unattached young people, to discover their interests and leisure-time activities and, following this, to help in whatever way seems appropriate to provide some of the facilties required.

The N.A.Y.C. decided to appoint a small central group to undertake responsibility for the scheme and appointed us, whose names follow, as its members: Mr Robert Beloe, Chairman; Mrs Joan Burnett; Mr Richard Davies; the Rev. H. A. Hamilton; Mr Penry Jones; the Lady Jean Mackenzie; Mrs Katherine Russell; the Rev. David Sheppard.

We were very fortunate in having as our Secretary Miss Lesley Sewell, the General Secretary of the N.A.Y.C. The fact that the Association allowed us to have her is evidence of the importance which it attached to this subject. We are most grateful to her for putting at our disposal her great wisdom and experience unstintingly. We are also very grateful to have had the constant help of the Assistant Secretary, Col. R. T. Brain. A number of other people have kindly given us the benefit of their experience and we are particularly grateful to Miss K. M. Slack, lecturer at the London School of Economics, for her comments and suggestions on the first draft.

Our group is referred to in this book as the Central Advisory Committee.

The Central Committee's first tasks were to find the areas for research and to appoint the workers. These tasks went on together. After consulting local Associations of the N.A.Y.C. twelve areas were considered. The object was to find four areas that would offer contrasting physical environments, economic and industrial backgrounds, and types of young people. A wide geographical scatter, urban and rural areas, the special problems of new towns, seaports, and housing estates were all taken into consideration. Local Education Authorities and voluntary organizations concerned with young people were consulted in confidence. The areas eventually chosen were a northern industrial town, referred to throughout this book as Northtown, a coastal resort in southern England to be referred to as Seagate, and an industrial town also in the south to be referred to as Hilltown. The fourth area, a town in the east of England to be known as Midford was added in 1961, when a fourth worker was appointed.

The work in Hilltown was terminated after eighteen months and another worker was appointed to an industrial town in the south of England to be known as Southtown. Since the work in Hilltown and Southtown was undertaken for a much shorter period, and invariably supported the findings and experiences of the Seagate, Northtown, and Midford workers, it is not reported in any detail here.

We had, after much careful thought, already come to a very important and far-reaching conclusion. We decided it would be impracticable for the workers to make effective contact with the young people in question and really to discover their interests and leisure-time activities, if it were disclosed that they had been sent down for these purposes by a central youth organization with the help of government funds. This made it necessary, in our view, to have in each chosen area suitable people who would act as local advisers. One of the factors in choosing an area, then, was the existence known to us of experienced and sympathetic people who would support the workers in the inevitable loneliness of their work, the considerable mental tension that it seemed likely to involve, and the possible local difficulties which could arise. We saw their function as helping to iron out local difficulties and, when necessary, to explain the worker's position to individuals and groups in the area.

In the workers themselves we looked for the following qualities, so far as we could judge them: a capacity to be out on their own; a sympathetic attitude to the unattached, yet one not unduly coloured by previous training and experience; an ability to observe and to record, and also to perceive possible ways of helping; finally, the fresh approach of youth.

We proceeded by means of personal search and advertisement. In all, we appointed five workers. Four started work within nine months of each other; the fifth much later, when one of the four retired for personal reasons to take up other work. The main part of this book tells of three of the workers – one a woman of twenty-three, unmarried, holding a social science degree and having worked for a year in a probation hostel; one a man of twenty-two, married, holding a degree in sociology; the third a schoolmaster of twenty-eight, married, with five years secondary-school and previous farming experience. The two others were a woman of twenty-two, married, with few academic qualifications but considerable experience in youth-club work, and a graduate schoolmaster of twenty-six with four years grammar-school experience, who married after becoming one of our workers.

The framework was:
(i) The *Central Advisory Committee* which had invited a few people in each area to act as
(ii) *Local Advisers*. With these informality was the keynote. They had no executive responsibilities. No minutes were kept and they gave their help collectively or individually when

asked. Most of those invited were interested and keen to help and gave the workers invaluable support. With this background and with the knowledge and confidence of the Local Education Authority,

(iii) the *Workers* started out. Almost complete freedom was given them, although emphasis was placed on the vital importance of consistent and adequate reporting. A day-to-day diary was kept and regular monthly reports submitted. Every three months or so the workers met the Central Committee at the headquarters of the N.A.Y.C. Occasionally one or more of the local advisers from each area would also come and meet the Central Committee.

(iv) As more experience was gained of the workers' needs, it was realized that they needed visiting from the centre and that they gained more from meeting each other and discussing their problems than from meeting the Central Committee. A *Supervisor* was appointed who visited the workers and had regular meetings with them. She also helped them with their recording of information, which was ultimately kept under the headings of young people's attitudes towards home, work, money, sex, leisure-time activities, the Youth Service, and moral and social values. Additional records were kept of meetings with various groups of young people. Individual case studies were carried out of a limited number of young people in each area.

Using the records and reports the supervisor, Miss Mary Morse, has written the chapters that follow, including Chapter 7, which sets out our conclusions and recommendations.

Some of the things recorded in this book are striking. Most striking, perhaps, are the failures. This book was bound to be a record largely of failures, because of what the inquiry set out to discover. The chapters that follow are about young people, many of whom our present society does not fit. We do not write 'who do not fit our present society', for the book shows that though these young people may very often appear wrong or stupid or intolerable – and must accept some, at least, of the blame for being so – yet, it is also our present society that is partly, often largely, responsible. Parents, teachers, youth leaders, education authorities, housing authorities, churches, management and workers in industry and commerce (including the entertainment and catering industries) have not helped these young people to feel that they 'belong' – or have not helped them enough.

If our recommendations do not seem exciting, we are sure that they are nonetheless necessary, and we put them forward with a sense of urgency. Carrying them out need not be a dull operation, though it may be exacting and costly. The three workers, one young woman and two young men, whose work this book mainly records, have surely shown the way. For each of them, isolated and uncomfortable as they were, was forced to think, as Miss Morse, herself a young woman, says, 'honestly about his own values'. Yet, they were able to get on terms with the 'unattached', because each had 'a willingness to like and a readiness to understand'.

This is surely what our present society must try to do. It will not achieve much by Acts of Parliament. Only if a great many individuals – old, middle-aged, and young – take their parts, can we tackle this problem successfully.

That is why we, who started and controlled this inquiry, hope that a great many people will read this book. If they do so, they are sure to join us in our gratitude and admiration for the achievements of those whose work is described so clearly and sympathetically by Miss Mary Morse.

ROBERT BELOE

1 Seagate

Seagate is a coastal resort in the southern half of England. It appeals as a holiday centre to people all over the country and is a residential area for the retired and the leisured. The history and characteristic atmosphere of the town has generally been one of ease and comfort, and the tradition of working other than to serve the interests of leisure has been slight. In recent years, however, there has been some increase in light industry on the outskirts of the town, but the predominant employment is casual and unskilled and still confined to service occupations.

The coastal-resort function of Seagate is such that there is an unusually good provision of commercial entertainment in the town, and in the main this is designed for the teen-age market. In Seagate there are some thirty coffee bars, in addition to numerous cafés, several cinemas, some jazz clubs, two bowling alleys, a pier, amusement arcades, two theatres, a concert hall, an ice rink, clubs, snooker halls, public houses, and several excellent dance halls. There is almost a surfeit of high-standard popular entertainment. Top artists are frequently booked, and latest fashions, for example in clothing or dance styles, are quickly seized upon. One important effect of this is that young people are apt to develop very high standards of comparison with which to judge the existing youth-service provision. There are, however, no youth clubs in the main centre of the town except for three voluntary-organization clubs on its fringe.

In December 1960 a male research worker, aged twenty-two and married, took a flat in the centre of Seagate and began to survey his neighbourhood in order to make contact with some of the unattached young people in the town. It was an accepted fact from a recent reliable publication on Seagate that the majority of young people frequented the centre of the town some time during each week and the worker decided, as a first step, to concentrate on the commercial places of attraction. During the first few weeks, he visited at least three times each twelve coffee bars, two jazz clubs, two public houses, one dance hall, and an amusement arcade. He found that the Seagate coffee bars functioned more as clubs than as mere places for drinking coffee. He found almost at once too that the major problem of talking informally with young people was how to answer the inevitable question about his occupation. He chose to explain that he was a writer, receiving an income from a sponsoring body and writing about Seagate in the form of reports, articles, and plays. This met a dubious reception ranging from disbelief to uncertain curiosity, but he felt instinctively it was still preferable to announcing his real identity. A writer was near the complete truth and might suffice to explain his interests and apparent freedom from daily work.

The difficulties involved in such an explanation and approach were quickly revealed on the second day the worker was in Seagate. His first contact began in a coffee bar with a casual comment about how crowded the bar was to a lone individual sitting at the counter. His name was Bob, he was aged twenty-one and was at present working for a furniture firm. The conversation moved lightly over his previous jobs, his travel in the Navy, his opinions of the countries visited, his views on marriage, politics, religion, and his general philosophy of life. Afterwards the worker wrote:

This meeting seemed at the time quite momentous, having spent about two hours with somebody who is obviously unattached and who apparently knows several other young people. I had high hopes of meeting him again and as such, in my enthusiasm, I invited him back to my flat to listen to some jazz records some time later in the week. Despite his sincere acceptance at the time, he did not keep the arrangement. It was clear, I think, that the invitation was made too hastily. Two days later, I met him again in the coffee bar and he apologized profusely. His excuse however was not explicit – concerned with a busy week-end and an 'extra commitment' on the Monday.

The contact with Bob was maintained spasmodically and the worker, realizing that he had been too eager, concluded that only through a series of unarranged casual encounters in the coffee bar could any form of friendship develop. Five other contacts were gained in this way during the worker's first month in Seagate. But since he had met relatively few young people and been unable to develop existing relationships very far, he concluded at this point that the coffee-bar approach was not very effective. He recorded that he found it difficult, for example, to start a conversation with someone completely unknown who happened to be sitting near by. Such a person was either a member of a group of people, in which case he was probably not interested in the outsider, or he was – more rarely – by himself, in which case he was wary. The general reaction to the irregularity of a stranger initiating a conversation was a mixture of curiosity, disinterest, fear, and embarrassment; the first feeling usually predominating. In addition, suspicion of strangers was probably intensified in Seagate where, because it is a holiday resort, the other man might sometimes not be as 'straight' as he seemed. The worker also felt that a brief meeting in a coffee bar often bore little relation to what people did outside, so that there was inevitably some vagueness and lack of structure in the encounter. Finally, the worker began to feel that probably the explanation of himself as a writer was not helping to allay suspicion.

Indeed, the term might well induce more doubt than if not mentioned at all, since the description is unspecific as well as tending, perhaps, to connote something dangerously uncertain.

It is clear that the worker did not feel the coffee-bar setting to be a particularly useful or easy way of making contacts, even though it was gaining him a reasonably accurate picture of where different groups of young people spent their leisure time, as well as a less clear picture of what they did and thought. He decided at the end of the first month to focus his efforts on three tasks. The first was to try and find some job in Seagate – in industry, a coffee bar, or in teaching – which would provide better opportunities for making contact with the town's youth. Secondly, to concentrate on collecting data and information needed to compile an accurate picture of the youth service in Seagate. Thirdly, he hoped to follow up existing contacts and try to make new ones by continuing to visit coffee bars, although probably less frequently than in his first month.

Difficulty in finding employment initially thwarted these plans. Attempts to find a job in a record shop were unsuccessful both because of his lack of experience and the lack of any vacancies. A further effort to obtain employment with a large electrical-engineering firm known to employ a great many young people was also unsuccessful; the management considered his inexperience would create obvious difficulties which could not be overcome. Teaching seemed a promising possibility, and while this was being investigated the worker began hanging around coffee bars again.

During the first two weeks of this period he noted somewhat despondently that the only contact he had seen was Jeff R., a seventeen-year-old youth who said he was a student at the local arts college. Since Jeff hardly took part in the social life of the arts college nor belonged to any recognized youth organizations, the worker considered him unattached and worth following up. The initial contact had been similar to the one with Bob but it was in a different coffee bar, the Mardi Gras, which was above a shop. It was pleasantly decorated, with good soft lighting, and crowded every evening with regulars who used it as a club. First impressions were that the young people were neither particularly tough nor necessarily problematic, although it was doubtful whether they were members of any youth organization. Ages seemed to range from thirteen to twenty-four, with the majority between fourteen and nineteen. Occupations ranged from students at school or at the arts college to shop assistants. How further contact with Jeff was sustained and developed in the Mardi Gras is shown by this 'typical evening':

Our meeting [Jeff and the worker's] in the Mardi Gras was casual, brief, and sustained – as is now customary – and I felt that the evening was well spent in the sense of adding a little more to what is, I think, a gradually developing relationship. I had a book with me which I lent him and this gave some purpose to the meeting as well as leading to quasi introductions to other people sitting about. The book was a 'beat' review which includes 'avant-garde' writings and which proved to be very popular with Jeff and his friends. In fact, simply on the basis of ownership of this book it is possible that my status has improved considerably. However, even if this is doubtful, his attitude towards me was certainly more positive and friendly than before. We talked mainly about the book and various articles which he had read in another review that I had already lent him. . . . The meeting with Jeff lasted about thirty minutes.

It is worth noting that the worker's initial contact was with an art student, and later, through him, with what may generally be described as a 'pseudo-bohemian' type of older adolescent with a middle-class social background. Nor was concentration on such a group as fortuitous as it may seem from the casual way in which contact was made. Within six weeks of being in Seagate and commencing work of this nature, the worker came to the conclusion that 'youth' was a term so composite and covering such a staggering variety of people that it was difficult to believe he could make himself known and accepted by everybody in each coffee bar he visited, let alone by those who were apparently not attached even to coffee bars. He therefore mentally divided them into the purposeless, meandering but not 'tough' type of youth, and the 'tough', disreputable type. Using this broad distinction, he stated somewhat tentatively but quite early on in his stay in Seagate that he was uncertain whether in practice he could ever extend his interest properly to the second category and whether he could ever feel comfortable trying to contact this 'tougher' type of youth.

In cafés, where they [the toughest type] meet, I must confess I feel very conspicuous and somehow very remote . . . I think that my own youth is not sufficient qualification to be accepted in these places and that to act as if it were, by trying to be 'just one of them' is essentially dishonest and will eventually prove inadequate and virtually impossible. Class, education, occupation, and emotional background are all important factors in the grouping of people; the mere fact, for example, of being relatively articulate is enough to differentiate me and it is doubtful whether the fact of being different is in any way helpful. I feel limited then because of my personality and my interests. I can enthuse and affect only those whose basic personalities are similar to mine and in only those activities which interest me personally. . . . The limitation suggested here applies not only to the 'action' aspect of the work, but also, the investigation. Both time and personality will limit my activities and although investigation can be made objectively in far wider circles, it too will be limited in the sense that the profound observer is the participant.

The local Advisory Committee were reluctant to accept this view, principally on the grounds that it was much too early for the worker to conclude anything, least of all the sphere of the work. The worker was moreover discouraged from believing that the emotional background of a person is a source of an impassable barrier to friendship with a person from a different background to his own. The Committee reasoned that even if a close, intimate knowledge of people with different backgrounds and personality were not possible, there could at least be an objective awareness of them. In view of this, teaching in a technical college or secondary modern school seemed the best solution to the worker.

Meanwhile, he was sent back – this time with the Advisory Committee's support and perhaps a little less despondently – to a renewal of coffee-bar sitting. The Mardi Gras again proved the place in which most progress was made. Here entry was at last achieved into a certain group which gathered regularly. It began with the worker meeting Jeff casually one evening and then being joined by Alan, a friend of Jeff. A few evenings later the worker again met Jeff in the Mardi Gras, this time by arrangement. Jeff introduced the worker to Larry, another friend, and for about an hour they talked with several others of Jeff's friends who were sitting near by, when the whole group, the worker included, left for a jazz club. Most of the time there was spent talking with Larry and another friend, and at the end of the evening the worker walked home with Larry.

As a result of making this one initial contact – with Jeff – several other acquaintances were developed, even though it later transpired that Jeff himself was only marginally accepted by most of these other contacts, and the worker found himself becoming a familiar face in a loosely associated crowd of un-attached youth aged mainly between sixteen and twenty. Many of these were full-time students at school, the arts college, or the technical college; some were part-time students trying to pass enough 'O' or 'A' levels to qualify for some form of advanced study; others were engaged in various temporary jobs.

Some forty or fifty young people of this type subsequently

became known to the worker through Jeff and his friends. But at no time nor in any sense could they be called a gang. There was never an obvious leader who set the pace nor any sense of group loyalty, merely an awareness that the Mardi Gras was a common centre and a place where news of forthcoming parties could be gleaned. The almost frantic preoccupation with parties, especially at week-ends, was one of the few characteristics which was common to all. In spite of the nebulous character of the crowd the worker felt that there was some binding force, even though it was nothing greater than that they were all associated with the Mardi Gras. He felt further that he must also become recognized in the same way, and within a week or so of being introduced to Larry and Alan he had succeeded. He reported:

My face has been, no doubt, recognized for some time since I have made several visits to the Mardi Gras. But it was not until tonight that, I think, I became noted as being connected to some of the people within the group. There was one moment in particular when my discussion with Larry and a few others became noisy and rather amusing. The burst caused attention and even comment, and the important thing was that I was associated with it. I know three of the group quite well (Larry, Alan, and Jeff) and several others on the basis of a few casual exchanges. Eventually, I hope to know most of the others through recognition such as that described.

Recognition of this kind was in fact achieved, and following close upon it came invitations into the boys' homes which the worker was able to reciprocate. A striking feature of all the work with the unattached, irrespective of area, were the occasions, often unexpected by the workers themselves, when a transition took place in the worker's relationship with the unattached from being an unknown entity to being 'someone whom it was all right to know'. The causes of such a transition seemed to lie either in the worker's sharing an experience of considerable significance to the unattached, or in the worker being accepted by an influential segment of the group. In Seagate it was a combination of both. The process whereby this transition takes place is crucial, and because the worker's account of it is such a brilliant illustration, the whole report of the evening when it occurred is given here:

My gradual acceptance into the 'group' was accelerated last Saturday evening, when I found myself, as one of many others associated with the Mardi Gras, in search of a party. I met Jeff and Larry at 5.30 p.m. in the coffee bar where they had apparently spent most of the afternoon, and from there went with them to Larry's flat. Here we sat quite passively for about an hour and a half, listening to records, perusing odd books, and occasionally fooling about; conversation was limited to general remarks about clothes, hitch-hiking, and numerous jazzmen. The effect of the varied collection of objects which decorated Larry's room – including a tiger's head, a bongo drum, a zither, some abstract paintings (composed by himself), about fifty LP records, and a variety of second-hand books – was chaotic, haphazard, and inconsistent; a touch of anarchy which, no doubt, pleases Larry very much.

Eventually, we moved back to the Mardi Gras. Larry rushed off on somebody's motor-bike to 'reconnoitre', while we sat around with a collection of other people, all waiting for the expected news of a party. Jeff, it appeared, was looked to for the necessary information, and since I had the privilege of sitting next to him, I conveniently became involved in brief conversations with a number of inquiring people. Amongst these was one particularly vociferous individual who somehow knew that I was married and began to accuse me of being unfaithful; infidelity, he told me, he abhorred. A few near-by people joined in and I became involved in considerable trouble in (a) convincing them that I was married, (b) that my wife was working at the time, and (c) contrary to their concept of marriage I did not consider it a 'drag' at all.

However (thankfully) the subject came to an abrupt end when suddenly a girl appeared and whispered the address of a party in Ridgetown. Whether it was intended for general reception or not was beside the point; within minutes, we were out of the coffee bar and deciding on the right bus; Larry was forgotten. We met up with another group and eventually arrived in the appropriate vicinity, wandering impatiently in search of the right road and the correct number. Before our quest was completed, however, we were suddenly joined by two more groups, both descending upon us from opposite directions. It became clear, as we all converged in the middle of the road (a group forty to fifty strong) that the party to which we were all on our way was 'useless' and 'full of — playing cards'. Somewhere else was needed, and suddenly, from apparently nowhere, an address of another party began to circulate; gradually we began to stir and then, on mass impulse, we were all charging down the road in pursuit of a bus that was just about to leave for . . . somewhere. The bus conductor was very annoyed that none of us happily monopolizing the top deck had any idea where we were going, and began to threaten to ring the bell and throw us off. In the end, however, there was general agreement that we would go back to town and think again there; to the conductor's relief, we eventually poured off the bus and congregated in the centre of the pavement for further conclave.

At this stage, under pressure of increasing feelings of general discontent and boredom, including in particular a growing scepticism of there being any party at all, anywhere at all, there began signs of a gradual dispersal; some moved off to the pictures, others to the fish and chip shop, and others to a pub. A small group remained there, quite differently composed to that which started off earlier in the evening at the Mardi Gras, and stood waiting at another bus stop, still dedicated and undaunted – yet unsure in remembering (or making up!) the address to which it was aiming. In desperation, probably to make things more definite, there evolved a consensus that the right number of the road was 160 (not 56, 84, or 110!) and so, happily refortified, we jumped on the next bus and made towards our new destination. Having reached the next field of action, we met yet another group engaged in the same search. A van pulled up containing a collection of grinning and familiar faces and caused a big powwow; eventually, it moved off and, contrary to what we had hoped, left us more confused than before and straggling behind in the direction in which it had gone. Eventually, after a long walk, we arrived at number 160; it was perhaps frustrating, to say the least, that all that could be seen through the gap in the front-room curtains was a peaceful and ageing couple, quietly enjoying the delights of television!

This anti-climax, which I felt was almost half-anticipated, brought the group, now thirty strong, to a static cluster in the midst of the pavement. There were no more addresses left tonight, and if another one were to have been mentioned I doubt whether it would have been believed. Suggestions to do something else were not enthusiastically received; the arts college dance was favoured by some, but as one forlorn individual pointed out, he'd spent all his money on bus fares; the Mardi Gras (on a Saturday night) was a last choice. Gradually we shifted down the road and began to scatter; in the end a small group of about ten, curiously similar to the one that had started out three hours before, was left. One of the members, who by now had his arm around the girl mentioned earlier, began tentatively and quietly to whisper that we few might care to use his flat for a small party. We might indeed have accepted had it not been for the slight distraction at that moment of about eight little girls waving at us from a passing bus. His offer was tacitly rejected, as we, again, rushed in pursuit of a bus. Seated however with these new attractions (average age: sixteen), we discovered that they were not going to a party, and resignedly we returned with them to the Mardi Gras. It was no surprise that there we should meet fellow lost travellers; there was no more information, or hope of information – except perhaps the fact that Larry was drunk on a park bench.

At Jeff's insistence, we both left the Mardi Gras, deliberately leaving the rest behind; there was just one more possibility, Jeff whispered, which would be lost if we went in a crowd. We avoided the occasional straying groups returning from their unsuccessful quests and arrived at the back door of a public house. Having failed, however, to get any reply, we met two 'strays' who told us where to find the person we were looking for. After waiting in a bus station for a quarter of an hour, we found him, together with a host of other people who similarly had secretly planned to find him. It was disappointing for all of us that he should want to take his girl home!

Jeff and I moved off to the public house near to the Mardi Gras. A few odd people came in and out, but we both knew that the evening was exhausted. Having played a game of darts, listened to the barmaid telling us of her war-time experiences, and finished our drinks, Jeff went home at ten fifteen and so did I, owing to pains in my feet!

In all, the evening, like so many others apparently, was quite mad, very comic, and at times rather pathetic. Hardly anybody had been personally invited to the two places upon which we, in increasing numbers, had advanced, yet the dedicated trek was made in the hope that all would be accommodated. The craze for parties is fanatic; the week-end seems simply not complete unless there has been one, or at least an attempt at one. Stories pass around in the post-week-end quiet of even windows being broken in order to get in. I have yet to experience one of these parties but I wonder whether they really warrant this excess frenzy. Perhaps 'being at a party' is a qualification for being 'in'; regular attendance at no-matter-who's house is as necessary to the 'already-in' as the initial achieved appearance is to the new status-aspirer.

This episode marked the turning point of the worker's acceptance by this group. From then on he searched with them for other parties, met and talked easily with them in the coffee bars and pubs, entertained them in his flat, and was entertained in their homes. Still later he was able to combine his own enthusiasm for drama with their latent interest and aptitude for it to weld them into a highly successful drama group. He was also able to help them over many personal difficulties. Some of these youths were on the delinquent fringe at this time. Some later became 'officially' delinquent when they were apprehended by the law; others became delinquent and were not apprehended; still others did not become delinquent at all and there is some evidence that the worker may have been instrumental in preventing this.

Gaining admission into this group then was a direct result of hanging around in a coffee bar, and it is particularly interesting that this should have happened despite the worker's initial lack of faith in such a method. The possibility will always remain that a more direct approach would have been successful with this group but there is considerable evidence, gained by the worker's subsequent knowledge of these youths, that any but a sensitive approach would have been doomed. An incident which occurred after the worker had been with them for more than a year illustrates the point:

Outside the church opposite my flat one evening, there was a display of a nautical organization for young girls. When I asked Nina in a non-committal voice why she didn't belong, she simply laughed as if I was being funny. Frank asked what it was all for. I suggested that it probably had something to do with Youth Sunday. He grinned and wondered why 'they' didn't do something for 'the likes of us'. It was more a mischievous thought than a serious one. I had the feeling that Frank, Andy, and Paul and possibly some of the others considered it amusing that people should be concerned about young people. They were able to look after themselves well enough; if the opportunity came, they would enjoy fooling the intruder.

This group of youths centred on the Mardi Gras came to be the most important part of the project in Seagate, but initially this was not foreseen by the worker nor was it in any way a predictable development. Indeed it was considered undesirable at this time that he should limit his attention to one group only. Consequently, the idea of teaching was pursued, and in the spring he began teaching part-time in an establishment run by the Local Education Authority offering recreational courses, full-time commercial classes, and part-time day-release courses. The majority of the students were part-time day-release and evening students and the college was in fact a centre where a great variety and number of young people attended some time during each week. It could reasonably be assumed that large numbers of these young people would be unattached.

The main subject which the worker taught for six forty-minute sessions was English, with an additional session of Social Studies. A total of one hundred day-release boys was taught each week, with ages ranging from fifteen to nineteen and occupations from G.P.O. messenger boys to factory machine workers and shop assistants. The worker's immediate reaction to the teaching situation was one of ambivalence. While he realized that it would allow direct contact with a large number of boys in a structured setting, he felt that the image of a teacher was inevitably somewhat authoritarian. It was a continual jar on his mind to be called 'sir' since he was aiming for an informal atmosphere. However he hoped that his age would be conducive to the development of informal relationships outside the class. And it was not only the boys inside the college whose suspicions had to be allayed. Jeff, for example, was so obviously intrigued and incredulous when the worker told him that he was to begin work at the technical college that he went so far as to check on what he had said.

Jeff waited for me one Monday morning to see whether I came out of the college. It took a great deal to convince him that a 'bum', as he so charmingly referred to me, could also be a teacher.

Wishing at the same time to broaden his contacts with a younger age group the worker then arranged to take part-time jobs in various secondary modern schools, where he was responsible for leading small groups in informal discussions on such subjects as Careers, Social Studies, and English. He was attached to three secondary modern schools for a total of eight hours a week. The ages of his pupils ranged from fourteen to sixteen, and he was able to teach his subject in whatever way he thought would be most beneficial to the aims of getting to know and establishing an informal relationship with his class. It soon became obvious that in one of the schools the general authoritarian atmosphere and the size of the classes (fifteen to twenty pupils) were not conducive to these aims. He therefore invited those interested to continue group discussions outside school hours. For the first session eight attended, then nine, then five. Having established a small nucleus he suggested moving away from the school atmosphere to a small hut which was used as an additional classroom by the technical college. Unfortunately the group never really became established. This was partly due to the worker's justifiable anxiety not to mix the school group with the Mardi Gras group which was now showing a promising interest in drama. He felt that there was such a difference in age and social backgrounds of these two groups that if either found out about the other a great deal of explanation would be called for, particularly to the Mardi Gras group who had been kept unaware of the worker's association with the secondary modern schools. These older youths might well have lost confidence in him had they known of his interest in a group of young boys unknown to and totally different from them.

It might perhaps have been possible to have worked with the two groups separately and discreetly, but any such likelihood was quickly ruled out. For the convenience of people in both groups he arranged to meet each on the same day at the same place – the technical college hut – but at different times. He was to meet first with the school group and two hours later with the Mardi Gras group. Just as he was about to leave to meet the younger group, members of the older group arrived at his flat. On the pretext of urgent business he left the older group in his flat and raced to the hut to postpone the meeting with the younger school group. Either because the latter felt that the worker had let them down or because they were not over-enthusiastic about the idea itself, the younger group did not attend their next two meetings and the worker was forced to abandon the attempt. However he recorded that this may have been desirable in any case. It seemed that the attached of the class were staying on for the discussions while the relatively un-attached were not. Of the nine who first attended the meetings, all but two went to a youth club. Four of this seven were only loosely attached, occasionally visiting a local boys' club for something to do on an off night. The two who did not go to any club were interesting; they seemed to spend most of their time at home, often alone, making things or watching television. It

was perhaps fortunate therefore that the meetings came to an
end, since the trend was for only the actively committed to
attend. The four who occasionally went to the boys' club formed
a reasonably well-defined sub-group; either they all attended
or none. The worker doubted if they would have attended any
further meetings even had it been possible to continue, since an
hour's group discussion – especially in the summer months –
was hardly an attractive prospect for this kind of boy. More
appealing activities such as visiting the worker's flat, playing a
tape recorder and records might have been an improvement but
they would create again the difficulty of mixing the groups
since the older, drama group had developed the comfortable
habit of just dropping in.

Thus for a number of suggested reasons, including large
classes, the authoritarian atmosphere in one of the schools, difficulty in attracting the type of pupil of most interest to the
project, and the dangers of mixing two entirely different groups
at the expense of losing both, the school-teaching approach was
not successful in Seagate. But the teaching approach was by no
means useless as a method of finding out about young people,
and for this reason the worker continued to teach at the school
and the technical college for over a year. By then, the time and
attention demanded by the drama (Mardi Gras) group was so
excessive that the worker was forced to give up school-teaching.

THE SEAGATE DRAMA GROUP

After two to three months in Seagate, by virtue of his acquaintanceship with Jeff and Larry, the worker became aware that he
was on the fringe of a large, incohesive mass of young people
best described as purposeless, being neither noticeably club-
able nor extremely delinquent. Most were aged between fifteen
and twenty and were the sons and daughters of a middle class,
'*nouveau riche*' parentage. Parents' occupations included night-
club owner, draughtsman, author, owner of a small business
firm, hotel manageress, and ex-professional sportsman. The
homes from which some of these young people came were
wealthy and comfortable and yet, in many cases, they seemed
to afford little affection or emotional security. Many of the

youths were irregularly employed in a variety of jobs from car-washing to hospital portering. Of the rest, some were art students and others were still at school, usually grammar or public schools. The older youths were largely the educational drop-outs of these schools and as a result their prospects for the future were extremely uncertain. A sense of boredom, failure, and restlessness characterized many of them and found expression in a quite definite identification with a rebellious, layabout, mildly delinquent way of life.

Approximately one hundred youths made up the larger mass. Thirty or forty of these became known to the worker. Ten members composed a central nucleus which seemed to epitomize the rebellious way of life and provide the extreme expression with which other, less venturesome members could identify themselves. These young people had rejected the local youth service, there was no doubt about this, and their wild, disorganized spirit seemed incompatible with the relatively confined atmosphere of the youth club. There was an almost complete dissociation from the world of youth leaders, subscriptions, committees, regular meetings, and organized activities. The most noticeable differences from the local 'attached' youth were the degree of rebelliousness and antagonism towards society and their refusal to accept limitations, whether their own or external. Brief descriptions of the central characters of this central nucleus are enough to display their main attributes.

Howard P. was aged seventeen when the worker came to know him and already had one court conviction for vandalism. In addition he had received a summons for being in possession of a dangerous weapon. He had left school at the age of sixteen with two G.C.E. 'O' levels. His failure to obtain more 'O' levels convinced his parents that he should leave school and Howard became a clerk. After two months, he left because 'he couldn't stand it'. It was 'lifeless', 'secure', and 'conforming'. In the first three years after leaving school he held no job for longer than two months. An only child, he was showing increased hostility towards his domineering mother and indifference towards his father's discipline which had become progressively weak and ineffectual. Generally too preoccupied with managing a hotel, his mother failed to give Howard more than nagging attention. From early adolescence he had been allowed to take part in the general life of the hotel and apparently had access, by various means, to whatever drink he wanted, probably without his mother's realizing it. As manageress, she was frequently so busy that Howard found himself virtually free to do as he pleased. He was even able to stay out at all-night parties without his mother realizing. His parents were concerned about his educational failure and inability to hold a steady job, but their interest was unsympathetic, intermittent, and without direction. Howard himself showed considerable evidence of discontent with his way of life. His ambition was to be a writer; he claimed to value not being tied down to any job, and intended to get as much experience as possible of life in general.

Paul W., aged seventeen, was similarly on the fringe of delinquency at the time the worker met him. He had left a public school the year before with five G.C.E. 'O' levels, after his father had refused to pay any more fees. His home was outwardly more affectionate than Howard's and his father, a businessman and the dominant figure in the household, had definite ideas about his son's future. Paul's failure to live up to them led to friction. Mr W. had found a job with good prospects for him as a trainee salesman, a job to which Paul, however, felt totally unsuited, both in temperament and in qualifications. He left after three months and by chance managed to get into the local arts college. Mr W. reacted strongly. He refused his son any economic support, discriminated in the home in favour of Paul's younger sister aged fifteen, and Paul came in for a good deal of harsh physical treatment. Paul's reaction was to rebel against these conforming pressures. He talked of getting on a boat and leaving the country. At this time, he, like Howard, placed a strong emphasis on experience – travelling, hitching, meeting new situations and different people – rather than on mildly conforming within the security of a steady job. He was intelligent and sensitive and possessed considerable artistic ability. He seemed to attach more importance to being creative than to merely earning money. His apparent disdain for it and for security led to an almost complete identification with the 'bum' way of life and this was linked, no doubt, not only to his preference to remain as independent as possible of his father but a desire furthermore to thwart him by becoming the antithesis of his hopes.

Andy S. was placed on probation for theft when he was fifteen. He was still at school where he had already successfully passed six subjects at 'O' level and stayed on to take three 'A' levels. The S. family consisted of Andy's father, a professional man, his mother, the owner of a fashionable hair salon, and his brother, aged fourteen. Andy's attitude towards his home was superficially emotionless. However, considerable evidence of defiance and rebellion became apparent on closer acquaintance. There was little discord between his parents and neither was dominant, their relationship was one of equality. However Andy showed a mild disdain for his father, who was the main disciplinarian, and in general the home seemed somewhat fragmentary, with each member of the family – particularly the parents – pursuing separate lives. Both Mr and Mrs S. were concerned about Andy and the way he was developing. They also felt that he would not listen to them any more. Andy's adjustment to school and school discipline was similar to Howard's and Paul's; all three constantly found themselves in trouble. Andy had a poor relationship with his headmaster, a contempt for school activities and for being treated as a schoolboy – a role which he felt to be beneath his level of sophistication. When he left school, having failed his 'A' levels, he displayed acute feelings of failure, becoming listless, sullen, and unhappy. Like his close friends, Howard and Paul, he also began to practise the 'bum' philosophy. He took two jobs, one as a lorry driver's mate and the other as a barman. From the first he was dismissed after two months and the second he left after three days because it was 'uninteresting' and poorly paid. He began to bet heavily and professed a generally careless attitude, expounding grandiose schemes for making easy money and making plans to leave Seagate.

Sally R., aged fifteen, was the youngest of three children. Her father had been chronically sick for a number of years and her mother, a charming, well-spoken woman, neither *nouveau riche* in attitudes nor taste, was the dominant parent. The home was wealthy and all of the children had received a private education. Sally said she had been expelled from school because of her pro-

vocative behaviour with some local boys. Her academic record
was poor. Neither Sally nor her parents appeared to have been
perturbed by the expulsion and since then she had a record of
irregular work. This was characterized by bouts of enthusiasm:
she started modelling, began training as a hairdresser, served in
a café, and spent a short period at an arts college, and these
efforts were interspersed with dissatisfaction, idleness, and restlessness. Sally seemed affectionate toward the rest of the family
but rarely mentioned them, least of all her father. She was very
fond of her mother and referred to her almost exclusively.
Occasionally she was rebellious and defiant. Mrs R. was worried
about Sally's staying out late, idling at home for most of the
day, and refusing to accept a steady job. At times she expressed
a little annoyance at Sally's behaviour, but more often it was
bewilderment. On the surface there was not so much friction
between mother and daughter as a constant but concealed
difference. Amongst her own age group, Sally was popular but
essentially flirtatious. She was a highly vivacious, polite, and
excitable girl. Of average intelligence, she sometimes regressed
to childish behaviour and seemed unable to sustain a deep or
lasting relationship with any boy, changing her affections frequently and seeming generally flippant about any hurt she
inflicted.

Celia M. was also aged fifteen when the worker first met her.
She had recently left a private school in order to take a one-year
secretarial course. She seldom mentioned school but seemed
quite happy at the secretarial college and anxious to pass her
examinations. Like the others in the group, she placed implicit
value on making money, but unlike the others she was prepared
to work and sacrifice for it. Her parents owned and managed a
small business, the importance of which seemed to have had a
pervasive influence throughout the home. A high value seemed
to be placed both on financial success and on upward social
mobility. These aspirations led to anxieties which in their turn
fostered tensions within the family. Mr and Mrs M. often
seemed edgy and querulous. Celia's attitude towards her family
was basically affectionate but she frequently complained of her
parents' nagging and strictness, and at times she was hostile
and resentful, demonstrating her defiance by her choice of

clothes and by staying out late at night. Usually, however, she deferred to her parents' wishes in the end. Celia referred most to her mother, who seemed to be the dominant parent.

Although of average intelligence, Celia possessed considerable acting ability. Physically attractive, she was often unpopular because of her childish behaviour, affectations, and self-centredness. Perhaps out of frustration at not getting attention she she occasionally behaved erratically, wildly even; for example, by punching people. She was frequently restless, quickly bored, and did not seem particularly happy. With boys, she tended to have a series of temporary relationships and seemed resigned to the fact that 'none of them would last'.

Nina F., aged sixteen, was the eldest of four children. The family was much less wealthy than the others so far described. Mr F. was a semi-skilled worker and regarded as apathetic and unaspiring by his wife, who was anxious to improve her standard of living and social status. Mrs F. had a full-time job and seemed financially independent of her husband, and since she owned a car she also went out in the evenings and away for holidays without him. Mrs F. was therefore the most influential figure in the family. According to Nina, Mr F. liked her the least of his children. In return, Nina was openly hostile and even contemptuous towards her father. By contrast, she was respectful towards Mrs F., wanting approval and support and sympathetic towards her mother's impatience with Mr F.

Nina had attended a secondary modern school until she was fifteen. She then took a secretarial job but gave it up in less than a year because she found office life too dull. She began studying part-time for G.C.E. 'O' levels but was unsuccessful, partly because of her reluctance to work and partly because of her mother's demands that she help in the home. Mrs F. was not enthusiastic about Nina's attempts at further study. It did not conform to the pattern of life of most girls in the neighbourhood and she expected Nina to supplement the family income. Nina herself felt disturbed that she was different from the other girls but she was concerned to live life to the full and the prospect of having an 'ordinary' job and settling early into married life was extremely unattractive. It would be exciting and glamorous to be a model, an art student, or an actress, but all required qualifications which she did not possess. Her solution was to take a series of temporary jobs and hope that somehow something interesting would turn up. Not only was this situation frustrating to Nina but it began to conflict with her mother's expectations and values. She began to nag about Nina's way of life. Rows arose between mother and daughter, although there was no bitter antipathy and basically they remained affectionate towards each other. Mrs F. seemed genuinely anxious that her daughter should be happy.

Nina was a very sociable person and her sense of fun, attractive physical appearance, and spontaneity made her popular. In general she was law-abiding and her sense of right and wrong seemed to have been well-instilled by her mother. But her thoughtlessness, lack of application and self-discipline were striking; completely absorbed in the present, she showed no ability to think ahead or to conceive the implications of what she was doing, and the effect was to make her seem irresponsible.

In many ways, these young people seem remarkably like any others of their age, passing through a typical phase of adolescent development with its characteristically rebellious and unsettled behaviour. However, they were different and they were different in two important respects. There were the inconsistencies in their family backgrounds. The parents of most of them had achieved middle-class income level, but this upward economic mobility had not been accompanied by a commensurate rise in educational status, nor even always by a rise in social status. This sort of situation is recognized as a potential cause of conflict between the parents and of conflict between the parents and their children. The tendency for these Seagate parents to try to pull themselves up by means of their children's educational boot-straps may explain both the high educational aspirations they held for their sons and daughters and the latter's acute sense of failure when such aspirations were not realized.

The other important way in which these adolescents, especially the boys, differed from the 'normal' was the violence of their rebellious behaviour, both against their parents and against society in general. Their rebelliousness was marked in almost every sphere of their daily lives. Towards work, for example, their attitude varied from regarding money as the sole motive, to explaining away their frequent changes of job by the value they placed on the new experiences this brought them. Even in the long run, their ambitions centred around highly paid occupations such as those of actors, artists, models, and writers, all of which they believed gave a high return for little effort. Paul W., who felt he was being creative at the arts college, was the only one during the three years that the worker heard admit to enjoying his work. A typical report on the employment situation of the group is the following one for May, 1962, written by the worker:

Howard with characteristic carelessness continued during the month to shift from one job to the next. At the beginning of the month, he was complaining that the delivery van job was 'a drag'. Within two weeks he had given it up. Five days later he had got a 'good' job selling ice-creams on a push-bike. Here, he hoped to earn £8 a week plus bonuses. After about a week, however, he gave it up: 'I got fed up, dragging around the streets on an old bike, bawling "ices" and ringing my little bicycle bell.' At the end of the month, he was talking about working in a photography firm. He needs money from time to time; therefore he gets a job – the one with the best wage. It becomes 'a drag'; therefore he gives it up. He laughs at his own repetitive course of changing jobs. He jokes about the 'crumby' way he earns his money; he almost boasts that he has never held a job for more than two months. Moreover, he does not seem to have any sense of obligation to an employer.

Despite his overt show of carelessness and his constant rationalizing that he would either fail or pass easily, it was evident at the beginning of the month that Andy was anxious about his examinations. He was suffering from asthma during the first week of the month. After the exams had finished, Andy resumed his affected nonchalance, bragging that he had failed but could have passed if he had worked.

At the beginning of the month, Kevin thought that a place in the arts college was in effect an opportunity to skive. He didn't want to work and therefore intended to try more colleges once he had left this one. He could foresee himself avoiding work until he was thirty – an attractive prospect. 'If you've got the talent, why not?' However, by the end of the month, it was clear that Kevin had not even bothered to attend college. He realized that to be absent for four weeks was dangerous, but he didn't know what he would do instead, if he were 'chucked out'. Why then should he act in this way and take the risk of being expelled when he recognized himself to be well-off? He slowly replied with a broad grin 'emotional troubles' and then laughed at the uncomfortable and half understanding responses that this phrase elicits from people, in particular a teacher at the arts college.

Generally, in the large group as a whole, this careless attitude towards work is shared. With some, the lack of concern is real; in addition to Howard and Kevin, Mark and Nina seemed during the month to be unworried. Mark worked selling ice-creams for a few days, tired of it, and gave it up. Nina, despite her former anxiety about her 'O' levels, showed little evidence of doing much work. She sunbathed a great deal, when not working as a housemaid.

This type of report could be repeated *ad infinitum*, with the prevailing attitude towards work invariably one of apparent indifference and apathy. This is not surprising, in view of the nature of the jobs which were nearly always below the educational levels of the young people and certainly fell short of their own high ambitions. Their feelings of inadequacy and their inability to concentrate for any length of time rendered them unable to work for the further qualifications on which the realization of their ambitions depended. They were caught in a vicious circle and, rather than compromise their unrealistic hopes by taking some 'secure' job with prospects they preferred the 'bum' role which at least afforded them a certain amount of prestige through its feigned indifference and blatant disregard of accepted social standards.

Their attitude towards other teenagers outside their own immediate group was one of intolerance and condemnation, generated partly by their insecurity and the rationalization of their own shortcomings. According to these young people, most other youth in Seagate fell into one of three categories – 'thicks', 'snobs', or 'hearties'. The thicks were the low, tough type of youth with working-class accent and secondary modern education, the type who preferred rock'n'roll to modern jazz. Thicks were to be derided; they were also to be avoided. As Jim once said: 'They'll punch you even if you just look at them – they must have guilt complexes or something.' He claimed to have been beaten up by them because he had laughed at them.

Howard was greatly amused by 'thick' terms, for example, 'Oo's yer', 'Let's turn 'em over', 'Cut 'em up', and 'Push a boot in his face'. He admitted, despite his amusement, that he would be scared if they tried it on him. Occasionally, this reaction to thicks directly affected behaviour. For example, Marlene, a girl on the fringe of the group, ceased attending a course at the technical college ostensibly because she could not 'stick' the 'ton up boys' with whom she studied. This was a purely snobbish attitude, she admitted. There was ample evidence from the other side that the thicks were equally intolerant, deriding the drama group for its 'intellectual' and 'posh' pretensions.

The second group these young people felt contemptuous about were 'the snobs'. These were the 'Young Conservative' types, wearing cricket sweaters and smoking pipes. They were considered dull, lifeless, and conformist, enjoying their sub-urban homes, their telly, and their little garden. Howard, who believed very definitely that the way to live was either 'high' or 'low' was strongly resentful of this type. Finally there was the derision aroused by the 'hearties'. A hearty was any keen, com-mitted, naïve person of the sort most frequently found in youth clubs but of course sometimes elsewhere. Their antagon-ism toward hearties was not solely aroused by outsiders, but also occasionally by some of their own fringe members. Larry, for example, was considered by most of the group to be a hearty, childish, and – in particular – self-centred. It was par-ticularly noticeable how this sort of antagonism was awoken by Liz, an outsider, when she was included in the group, largely on account of her acting ability, to make up the cast for a play. It was increasingly felt by most of the group that she was too respectable and rather naïve in relation to their own sophistication. Liz, like Larry, was aware of this 'unfriendliness' and one evening broke down and cried. She later told the worker that she felt she didn't have any contact with the rest of the group and was alone.

The rejection of the hearty came out more specifically in the attitudes of the group towards youth organizations. One four-teen-year-old fringe member who was an ex-scout considered all scout masters as 'overgrown schoolboys still in short trousers'. Kevin had belonged to a church drama society shortly before

meeting the worker. He had left mid-way during rehearsals and
let the producer down badly. His reason for this was that he
considered them all 'a load of twots'; he hated their patronizing
attitude and suspected hollowness in their thanks to him for
designing a set. He felt that the church members looked after
their own and he especially disliked their attitude towards him
as if he were a delinquent that they had cleverly caught.
Howard, after seeing the film *Some People*, said he thought the
Duke of Edinburgh Award Scheme stupid and designed for 'a
load of hearties'. He supposed he himself could run a hundred
yards if he tried, but he could see no reason for doing so. He
then talked about the women who belonged to the Salvation
Army and concluded that they belonged because they were
unattractive and stupid. This attitude towards the youth service
cannot be lightly dismissed as a prejudiced one developed by
people who have never been near a youth club to see for themselves. Later on in this report there is an account of how the
group, through the worker, came into prolonged contact with
youth officers of various voluntary and statutory bodies. The
experience only served to confirm for some of them that the
youth service was for 'the kiddies' and 'nig-nogs', and operated
under a system of petty rules and regulations reminiscent of a
younger, school atmosphere. For others, however, a change did
in fact begin to take place.

So far individual and group attitudes have been described
negatively. Work, many of the group's peers, and all youth
organizations were actively disliked, and home, religion, most
adults, and any form of authority can be added to that list. However, it may be refreshing at this point to consider if there was
anything they felt enthusiastic about. The simple answer was
'the party' and all it represented. Parties were held not only in
Seagate but also in neighbouring towns and villages. The
amount of effort necessary to get to them and to locate them
gave an indication of the great value placed on being at a party.
The feeling was that 'you've got to find them because everybody
else is going. It's a terrible feeling missing out, especially if
everybody else has gone and had a good time'. To be excluded
meant a loss of status; to find a party required one to be 'in',
and the process of locating the party and the hope of something

grand or unexpected happening were sufficient to attract people, uninvited or not. One account has already been given of a typical attempt to find a party. Many of these attempts ended in an anti-climax, with large numbers of young people drifting away either in couples or in small groups from what was to have been the scene of a 'great' night. In general, however, parties on a smaller scale were held every week-end and were eagerly antici- pated as a break from the relatively inactive week-day life. The party was the occasion, with the aid of drink and sometimes of drugs, for the release of latent feelings of rebellion amongst the core of the group against middle-class adult values. The most anti-social behaviour occurred at week-ends, either at parties or elsewhere where it was possible to get high. At a party given by Mark, for example, there was a characteristic lack of regard for property, with Andy and two others trying to break into a house. Paul displayed a similarly careless attitude when he, Andy, and three others 'borrowed' his father's car, exhausted the battery, scratched the paintwork, and covered it in mud. This kind of behaviour was considered remarkable, exciting, and good fun. Most parties were generally evaluated in these sort of terms.

The considerable time spent each evening in looking for the parties was an essential part of the fun – the strange territory, the random questioning of passers-by, and the sense of expecta- tion. Once inside, the success of the party depended on the number of people present, the supply of drink, the numbers of each sex and the amount of music. Here is the worker's account of two parties held in October 1962 which were both rated good by the group.

There was plenty of drink and according to Les, 'everyone' got drunk. There was incident too. Howard, because of loud singing, got involved in a fight with a thick, who resented the drama group's monopoly of the party. Paul, very drunk, tried to intervene but only managed to wildly miss the thick and instead punched the door – thereby causing his hand to bleed a great deal. Eventually the police were called in and the party came to an end. The account of this party was given to me by Les, who perhaps is one of the more stable members of the group. To him, however, the inordinate and liberated nature of the evening was very highly valued.

Nina had wanted to celebrate her nineteenth birthday by having a party, provided she could find a place to hold it; her own house was out of the question in view of the restraining influence of her mother. In the end, Nina held the party at her friend Vicky's house. It was attended by a large number of people, including several who were not invited, and went on all night, Vicky's parents being away on holiday. The principal activity was dancing. I saw little drunkenness, although I left at about twelve thirty.

The sequel to Nina's party was rather serious. The noise and behaviour caused considerable annoyance to neighbours in the road. In particular, one or two complained of 'very immoral' behaviour in one of the bedrooms, the curtains of which had not been drawn. The result was that Vicky's parents were very annoyed and told her to leave home. The fact was that the party had gone on through the night and that some degree of sexual behaviour had caused offence to neighbours. This was not considered unusual by most of the group – it was a general facet of party activity. Les told me that at the party mentioned earlier most of the bedrooms were occupied. In particular, Jo was very drunk and spent most of the night in bed, visited in turn by a series of boys. How exaggerated this is, I am uncertain – Les does not usually exaggerate. His attitude towards this sexual behaviour at parties was quite approving – accepting it as part of the general 'release' characteristic of a party.

The extent of sexual promiscuity amongst this group is difficult to assess with complete accuracy. On the one hand a fair amount of promiscuity is evidenced not only by the above account but also by the worker's own reports of parties he had attended where couples retired to bedrooms.

In general, sex did not dominate the conversation of the group; in fact, it was rarely mentioned. What the worker learned about sexual behaviour and attitudes was derived mainly from casual and incidental comments. At most times, whatever comments were made on the subject were said in an apparently casual and blasé fashion. The youths in particular seemed to have completely rejected as irrelevant any question of whether it might be right or wrong to have pre-marital intercourse. For most, there was no doubt: it was permissible – 'everybody does it'. The attitude of the girls is less clear. Occasional complaints were heard from the males that some of the girls in the group were virgins, and both within and outside of the group girls were sometimes dropped by the boys because they weren't 'getting anywhere'.

The character and quality of the personal relationships between the youths and their girl-friends varied from an almost nonchalant disregard to quite genuine affection. Kevin, for example, adopted a very superior attitude towards his girl-friends and expected them to chase him. He exploited one girl, who was obviously very fond of him, by frequently ignoring her and ordering her to do whatever he wanted. By contrast, Howard thought that Kevin treated the girls abominably. Howard himself was usually less superior towards his girl-friends, but showed a strong need to dominate them by demanding an excessive amount of attention and affection. Marlene frequently confided in the worker that she was worried by the pressure made on her by her boy-friend to have intercourse with him. He quoted 'all the other girls' he had been with and interpreted her attitude as a rejection of his affection. He was impatient with this attitude and Marlene began to doubt her own values and wondered if she was being unnecessarily prim.

Both the boys and the girls were subject to the rapid changes of affection that might be expected of this age group. Few of them were interested in marriage, and the general feeling was that they were too young to commit themselves, preferring to 'achieve something before settling into domesticity'.

Finally, one or two other attitudes held by the group should be mentioned. With few exceptions the members held little respect or regard for adults and the adult world as they saw it. In some measure this was due to the feeling held by the main group that there was in adulthood a strong element, often tacit, of superiority and disdain for the way of life the group led, which was expressed frequently in an aggressive and disapproving way. The individual who refused to be served a drink by Howard because he (Howard) wore a beard, the bar-tender who wanted the group 'to get out of my pub', the caretaker who assumed a rather strict attitude before a rehearsal, the policeman who for no apparent reason told the group to move along the street – all these were representative of an unsympathetic and disagreeable, older, more conforming public – a public whose demands seemed frequently silly and capricious. Even when the demands or criticisms of adults were justifiable, the group had become so over-sensitive that these were interpreted as unwarranted hostility.

The general attitude to life also is worth mentioning. For most of the group, a leisured existence with periodic opportunities for acquiring large amounts of money, preferably easily, was highly valued. In keeping with this philosophy they made no sustained effort to work. When they had money, the tendency was to spend it immediately on such things as large meals, drinks, or clothes. It was also characteristic that those without money were supported by those who were flush. They saw no wrong in 'conning' from others, whether on the small scale of buying drinks or, more dramatically, hitch-hiking around Europe dependent for their meals as well as their transportation on the people who gave them lifts. The attitude towards the generosity of such people was a mocking pleasure at finding them to be so naïve and easy to exploit and deceive. While money itself was highly valued for maintaining a middle-class standard of living, the traditional middle-class values of attaining money through honesty, sobriety, and industry were completely ignored. One of the principal complaints was lack of money. Jazz clubs and cinemas were frequently entered without payment, train fares were seldom paid, and a great deal of time was spent in coffee bars and pubs, avoiding as much as possible the obligation to buy anything.

Such were the main characteristics of the unattached in Seagate with whom the worker found himself becoming increasingly involved. Their rejection of the local youth service was quite unmistakable. If they had wished to do so, all could have belonged to a local youth club. The total adolescent population of Seagate in the fourteen-to-twenty age group in 1961 was approximately eleven to twelve thousand, and this number was served by about one hundred and sixty youth organizations of various kinds, including specialist clubs, church clubs, open clubs, Local Education Authority and voluntary clubs. Eighty-nine of these organizations were church clubs, the majority of which held meetings for members only on the one or two nights that their church halls were free. Other church clubs that attempted to run an 'open' evening were generally insufficiently equipped with leadership and facilities to cope with the demand. Ten clubs had their own premises, and these included three Local Education Authority youth wings and four voluntary organization clubs. The remainder of the organizations met in school premises. Only eight clubs were open five nights a week, the majority opening for one or two nights.

It was clearly the belief of the unattached described in this opening chapter that the youth service, as represented by these various organizations, had nothing to offer them. It remains yet to be seen if a detached worker of the youth service could succeed where more orthodox approaches had apparently failed.

TRYING TO HELP

From the autumn of 1961, the Seagate worker tried to become increasingly accepted by the eight or ten youths who formed the nucleus of a larger mass of thirty or forty young people, all aged between fifteen and nineteen years. As explained earlier, the 'mass' consisted of individuals and small groups of two or three people who were held together as a whole by the seemingly superficial fact that they all attended the same parties, jazz clubs, and coffee bars. Many of the individuals and sub-groups hardly knew each other so that the 'mass' was in no sense cohesive or structured. Most of them were middle-class in home background and education and all were involved to varying degrees in an adolescent rebellion. Through identifying with those nucleus members such as Howard and Andy whose behaviour was the most notably defiant, members of the 'mass' could contact and occasionally take part in a segment which was in genuine revolt against the respectability which all of them periodically resented: at school, at home, and at work. To some extent the members of the 'mass' wanted to be accepted and included in the nucleus. To compensate for being rejected, as they invariably were, they needed to be independent and in rivalry.

In the light of these groupings and sub-groupings the worker decided that he must become accepted by the members of the nucleus. Howard, from all accounts, seemed to be the most popular and notorious character of this central group, and it was with Howard that the worker started. After a period of tentative suspicion and testing out, Howard began taking an interest in the worker and invited him to various functions in the town. The development of a close friendship with Howard led in turn to close friendships with members of his group such as Andy, Paul, Frank, and Ray. Three factors were of importance in furthering the worker's acceptance with Howard and the group: his knowledge of jazz, his ability to play jazz piano, and his impartial and non-judgemental attitude. Talking jazz was, of itself a means of communication. It allowed the worker to show that he was knowledgeable and 'with it' and it also gave the members of the group the necessary time to assess him. Jazz is an impersonal and emotionally neutral subject, it was a safe topic and served as a kind of defence to keep the conversation away from a more personal focus during the early stages of the worker's introduction to the group. Further, the members began to feel a sneaking pride at having a pianist in their group, and on numerous occasions the worker played at public dances in jazz clubs. The group usually clapped noisily and enthusiastically as if championing their own star. Finally – and without doubt the most important factor – the worker's manner during the autumn was unassuming and unobtrusive; he was casual, quietly interested, and non-judgemental. He did not try to influence or direct anybody; he said little and was essentially peripheral, mildly amused, and always following. Within these limits he endeavoured to encourage people to express themselves to him without any risk of a rebuff such as the habitual sarcasm which was characteristic of the group. Meanwhile, the worker became more and more included in their activities and involved in the routine of the members. He found that he was expected at local meeting places, and invited to parties and jazz clubs. However, the knowledge that he was a school teacher lingered a long time and though seldom acknowledged, was rarely forgotten. Even his closest contacts such as Howard, Andy, and Frank displayed an element of deference towards him that was unnatural. They found it a little odd that a person of the worker's calibre should want to spend so much time with 'a crowd of bums' such as they considered themselves. As Howard told the worker: 'You don't look like a teacher – no tweedy jacket with leather elbow pads, no pipe, no chalk in your fingers.' Understandably, the group was cautious, and yet they already liked the worker sufficiently not to want to forgo his friendship.

In spite of the ambivalent attitude of the group caused by his teaching role, the worker judged by the end of December 1961 that his relationship with Howard and the others was secure enough for more positive action. For example, whereas before Howard had concealed his absences from the technical college from him, now he was able to discuss the college and explain why he disliked it. Equally the worker could show his disapproval of Howard's action without having this interpreted as a form of rejection.

The way of life of the nucleus was essentially static at the beginning of 1962. They were basically dissatisfied, bored, and resigned, with few prospects and no direction. A series of jobs were tolerated for the money and the prolonged intermissions of unemployment were filled with daydreams. There was an almost self-destructive resignation in the 'bum' existence. It was as if the boys had got stuck and were incapable of moving forward. Perhaps because of their individual insecurity and lack of affection at home they needed group support and recognition. Afraid of change, they placed heavy expectations on each other to remain the same. There were further pressures on them by the mass to continue their familiar roles of extremists, failures, and rebels – roles that they were known to play so well.

This was the setting early in 1962 when the worker tentatively sought to interest the nucleus group in drama. He had thrown out, half in jest, the idea of doing a play once or twice during the autumn. Although intrigued, the group dismissed it as impracticable. The worker did not push the idea – he decided to wait until he could present the script of a highly unconventional play that he particularly thought might catch their imagination and thus make the idea slightly more concrete. The following is the worker's account of the evening the play became something of a reality :

Frank, Howard, Paul, and Brian came round to my flat at eight p.m. We listened to the jazz record that Howard had brought with him and made a few comments on this. We talked about jazz musicians, Paul's chances of getting into arts college, and Frank being thrown out of his flat by the landlord.

Earlier in the evening, I had decided to leave a copy of a play by Ionesco on the table and hoped that someone might pick it up. Whilst I was playing the piano, Howard did so and began to read out particularly 'mad' passages. I stopped playing and Howard carried on reading. It was something to do and a laugh. Paul, Brian, and I listened for a while and were amused. Frank half listened but seemed more interested in playing his guitar. After a while, Paul joined Howard and they read out odd passages together. Howard, who at first had been enjoying the book in a ridiculing and dismissing kind of way, asked me what the play was about. At this stage, I began to show that I thought the play was more than just a laugh. I explained that I had seen it a long time ago and, without making any implied comment, I added that I had always wanted to 'have a go at it'. I said that I thought it was a terrific play. At this, Paul became more interested and I suggested that we might read a whole scene together. Howard thought this was a good idea and although Frank had subsided into playing blues to himself, Howard insisted that Frank should read a part because the character in question was just like Frank – 'thick'. Brian followed and we all read the first scene. The play had an exciting, staccato quality about it and really was great fun, with plenty of shouting and singing.

It was clear that all of them were very enthusiastic about it. I then asked, 'Well, why don't we put it on?' Immediately, they all agreed, and began to speculate wildly on the prospect of presenting it at the largest concert hall in Seagate and making lots of money. I joined with their enthusiasm; I showed forcibly that I thought it was a realistic possibility. Having speculated wildly for a while, Howard wondered whether we could really do it. They were clearly uncertain. I firmly made it clear that I thought it was possible – 'anyway what's wrong with trying?' I said that the first problem would be to find a rehearsal centre and I asked if they knew of any place. They were all rather vague. Howard mentioned some church hall but seemed surprised when I asked if he knew how much it cost to hire. For the rest of the evening, they had fun thinking of people to play the eight characters in the play. They cast themselves in leading roles. Howard said there would be no difficulty in finding more players.

I told Howard to keep the book and show it to anyone who was interested. Howard said he would do this and that he could get a girlfriend, Karen, to type some copies.

This was a slight but hopeful beginning. The careful choice of a play which would appeal to the group and the worker's unobtrusive manner of drawing attention to it had aroused enthusiasm and had got the project somewhat tenuously under way.

They liked the play because it was unconventional and apparently rather 'mad'. The atmosphere and theme of it also must have seemed familiar to individuals in the nucleus. Amongst other things, the play was about the release of a group of young people from their confined and disordered lives. It created a setting in which a few careless yet insecure characters were allowed to dream, play, tease, and torment amongst themselves. It was not difficult for the nucleus to identify with such a theme. In addition, the whole quality of the play was alive and tense and there was plenty of scope for improvisation, singing, shouting, and dancing.

It remained to be seen, however, if the play could become a reality or if it would fade out like other grandiose schemes of this group. The chances of success looked remote, but there were two favourable factors. The worker recognized that despite the apathy of the group the members had a fundamental need to break out of the rut, to be active and to do something constructive. Secondly, an external yet accepted adult was present who expected more from the group than it expected from itself. What was crucial at this point was the nature of the worker's relationship with the group. He was sufficiently close to be in a position to suggest something and have some attention paid to it, equally he was sufficiently apart to lead without being rebuked or ridiculed, which was usually the fate of most members of the group who suggested anything constructive.

Five days later a second meeting was held to discuss the play. As the worker's report clearly shows it gave some indication of the problems ahead.

Howard and Ray arrived . . . Ray was very excited by the play and assumed he would have a part. He predicted that it would be 'great'. He assured me that when he does anything, he always does it 'a hundred-per-cent right'. He scarcely applied his mind to anything, he told me, but when he does he has to do it 'right'. I listened and accepted his bravado.

Ray then went on to tell Howard that 'We've all got to pull our weight'. He began to accuse Howard of not organizing things as they should be and say that he was already messing things up. 'Have you rung up everyone about this evening?' 'Have you rung up Paul?' Finally he accused Howard of being in this for the wrong reasons – for his own self-adulation. Howard denied this angrily.

Frank and his new girl-friend and Paul arrived. They were excited about the play and a new discussion of it began. Ray started again. The part he wanted to play was that of a drummer. He began to theorize about acting, of absorbing himself into the part, like Brando, and of being able to say just 'yes' in a million different ways. He said that he would buy a £120 drum kit and practise all night. Ray will be the most difficult person to help accept reality. It is doubtful whether he will accept rebuff or understand criticism. . . .

The idea began to take shape, but the members remained uncertain. Throughout January, to cover their fear of inadequacy, they repeatedly invented wild fantasies of the final glory. This was a characteristic reaction – high aspirations without the ability to apply themselves to realistic details. As a result the worker was forced to take a very positive role more quickly than anticipated. While he took part in the discussions about things to be done, he made a point of getting on with the work – arranging play readings, finding a rehearsal hall, arranging rehearsal times, inquiring about royalties. It was necessary that the worker should show that he was capable and able to lead. The members were clearly unable to organize themselves. They needed a leader and if he should falter so would they. The worker then assumed a very directive role and, although the group needed this, such an approach was dangerous because of the known intolerance of the members to any form of imposed discipline. The fact that such a firm approach by the worker was tolerated was due to the relationship he already had with the members. For example, during one rehearsal, which was held in a church hall, Howard accidentally spilt some beer on the floor. There was at first amusement and Howard seemed unconcerned. The worker decided to use this incident to establish a standard with reference to the use of rehearsal rooms. He shouted at Howard for being so careless. Everyone fell quiet. The worker briefly explained his point and then quickly carried on the rehearsal. The moment passed, but was forceful and effective.

The worker tried to interfere very little in the casting for the play, leaving Howard to choose people whom he, Paul, Andy, and Frank considered acceptable and talented. Of the eight characters, the three leading roles were filled by Howard, Paul, and Frank, who were involved in the idea from the very beginning. Howard was quite clearly the leading member and it was through him that the worker did much of his communicating to the group. Once Ray had been included, they only needed three girls to complete the cast. The group hadn't much enthusiasm for any of the girls they knew. Girls were generally thought of as peripheral and insufficiently positive for an active role in the life of the group.

Karen, aged sixteen, was the first girl to become part of the cast. She typed copies for the production and acted in the first set of rehearsals. At this time she spent a great deal of time at Howard and Frank's flat. Outwardly a very affectionate girl, she was also rather hysterical and seemingly in need of constant attention from the group. She did a lot of cooking and cleaning in the flat and to some extent was generous sexually. Easy to exploit, she became an object of contempt. Nor was her acting immediately adequate and the group became increasingly hostile. Eventually Karen told the worker that because of personal matters she would rather not carry on. He was reluctant to let her go but could see no alternative as there was little he could do to alter the attitude of the group at this time.

The group found a replacement in Celia. This was largely due to the worker's influence. She was one of the most attractive and lively girls in the 'mass', aged fifteen and currently taking a secretarial course. Like Karen she was not very popular with the group, who considered her rather 'mad' and inaccurately labelled her a 'nymphomaniac'. The worker's idea to include her in the cast was initially rejected by Howard and the others. Nevertheless and although he himself privately thought Celia quite eccentric, he judged her to have acting ability and quite strongly urged her inclusion. Eventually, after some reluctance which seemed general towards any girl that was mentioned, Celia was invited along. She proved to be so good at acting

that despite everything she was accepted for the whole production.

Three weeks later it became necessary to cast the second
female part, a childlike and innocent character. None of the
group thought they knew of any suitable girl. Then Paul suddenly arrived with Sally, a girl from the art institute, who fitted
the description. Paul had only known her a few weeks and there
was nobody she knew in the group. She was sixteen and at first
undecided whether to commit herself. The group however was
keen to include her. In turn Sally found the new company
attractive and she accepted the part. She attended regularly and
had a succession of affairs with Ray, Howard, Paul, and Frank,
which ended in disturbing the atmosphere of the rehearsals.
She also took charge of and ran the make-up department
efficiently.

It then became urgent to cast the third female part, one of the
most difficult and most important. The worker explained to
Howard that what was needed was someone 'big with long hair'.
With this crude specification in mind, Howard searched around
in the 'mass' and eventually brought Nina to rehearsals. She was
vaguely familiar to the group through parties. At first she was
very uncertain. She looked right, but the group increasingly felt
her acting was not to their standard and there was talk of finding somebody else. The worker disagreed. He felt that Nina was
keen and would develop ability during rehearsals. Once again
he intervened and his assessment of her acting ability was subsequently proved correct. Although not quite so sophisticated
and subtle as others in the group Nina was attractive, pleasant,
and fun-loving and gradually she became an accepted and
familiar part of the group.

In this way the cast was decided. Its formation had depended
largely on the preferences of the group, except when these con-
flicted with the worker's concern for the success of the play. He
had decided that this must receive priority since the group
would never get started again if the production failed. Similarly,
during this first play, he was not prepared to test the enthusiasm
of the group by demanding money towards the costs. He personally took on the financial backing of the production but did
not publicize the fact. To have done so might have given the

group the impression that he was doing it a favour. This might have involved feelings of indebtedness and obligation which would have been resented, and there was the added danger that the worker would lose the respect of the group if he were to appear so easy to exploit. As it was, none of the members had much money, nor was the matter raised very frequently or realistically. Generally they seemed to expect the worker to put up the capital. Many of the bills were clearly beyond their reach, but they were nevertheless sympathetic to occasional reminders of the importance of clearing costs. To some extent this was because they liked the prospect of making a profit once the costs had been cleared.

The general reaction of the group to the idea of producing the play had been enthusiastic, but it was natural, in view of the past history of individual members, that the rehearsals would be fraught with difficulties and problems. Early on there was a period of routine rehearsing spent in establishing the moves of the play. There were no spotlights, and the production appeared raw and angular and success remote. Whenever difficulties arose the whole production looked as if it would crumble and the members became extremely pessimistic. At such times the worker clearly showed that he believed the difficulties could be overcome. At others the group's underlying hope for success and exuberant interest came through. For example, the difficulties in finding rehearsal rooms were overcome by the group's deter- mination to rehearse anywhere – church halls, a youth centre, school classrooms, and even in the open air one very cold even- ing, by the glare of two car headlamps.

While remaining the moving spirit of the production, the worker was careful to ensure that his manner was quiet, pleas- ant, unassuming, and always casual. In many ways the play needed 'just to happen': too purposeful a driving force would have caused it to collapse, because everyone would have been too self-conscious. The worker therefore had to steer a middle path between being too careless, passive, and lacking in control over things, and being rigid, bossy, or aggressive. Although he made a detailed plan for each evening and generally managed to keep to it, he deliberately allowed for periodic breaks, for half an hour in the pub, and for people being a little late. He did not nag at people who were talking, laughing, or drawing on the blackboard, as long as the rehearsal was not seriously disturbed. Essentially it was a permissive atmosphere in which the worker persevered with the rehearsal plan, which everyone usually followed. Occasionally, if the group forgot its purpose and played about too much, it was necessary to do more than exude tolerance. Then the worker showed impatience, 'blew his top', and declared that they might as well stop if nobody was going to concentrate properly. Such outbursts, because infrequent, made the point and the group got on with rehearsing.

Most of the organization was left to the worker, particularly during the early stages. None of the members knew much about drama, nor indeed did they have a great deal of belief that the play would succeed. Later, however, as the success of the project was becoming more apparent and the performance dates were drawing near, the group took a much more active interest. The worker tried as much as possible to encourage this and to support any ideas that the cast spontaneously brought up. On several occasions, he deliberately presented the group with particular problems and waited for the reaction, problems such as the name of the group, the venue of the production, the number of performances, and the behaviour of Frank.

At the outset Frank was greatly enthusiastic, but gradually it emerged that the necessity to practise continuously in rehearsals was a discipline he found too difficult to accept. For the first month he pursued an idea of forming a jazz combo and seemed unprepared to accept the fact that its formation would seriously conflict with the play. The worker bluntly presented him with a choice and Frank chose the play. In February, however, he took a job which required him to work for a part of the week on evening shifts. Since he had been out of work for some time this was a good thing, but his inability to organize his time meant that he was either late for rehearsals or failed to attend at all. This was very inconvenient, particularly because Frank had a large and indispensable part in the play. Despite his general popularity the group was unamused and gradually lost sympathy with him. Frank's enjoyment also decreased. He lost the pages of his script, was restless at rehearsals, and continued to be late or absent. The worker first tried a patient, then a more irritated approach, both with no more than initial success. One month before the performance itself Frank was obviously finding the activity and the worker too demanding, and the cast too unsympathetic to derive much pleasure from the play. Still he did not leave, and it got to be a matter of choice between his continued inclusion or the success of the production. The worker consulted the cast, and it was reluctantly decided that although Frank was known and liked it would be better to find a replacement. Therefore at a rehearsal, in the presence of the cast, the worker gave Frank the option of attending regularly or leaving. It was unpleasant but necessary. It may also have been a valuable group experience. Frank chose to leave, giving as his reason that he could not do two things at the same time, work and play. Since he left his job about a week later, it was clear however that he had already lost real interest in the play. Nevertheless, despite this, he took a strong and unashamed interest in the group after the successful public performances three weeks later. He was very keen to be involved in the next production.

Meanwhile, with less than three weeks to go, the group was left without one of its leading actors. Fortunately Kevin had become involved in the production when Paul and Sally had asked him to design a poster for publicity. At the time of Frank's defection, the worker joined Kevin for a drink in a pub one evening. Instead of talking about posters, which they had met to discuss, Kevin began guardedly to talk about the production generally. It transpired he knew when the next rehearsal was and intended coming along, and it ended with his taking over Frank's part. His status was high in the group because of his age (nineteen), his clothes (which were immaculate and very much in vogue), and his casual, rather enigmatic manner. Accepted by the group and perfect in the part, he was the ideal solution.

By the last few weeks of rehearsing, with completion in sight, the group began a great drive to ensure success. Andy, who had been pessimistic, aloof, and sceptical, grew interested in publicizing the play. With the help of Nina, Paul, and Howard, he carried out a door-to-door ticket-sales drive. The group pestered local journalists so that there were articles in local newspapers, and posters appeared everywhere in town. The members had suggested these themselves, but wild suggestions were frequently being thrown out and there was a tendency to avoid details. It was only when the worker was insistent, making it clear that he wanted to get his money back, that anything was carried through. When the group did start, it became keen, and put ideas into action without any further prodding.

Finally the play was presented on three evenings in a public hall in Seagate. About seven hundred people – mostly under the age of twenty-one – attended, and a profit of under £10 was made after the total costs were covered. After the weeks of rehearsing – it had been laborious at times – and stimulated by an audience, the cast sprang suddenly and remarkably into life. They put everything into it and were literally hoarse at the end. The most frequent comment made by the audience afterwards was that the whole thing was 'too loud' – a fair but welcome criticism.

Without doubt the project had proved a success. 'Best bit of theatre for years', 'Remarkable', 'Brilliant' were some of the Press comments. Someone quite unknown to the group even wrote a letter to the local newspaper arguing that 'there was nothing wrong with young people today', having just seen the production. Finally parents of the cast expressed approval, particularly meaningful for Howard, Roger, Andy, Nina, and Celia. None of the parents claimed to understand the play, but as Howard's mother said: 'At last he's done something.' For the group, this apparently genuine acclaim was unprecedented and surprising. Many of the groups that were part of the 'mass' were also complimentary. They never thought that the group could 'get down to it'.

The drama activity was of value to the group in a number of different, though related ways. It gave a sense of achievement and a feeling of self-confidence to those that took part. This was especially valuable in the context of previous histories of failure. In particular, the fact of accomplishment was an assertion and demonstration of the group's worth *vis-à-vis* parents and other groups. It provided a means of expression and an opportunity to develop latent talents, important in view of the considerable potential which had been repressed by insecurity and a fear of

commitment. Then it established a relatively structured existence, giving a sense of order and security to what was formerly a
chaotic and timeless atmosphere. There was an element of
discipline, not overbearing but just sufficient to 'catch on to'
(Howard). Moreover, it was an experience of learning tolerance
in a group setting and of working together constructively.

It was no accident that the worker chose a play with a small
cast and one in which all the characters were closely integrated
into the action of the play. It meant that everyone was needed
at every rehearsal and each member was closely involved and
very much a part of the whole development. The sense of
belonging to a defined group was all the more pronounced. The
group had a name, an identity, and it became exclusive. Under
these special circumstances this was not a narrowing experience.
It was necessary in order to give the group a growing feeling of
pride and confidence. The security afforded by the smallness of
the group and the attitude of the worker enabled the individuals
to face up to some of the problems and frustrations that arose,
instead of pursuing their more usual course of withdrawing
from the issue. It was clear the group had much more to learn,
but at least this production was a beginning. For some of the
cast the play was a demonstration of the idea that personal
satisfaction was more important than the acquisition of money.
Eight pounds profit was negligible in relation to initial high
hopes, and yet there was little real disappointment. Other things
had mattered a good deal more.

Finally, putting on a play helped to bridge the gap between
this group and the adult world. Members realized the fairness in
paying royalties and paying for the hall. To some extent they
were conscious that they depended on public support. For the
first time, they had also won adult approval.

During the course of this first production the worker had not
been keen to make any move towards using the Youth Service
facilities because of the probable adverse reaction of the group.
However he discussed the possibility with the Organizing Secretary of the local Association of Youth Clubs. She mentioned the
Seagate Youth Drama Festival and the possibility of the County
Youth Drama Festival. The worker decided to sound out the
group and was surprised to find they were quite interested.

Despite a few sarcastic remarks about youth clubs, the thought of participating in the County Festival was absorbing. The group seemed a little incredulous that they should be allowed to apply.

The group accordingly rehearsed the second act of its play for the Seagate Festival. On the day of the Festival it transpired unfortunately that while the group could perform it was ineligible to compete because it was not affiliated to the appropriate local Youth Association. This was contrary to what the group had been told. The Youth Officer admitted this and apologized. The group performed and was judged by many to be the best of the evening. Needless to say the cast was bitterly disappointed at not being allowed to compete and the worker had difficulty convincing everyone that they were not being victimized because they were 'beatniks'. The whole question of affiliation was raised and the worker did his best to explain its purpose. The disappointment, however, had clearly added fuel to the group's antipathy towards authority and the worker felt the issue ought to be left for a while.

The unqualified success of the play led to immediate demands by the group for another and the worker suggested a similar type of production with plenty of scope again for spontaneity, singing, and dancing, but which would involve many more people. Howard and Andy took on responsibility for recruiting the large cast, distributing copies of the play, and notifying people of rehearsals. These two and to a lesser extent Paul and Kevin allocated themselves the four most important parts and accepted without question the inclusion of the remainder of the original group – Nina, Ray, Celia, Sally, and Frank. Considering the many tensions and bickerings that had characterized the rehearsals for the first play, this in itself was an indication of how group solidarity had been strengthened. The remaining fifteen people needed to make up the cast were recruited from the 'mass' which by now was eager to join the drama group. They were chosen, however, not only for their acting ability but also for their social status in the eyes of the nucleus group.

During the month or so it took to recruit the cast, the worker mentioned from time to time the advantages of affiliating to the local Youth Association. Rather reluctantly the group decided to apply. The official application form proved impossible to complete and the final application was made by letter in which it was argued that the group had never found it necessary to draw up a constitution nor officially appoint officers and a committee. The work of the group had been done efficiently and enthusiastically without the aid and support of such a structure. The letter went on to state that the group was a spontaneous and flexible one and that the element of formality implied by the form was contrary to the spirit of the group. As a result the Local Education Authority granted the group 'temporary affiliation', 'full affiliation' being subject to a probationary period of six months if the Youth Officer, having seen the group in action, found it to be acceptable. The principal motive in applying for affiliation was the purely selfish one of being able to enter competitions and use the L.E.A. equipment. The worker knew this but encouraged the group to become affiliated in the hope that if it became aware of the Youth Service and used some of its facilities without unnecessary interference or encroachment, a more positive attitude towards officialdom might ensue. This eventually happened, but initially the group was deeply suspicious and most unenthusiastic.

Rehearsals for the new play began in the early summer of 1962, but did not fully get under way until the autumn, when everyone had returned from the holidays. It was the worker's intention this time to delegate responsibility to a much greater extent than in the first play, to help individuals develop a capacity for leadership and to lessen the group's dependency on an outside adult. In the event the large cast of twenty-four actors and the problem of merging the original nucleus with the newer members into one effective unit proved so demanding that the worker was forced to resume his more directive role. The original members particularly missed the more intimate atmosphere of the first production and resented the additional people, occasionally implying that they were not talented or enthusiastic enough. The mood of each rehearsal varied enormously and depended very much on the attitude of the nucleus group, which tended to be critical of the rate of progress, as they were anxious to achieve high standards and repeat their success. Immediately before the three public performances in the late autumn, the shortage of time and the news that tickets were selling slowly depressed everyone. The worker concentrated on reassuring them and held a rehearsal in the theatre itself which heightened the sense of excitement. He also arranged for a short regional TV filming. In addition, with the increased sense of urgency due to the fact that time was running out, there was no lack of opportunities for everyone to become involved in all the other aspects of the production. Kevin, helped by Les, undertook the major task of constructing the sets. Andy resumed his publicity duties and with Howard's help arranged advertisements and articles in the local Press, distributed posters, and took over the house management, including the recruitment of usherettes. Nina found she did not have enough time to collect props because of work and Howard took over this with the help of Frank and his motor-cycle. The more marginal members also took on some responsibilities. However the final week brought problems and mixed feelings. The scenery was not properly finished, the lighting was imperfect, and the stage management was unpractised. As a result, the first night was virtually a dress rehearsal and was not considered a success by the cast. Morale was extremely low for the second evening although the televising of the film as a local news item before the start of the performance was slightly reassuring and the second performance was far more accomplished. The last night was even more successful. However, judged by the first production the cast was far from exuberant. Further, although over six hundred people had attended, it became clear, when all the ticket sales had been accounted for, that somebody must have embezzled about £20–£30. This was particularly unfortunate, since it gave rise to a rather uneasy mood of suspicion within the group. Despite its resentment at having been cheated of a due financial reward, however, the group generally seemed embarrassed at being associated with such a theft and silently disinclined to pursue the question of culpability.

The play was adjudicated for the County Drama Festival on the second public performance. The adjudicator was critical yet complimentary and in general most of the group accepted his comments. Later, when the final result was given for the county, the group found that it had been placed third out of fifteen adult entries.

After the usual round of celebrations the original group began impatiently to demand another production. In the meantime a small drama society in Seagate had become interested in the group and the possibility of a joint production was discussed. It was discovered, however, that the drama society was dedicated and intellectual; this attitude was unacceptable. The group valued drama less as an art form and more as an opportunity for achievement and pure enjoyment. Howard did go as far as attending one or two rehearsals of the drama society, but found the atmosphere so sombre, long-haired, and tedious that he quickly left. He also disliked what he considered to be the producer's paternalistic approach.

Everyone was anxious that the group's next production should involve a much smaller cast. The worker knew that he would be leaving Seagate during the next year and that the group was not yet experienced or mature enough to function without his leadership. The aims of the group and the aims of the worker became focused together in a series of one-act plays. In these the worker encouraged Howard and especially Paul to take on the responsibility for producing, and after some initial uncertainty they achieved it. Once again public performances were successful. Howard and Liz were awarded cups as the best actor and actress in Youth Festival performances and the group was placed first.

There could be no doubt that the original group of 'layabouts' had proved themselves highly skilled and successful in their venture into amateur dramatics. But what improvements had been taking place in the general way of life of the group and in the behaviour and attitudes of individual members? Because the group had become proficient and accomplished in this one activity of amateur dramatics it could not automatically be assumed that the whole way of life of the group would necessarily have changed. There were many indications that it had not. For example, while the one-act plays mentioned earlier were being rehearsed one of the group was placed on probation for three years for stealing electrical equipment worth over £300. Other members were at various times found guilty of driving vehicles without a licence, petty thieving, and avoiding payment of rail fares. Mark continued to bet regularly and Andy recklessly. The periods between drama productions were usually spent as indolently as before in jazz clubs and coffee bars, and the members continued periodically to be thrown out of them. Strained relationships with parents continued in many cases and only a few individuals settled into a regular job. In spite of this there were some definite indications of improvement which could be traced back to the worker's influence.

One of the most obvious was a perceptible change in attitude towards some adults in the Youth Service, which had been brought about by meeting them frequently at the various Youth Drama Festivals. It wasn't that there was any greater acceptance of the Youth Service so much as that some individuals grew to like and respect a few local voluntary or statutory youth officers sufficiently to be able to approach them for advice. Generally at the Drama Festivals the group was impatient at having to compete with young people and being subjected to officious supervision. They tended to remain aloof and unidentified with the festivals which had been designed for 'youth'. The word itself was much disliked. In their minds it connoted a strong feeling of paternalism which was profoundly resented because it offended against the group's feeling of maturity and adulthood. The Youth Service, as far as the Drama Festivals were concerned, did not, in fact, properly accommodate a group of young people whose usual habitat was the 'teen adult' world of the coffee bar and jazz club. The group was part of a pseudo-adult class of young people whose presence in the less sophisticated and younger setting of the Drama Festivals was incongruous. But the group were able to like and respect the 'right' kind of adults in the Youth Service that they met there, the kind of adults who were talented and had something relevant to offer, and who were genuinely willing to assist or advise without a hint of paternalism or ostentatious concern for 'youth'. Before the worker's arrival in Seagate even this much of acceptance of anyone connected with 'youth' would have been most improbable, if for no other reason than that the group would have been unlikely to come into contact with the Service.

A most striking indication of this changing attitude towards some youth officials was the worker's success in persuading the group to take part in a residential film-making week-end organized by the local Association of Youth Clubs. To start with the group was amused and suspicious at the idea; but film-making sounded fun and the week-end promised to be a new experience, even if it did mean early bed on a Saturday night. At first also there were strong fears of 'being directed', of being surreptitiously introduced to 'religion', and of having to mingle with a 'hearty' crowd of young people. By the end of the first evening, however, none of these fears had been realized. A task had been set of creating a film script that was to be ready for shooting the next day. The group was allowed to remain intact, and complete freedom was allowed in the choice of subject matter and treatment. The process of working out the script proved to be arduous and stimulating and one that required the group to stay up till late into the night. The fact that there was no stipulation about bed times was very much appreciated. What was clear to the group at the end of the first day was the absence of any unnecessary restriction or oppressive organization. They recognized they were receiving positive encouragement to create and do something which they valued, and to do it by themselves and with considerable freedom. They came to see that adulthood – as exemplified by the leaders – could be genuinely helpful rather than restraining. This was particularly true of the two organizers. The group found them very sympathetic to its ideas as well as encouraging, unrestrictive, and uncondescending. It was also true of one of the tutors, whose artistic sense, knowledge, intelligence, subtle humour, keen enthusiasm, and understanding of what the group was trying impressed them. In complete contrast, the other tutor was considered embarrassing. Despite his obvious affection for young people it was quite evident that he was very much out of touch with this particular group. He was considered unimaginative, unsophisticated, and patronizing – 'God bless you, I've done this for twenty-five years'; 'I know what you young people are today'. Moreover they found it aggravating when he spent a lot of time simplifying relatively minor points.

By the end of the week-end the group had found film-making stimulating and exhilarating. Other young people on the course were completely disregarded and the conventional ideas they chose for filming were considered pathetic. The group's attitude towards the leaders on the course had changed from an initial distant politeness to varying degrees of liking and respect. The contact with the organizers was maintained after the week-end with the viewing and editing of the film at the local Association offices. An indication of the energy spent and the fun enjoyed was given by Nina and Paul when they commented, after the course, that they felt as if they had just returned home from an all-night party.

It could be seen then that the group did show some change in attitude towards adults during the three years of the project. There were also some marked improvements in the future outlook of most of the individuals in the group. It was still too early by the end of the project to predict how long such improvement were likely to last but there were many encouraging signs. After the first two drama productions, about nine months before the end of the project, it was already becoming obvious that many of the group were outgrowing it and anxious to widen their friendships and interests beyond it. Shortly before the project ended five of the group left Seagate to work or study in London.

Perhaps Howard had changed the most noticeably of all. He gained admission to a well-known college of dramatic art in Edinburgh. When the worker had first met the group Howard had been the leader more from the popularity his extreme 'bum-like' behaviour gained him than because of any particular wisdom or good sense. After his successes in the first two plays this role began to chafe him. He had proved that he was capable of achievement and he was growing tired of leading an aimless existence. The group's idea of him was slower to change. His suggestions for the plays were often derided by Paul and Andy and his first tentative thoughts of applying for admission to a drama school were greeted with giggles of disbelief by Frank. In a group situation such as this the worker had simultaneously to protect Howard from the ridicule of his friends and privately offer him what encouragement he could. Without this support Howard probably would have dropped the idea of going to a drama school. Howard had become very attached to Nina after the first play, and she confided in the worker that Howard valued talking to him. He was able to be natural and frank with him without risk of the typical group response of ridicule or a rebuff and as a result she felt the worker could be influential in persuading Howard to apply for drama school.

Through her affection, support, and encouragement, Nina was also a very good influence on Howard. One instance was when the worker suggested to Howard that he meet one of the L.E.A. youth officers (whom Howard had often met in connexion with the Drama Festival) in order to discuss the college prospects. Howard ridiculed the idea until Nina told him 'not to be so silly'. This reassured him sufficiently to consult the Youth Officer about suitable colleges of dramatic art to which he could apply and the possibility of an L.E.A. grant; later he sought his advice regarding test pieces to read for an audition. In spite of his more constructive attitude towards the future, Howard was usually unemployed throughout this time. He periodically took jobs, but for long periods lived on an allowance of five shillings a day from his mother. This was apparently sufficient to make him not bother about getting a job and the only time he did work was when his mother pressed him to do so. It usually lasted for two or three weeks. There was no radical or even marked change in his social values. He still believed the acquisition of money was the most important aim in life – despite his reluctance to work. He saw nothing very wrong in relieving the fruit machine in a coffee bar of £2 when the machine broke down or in keeping a purseful of money he found on a seat there, and he was still occasionally thrown out of coffee bars for rowdy behaviour. But the days of 'extreme' living were over. At a party where most of the guests belonged to the 'Young-Conservative type' of university students and young office workers, the worker noticed that Howard was accepted within this group and acclaimed for his recent acting performances. He was no longer expected to behave extremely or cause a disturbance. He was respected and his attitude had significantly changed.

None of the other individuals showed as great a change. However, most seemed to have benefited by knowing the worker, if only in the sense that their behaviour did not deteriorate still further as could easily have been the case had the worker not been available. Nina, for instance, frequently consulted the worker about personal problems, including family relationships, work, and her feelings about Howard. Like him she appeared to regard the worker as a young father figure. In the context of the attitudes and opinions of the nucleus group, Nina frequently became dubious of the value of chastity before marriage. The pressure to conform must have been considerable, and the worker often found himself alleviating her anxieties by giving her support for what she believed to be right and assurance that her problem was by no means unique. Nina also had difficulty in deciding on a job and was unemployed for considerable periods. Her ambition was to become an air hostess but she could not apply until she was twenty-one. Meanwhile she was unsettled and drifted into menial, unsatisfying work. Shortly before the worker left Seagate Nina left also to model clothes for a firm in London.

Paul W. also showed a decrease in anti-social tendencies during the three years. In 1961 he was planning with Howard to break into a store; by the end of the project he openly disapproved of Andy's attempts at crime. In all of the drama productions he was extremely enthusiastic, hardworking, and very imaginative. His achievements made him visibly more confident and proved even to his father that he was not a complete 'waste'. His personal characteristics of independence, detachment, and discrimination became increasingly pronounced. He remained one of the most influential members within the group, but outside his circle of friends widened. By the time the worker left Seagate in 1963 he doubted if Paul would keep in close contact with the others of the group. He no longer had any need of a close, exclusive friendship.

Andy's anti-social behaviour had shown no decrease during the project. But there were encouraging signs. The way in which he accepted the worker's authority and guidance in the plays was hopeful, as it showed he could accept authority, and his response to the worker's encouragement contrasted strikingly with his indifference at home. A gradual realization of the pointlessness of his way of life was dawning on him and partly as a reflection of this he, like Paul, was slowly dissociating himself from the group and developing a more purposeful attitude towards future work. By 1963 and with the help of his parents, he was applying for jobs in which he was particularly interested. During the drama productions, he had become more confident of his abilities in acting and organization and he began to look for jobs in theatre publicity, advertising, public relations, and film processing. He finally took a suitable job in one of these fields in London.

There was very little outstanding in the behaviour of Celia and Sally, though the latter had tended to become more stable in her work. Both were apt to treat the worker as a father figure and hold confidential discussions with him.

It would be impossible to give detailed accounts of the development of all the individuals, but it is hoped that that which has been outlined gives some indication of the way in which the worker was trying to help. In addition, there was one other important respect in which the worker tried constantly to help. It had become clear that nearly all the members of the drama group suffered a social isolation from the community as a whole. Consequently the worker was always looking for ways in which the group might be drawn into a closer relationship with local adults. Some account of how the worker tried to do this has already been given with the descriptions of the group's involvement in the local Youth Drama Festivals and its attendance at the film-making week-end organized by the local Association of Youth Clubs. In both of these cases, as in all cases where outside adults and the unattached were brought into harmonious contact, success was largely dependent on the extent to which the worker fulfilled a dual role. On the one hand the worker needed to find adults with an attitude sufficiently tolerant and understanding to accept the group for what it was without wishing to impose change or insist on conformity to narrowly defined standards just for the sake of it. On the other hand the worker had to help the members overcome the prejudiced attitude which caused them to dismiss most adults, within or outside the Youth Service, as officious, patronizing, or hypocritical. As a result the occasions when outside adults could be introduced into the group had to be selected with the greatest care. The worker invariably spent considerable time with the group pre-

paring them for such meetings, and again afterwards, interpreting to them why some adults may have behaved as they did
or trying to clear up any residue of hostile feeling aroused by
particularly dogmatic or unsympathetic individuals. The bitter-
ness of the group towards the Youth Service when it was not
allowed to compete in the Drama Festival is one example of an
attitude which had to be overcome before the question of affiliation could be raised again. Similarly, unless the local Area Youth
Association had been liberal-minded and able to agree that there
were good reasons why this group need not conform to the usual
standards of affiliation, no immediate progress would have been
possible. In this instance, the function of the worker was clearly
one of interpretation and mediation between the official Youth
Service and the unattached.

Apart from these attempts at closer association with the statutory and voluntary Youth Services, the worker encouraged other,
less formal contacts with other drama groups in Seagate in the
hope that some of the unattached would become members.
Sometimes such contacts did not work out, as in the case of
Howard's experience with the drama society which has already
been described. At other times, the outcome seemed more hopeful. One of the most interesting possibilities arose in February
1963. By this time the group was aware that the worker would
be leaving Seagate within less than six months. The occasion
was another Drama Festival where the performance of the group
had caught the attention of the producer of a private repertory
company in Seagate. The producer, Don Elliott, became interested in recruiting some of the members for his own company.
Howard was offered a leading role; Andy and another member
were offered smaller parts. All three accepted, and Nina accompanied Howard to rehearsals to support him. Their participation in the production was good, but the comparisons which
were inevitably made between Elliott's and the worker's direction were revealing and highly relevant to the whole problem
of transferring the group's relationship with the worker to an
outside adult.

In general they found Elliott to be amusing and pleasing, not
ostentatious or officious and 'pretty good' at producing. They all
seemed to respect his ability and felt associated with a worthwhile

production. However, when I suggested that he would be a good producer to introduce to the group in the future, they seemed not immediately enthusiastic. In part, I think this was because of their tacit acceptance that I was 'the boss' (Nina's term) and that the advent of an 'outsider' would break the general character and feeling of the group. I was the person whom they knew and on whom they had always depended for leadership, and because of this the introduction of any other producer was almost a threat to the identity of the group. As Nina explained, she was 'used to' me and felt that I was 'one of us' although 'adult' enough at the same time to tell them what to do – an unusual kind of adaptable person, whereas Elliott would be 'just an adult'. Similarly, Andy was dubious and didn't think that Elliott would be 'strong enough' to cope with 'all the bums' in the group – he quoted the frequent lateness and absence of Frank in the past. Nina too seemed to think that Elliott was too docile; she wanted more 'life' and bursts of temper at rehearsals that made them more exciting. These objections, however, were largely a reflection of the group's dependency on myself and I felt that basically Elliott would be acceptable, especially when I am no longer in the area. Before then, I think there would be a feeling in the group of my almost rejecting it.

Following this participation by three of the drama group in the repertory company's production, the company offered to present the entire group in its theatre, contributing whatever financial and technical help was necessary.

The actual performances were very successful and members of the repertory company were enthusiastic, judging the production on adult standards. However, even these generous adults did not seem to have realized the true nature of the drama group. In the advance publicity circulated by the repertory company was a short note describing the group. It stressed the group's vitality, its enthusiasm for drama, and its dedication to the theatre. This was the kind of impression the group gave to most adults interested in the theatre. But it was a romanticized impression, misinterpreting the reality of the situation. Far from being dedicated to the theatre, most of the members were principally attracted by the social activity itself and the sense of fun, purpose, and excitement which it gave. This distinction seems particularly important to note in connexion with the leadership of drama with a group of young people of this kind.

Meanwhile, it says much for the tolerance of the repertory company that the group's production went on at all. Many of the company's members were surprised by the chaos at rehearsals – the fact that parts were not learned properly until the last few days, that members of the cast rarely seemed to discuss the play or interpretations of their characters. In fact the company members were baffled that such a heedless crowd of young people should eventually be able to perform in a way that was satisfying. The wild jiving party on stage on the last night was symptomatic of the drama group – spontaneous, full of fun and movement. It was in complete contrast to the far more talkative and committed last nights that were customary with the company when there was usually earnest discussion about the play.

The attitude of the drama group towards the company's members is worth noting. In the main, it was distant and almost defiant against the theatrically-conscious, adult, rather pompous and respectable atmosphere of the company. The whole tone of the latter, especially in age and outlook, was quite different from that of the drama group. This did not mean that there was no contact at all. Indeed, both sides were apparently friendly. Perhaps the situation was most vividly expressed during the final-night party. One of the leading members of the company called for a close to the evening, walking into the midst of a rather phrenetic crowd of dancing and yelling youths and addressing them in a very refined voice as 'Ladies and Gentlemen'.

For many of the group, this production was to be the last. Howard, Andy, Paul, Nina, and two or three others intended to leave Seagate. For them the drama group had served its purpose and its dispersal was a healthy sign of maturation. But for those who remained, such as Kevin, Frank, Ray, and Sally, the prospect of the drama activity coming to an end was disappointing and frustrating. The one member whose leadership and direction would have been acceptable to all the others was Paul, whom the worker had encouraged as an assistant producer. Unfortunately he was leaving Seagate.

The worker spent considerable time without success investigating the possibility of some other adult person in Seagate taking over. Don Elliott seemed the most suitable but when the worker approached him, although attracted to the idea, he felt that his numerous commitments would not allow him enough time to spend in working intensively on a production with the group. The drama prospects for those of the original group who were remaining in Seagate did not seem good but were not without hope. There was a very strong wish amongst these members to continue the activity in some way and Kevin certainly had the ability to lead a production although he had so far refused to commit himself. However, Kevin's undoubted affection for drama, the worker felt, would sooner or later move him to make the effort. Before the worker left Seagate, he completed a number of arrangements, mainly with Tony, a member who had taken part in the last two or three productions, to keep contact between the group and local agencies, namely, the local Association of Youth Clubs, the Local Education Authority, and the Area Youth Drama Association. All of these agencies were interested in the future of the group; they knew of its history, nature, and way of life and would encourage it whenever possible. Tony readily agreed to have his address given to these agencies and was quite attracted with the idea of acting as a kind of secretary for the group. Through him the group would at least be aware of possibilities in the area. Then the repertory company sent members of the group invitations to attend readings for the next season's programme, making it clear that it was very interested to include some of the group in its own productions.

Some links of a tentative rather than definite nature were therefore established between the group and some agencies in the local community. It might be useful at this point to consider how the service might have continued had there been the opportunity. It is important to remember that the drama group was only part of a much wider group of young people who frequented the coffee bars and other meeting places in the centre of Seagate. Although the size and composition of the cast for each production varied considerably according to the play, there was never any problem in casting since there was always an enthusiastic fringe waiting to be included. It was certain that in this larger crowd there were a great many young people who were intelligent and talented and yet who were rebellious and unwilling to conform to the normal approaches of the youth service. Had the worker or some other detached worker remained with the drama group in Seagate it is conceivable that, while the membership of the group would vary as young people became attached to it, developed some of their potential within it, and then left, the actual entity of the group itself could have continued indefinitely. To some extent this may still happen if Kevin is successful in attempting another production and Tony obtains financial and other support from sympathetic yet distant agencies.

These attempts to strengthen the links between the drama group and the local community were made easier by the fact that the nature and purpose of the worker's job were known to some of the officers of the local statutory and voluntary youth organizations, most of whom were sympathetic to his aims and extremely generous in their willingness to help. In most other aspects of working with the community, the worker felt hampered by the lack of a clear identity. Particularly with parents. Strained parent–child relationships were characteristic of the unattached in all areas and anything that could be done to improve the situation would be of importance.

It was perhaps inevitable that on a project which set out to investigate young people, more knowledge should have been gained about the attitude of the unattached towards their parents than vice versa. Much factual information about home circumstances and parental relationships was gained and it is known that many of the unattached felt their parents to be unreasonable and harsh. However, there was considerable evidence that parents were often simply confused and bewildered by their offspring, to such an extent that reaction and repression seemed the only course left open to them.

Occasionally, an opportunity arose for the worker to talk with parents and a fairly full description of one such chance encounter in Seagate is included because it demonstrates both the parents' problem and the possibility that a detached worker can help.

I met Brian R.'s father by chance one evening. He recognized me from the play and seemed anxious to talk about Brian. Things had come to a head at home and Brian had decided to leave and live in a flat. Mr and Mrs R. were surprised, concerned, and upset about this and Mr R. wanted to know from me what to do about it.

The impression of Mr R. that I had formed from Brian was that he was a reactionary, physically brutish individual. . . . The impression derived from meeting Mr R. was quite different, although it became clear why there existed such a strong disapproval from Brian. Mr R. started in real poverty and has achieved materialistic success by hard work and perseverance. His standards are staunchly conventional and he naturally fails to understand how any other set of values can be worth while. In particular, he cannot comprehend the arts-college world, 'what it is for' and 'where it will get anybody'.

Mr R. has seen Brian's growth as simply bewildering and has accordingly attempted during the past four or five years to clamp down on it; he has forcibly tried to check Brian and does not deny instances of brutality. The result, however, has been unsuccessful. Mr R. is now aware of this but not clear what to do instead. Added to this lack of understanding is a strong element of irrational stubbornness, shared inherently by father and son, which has served to perpetuate the gap between them.

Brian had now presented a showdown by intending to leave home. Mr R. wanted a happy family and was prepared 'to rethink'. Because of this, he talked to me for about an hour. He considered me as a person who knew his son well and yet who was also approachable in the sense of being responsible and adult.

Briefly, I suggested that there was an immediate need for someone to relinquish his pride and break the deadlock. It was improbable that Brian would give way, and I attempted to show that his behaviour could be explained in terms of adolescent rebellion – which was not as abnormal as Mr R. seemed to think. I suggested that instead of being aggressive and cynical towards Brian's interest in art, it might well be helpful, if possible, for his father to show more sympathy towards what he was doing. . . . I then tried to put the case for the art student so that Mr R. would see that it is not entirely a wasteful way of spending time.

Mr R. seemed to accept much of what I said. Whatever the influence of this meeting, it was pleasing to hear a few days later that Brian no longer intended to leave home. Howard asked 'Why the change?' and Brian replied briefly that his father had altered his attitude.

Mr R. was known to be typical of many parents of the drama group members and there appeared to exist a genuine need for someone to whom the troubled parents of these adolescents could turn for advice. However, not all parents were as prepared as Mr R. to rethink their attitudes. While Andy S. was in prison for theft, the worker met Mr S. at the Court hearing. Mr S.'s apparent lack of concern was most noticeable. He seemed strangely untouched by his son's delinquent behaviour and tended to dismiss it as a rather tiresome and irritating piece of stupidity. He talked to the worker about the architecture of the court-room and expressed more interest in the workings and intricacies of the law than in the condition of his son. After Andy had been remanded on bail, Mr S. briefly arranged fares for Andy to get home and then left. There seemed in this meeting no emotional contact at all. Andy later commented that he thought there was a 'wall' between his father and himself.

Talking with Mr S. about Andy was a very different proposition from talking with Mr R. about Brian. Had the worker viewed consultation with parents as a regular feature of this work, it would have been necessary to reach out to some of them, such as Mr S., in much the same way that it had been necessary to reach out to the unattached. It is of course debatable whether the detached worker, whose primary concern is to offer a service to the unattached, is the most suitable person to work with parents. There are many indications that he is not, since the detached worker is essentially a group worker, making use of group relationships and activities to help individuals. A service to parents, on the other hand, would seem to demand a casework emphasis. However with some parents the need seemed to be simply for an opportunity to talk over their problems with a sympathetic outsider. It is noteworthy that the Seagate worker was in an excellent position to refer parents to other sources of help in the community, had they been available.

2 The Unattached

In accordance with the N.A.Y.C.'s terms of reference, three workers were appointed to contrasting areas of England to make contact with unattached young people, to discover their interests and leisure-time activities and to help subsequently in whatever way seemed appropriate. One of the areas studied was Seagate, and the information and impressions obtained by the worker over three years gives a remarkably detailed picture of some of the unattached and of the troubled, restless lives which many of them were leading. But this book is not only about the unattached and the areas in which they live. It is also concerned with the workers and their difficulties when they tried to approach the unattached in coffee bars, jazz clubs, at parties, in schools, and in factories – their experiences, because of the insight they give about the demands on anyone who undertakes this work, are as valuable as what was learned about the young people themselves.

This book sets out to answer three major questions. Who are the unattached? How can contact be made with them and what are the problems of locating the groups and individuals on their own ground, of getting to know them, and of gaining their confidence? And, what can be done to help these young people, not only by a worker who tries to establish a strong relationship with them, but also by other people and organizations in their neighbourhood?

WHO ARE THE UNATTACHED?

The term 'unattached' has been used in this book to describe those young people who do not belong to any kind of youth organization. Using this definition, every single one of the one hundred and seventy young people with whom the workers of this N.A.Y.C. project developed a close, personal relationship could be classified as 'unattached'. But unattachment is not itself necessarily an acute symptom of social *malaise*, and any youth suffering from it is not necessarily in need of help. It has never been assumed that every 'unattached' young person must, by definition, be 'maladjusted', 'a problem', 'anti-social', nor necessarily even 'difficult', and the workers soon confirmed this. There were those young people who had little time or use for an organized youth service because they were fully capable of filling their leisure time in other constructive ways. Then there were those who rejected their local youth clubs because the services were so inadequate that only the maladjusted could have enjoyed or tolerated them. One could interpret this in a back-handed way as a sign of social and mental health, with the implication that more imaginative youth-club premises, programmes, and leadership would have removed a major source of unattachment. However, the vast majority of unattached youth contacted in Seagate, Northtown, and Midford were in neither category. On all the evidence, they would scorn membership of any kind of organized youth service. But, far from spending their leisure time in any demonstrably constructive fashions, they were manifestly unhappy and frequently delinquent. These were the hard core of the unattached representing the focus of the project.

It is useful to narrow the term 'unattached' to those who do not belong to a youth organization and who are also unhappy and/or delinquent, and unless otherwise stated it will be used in this rather specialized sense. It must not, however, be assumed that young people in this narrowed category shared identical attitudes, problems, or emotional characteristics. Differences will be seen in age (eleven to twenty-five years), social class (professional-middle to lower working class), social value and aspirations, family background, vocational capabilities, and delinquent tendencies. These wide variations make it difficult to generalize about all the youth in all the areas. For example, in each locality it was necessary to discover the social norms for groups and individuals, and then assess deviant behaviour patterns and attitudes in the light of these.

But there were some similarities. After all the information

about the unattached had been collated, it could be seen that their inability to join a youth organization was no more than one expression of a much wider pattern of unstable behaviour. Other expressions of it were to be found in their attitudes towards work, school, leisure, home and family, money values, the opposite sex, and adult authority in general. Much of the unstable pattern seems to be due to frustrations of various origins, which could usually be traced back to a single or a combination of factors. These were emotionally poor home backgrounds; a lack of or poorly developed physical, intellectual, or social skills; some sort of emotional maladjustment. In some cases failure to achieve unrealistic or unattainable goals they had set for themselves or had had set for them caused frustration or boredom. Good examples of these were the aspirations of the Seagate group to become famous writers, artists, and photographers without accepting the need to work gradually towards these goals. In other cases part of the cause for frustration and boredom was the abject social and cultural poverty of the environment. In all cases there was very little ability on the part of any of the unattached to accept responsibility for what was happening to them. They saw themselves as unfortunate victims of circumstance. This, coupled with other factors such as insecurity and ignorance of the possibilities, helped to induce feelings of impotence and a general belief that little could be done to change their lot.

Another characteristic in all areas was a general inability to postpone immediate pleasure for the sake of future gain. It came out in attitudes towards money (saving and spending) and in an inability to undertake training for vocational advancement. With some young people, on the surface at least, 'bumming' had become a recognized, accepted, and valued way of life. But shame and discontent still crept through and there was considerable evidence that this way of life was yet another cover-up for insecurity and fear.

A hand-to-mouth philosophy governed the lives of these youths; leisure-time interests were short-spanned, constantly changing, and interspersed liberally with periods of boredom and apathy; friendships suffered because they were incapable of sustaining any effective feelings of obligation or consideration for others. Small close friendship groups were undoubtedly a necessity; they provided a measure of the support, security, and recognition that they all needed, but the existence of such groups was brief in duration because of this inability to sustain friendships. Another marked characteristic was a craving for adventure: youth clubs were usually rejected as being too tame, and excitement was often sought through delinquency: avoiding payment of rail fares, petty thieving, entering cinemas and dance halls without payment, violation of property, drinking, and experimentation with drugs. Sexual promiscuity may also be included here, but there was evidence that this was as much an attempt to resolve conflicts over personal relationships and sexual roles as it was to satisfy any craving for adventure. A less extreme example of the craving for adventure was a reluctance to spend even a single evening a week at home, or the frantic search for parties. The spontaneity which accompanied all this was an outstanding feature. With the exception of some older coffee-bar youths in Northtown there was very little premeditated delinquency or any planning behind the various escapades.

Finally, the unattached showed pronounced hostility towards adults. This was directed particularly towards adults in authority: parents, teachers, employers, and the police. As a result adult discipline, including parental discipline, was often quite ineffective. There was also the feeling that adults did not understand them. All adults in authority were classed as 'them' – those who were opposed to and against 'us'. The coffee bar's freedom from adult demands and control explained much of its popularity. Conversely, the reluctance to enter a youth club was often a revolt against being organized and being told what to do by someone who was perceived as being a patronizing, interfering, or hostile adult.

This is a generalized picture. Seldom did one individual show all these characteristics. Nevertheless much of the description holds true for a large number, particularly among the older groups in Seagate and Northtown. Age was an important factor affecting the extent to which the attitudes and problems had become crystallized. Many of the symptoms were already visible with the younger groups, but the problems really began to express themselves by about the age of sixteen or seventeen when the novelty of the first job had worn off, work was becoming boring, and the question of adult authority had become particularly acute. Many of the attitudes and feelings voiced by older groups in Northtown and Seagate could be described as cynical or even embittered and it became painfully clear that attempts to attach this type of young person to any of the usual youth clubs would be unlikely to meet with much success.

MAKING CONTACT

When the project was originally conceived none of this information about the unattached had been established. Nor could valid information be gained about them or help of any real or lasting kind be given them unless the workers could find a way to approach them, gain their confidence and trust, and ultimately be accepted by them.

Opportunities for contacting young people within the terms of reference, it was reasoned, could be found at a number of points, classifiable generally into situations of work, school, and leisure. In the work setting contact might be possible either in working alongside the unattached, or in occupying some sympathetic position such as that of a personnel, welfare, or sports officer. In the school setting the only possibility seemed to be the direct approach offered by the teaching role. In the leisure setting the possibilities were as variable as the young person's capacity to devise ways of spending it. Coffee bars, dance halls, cafés, public houses, parks, recreation grounds, and street corners were just a few venues which suggested themselves. In view of the exploratory nature of the project the Central Advisory Committee felt it valuable to investigate as widely as possible all three approaches – work, school, and leisure – to enable an assessment of the relative merits and demerits of each as a practical means of making contact. The test of whether a given means of contact had been successful or not was to lie in the nature and quality of the relationship which developed out of it. A 'successful means of contact' was one which permitted the development of a strong relationship with unattached groups or individuals. A 'strong' relationship in turn was defined as one which was basically characterized by warmth and by holding the trust and confidence of the unattached, in contrast to a 'casual relationship' which permitted no more than a superficial expression of pleasantries or hostility.

Although existing research in this whole field had been extremely limited, both the Advisory Committee and the workers recognized that unattached youth had been observed to have certain characteristics which it would have been most unwise to ignore. There was their suspicion, if not derision, towards everyone who would 'do good to them'. The following report of a female worker in an earlier café experiment with similar youth aged sixteen to twenty in Chelsea illustrates this clearly:

The local youth clubs are sometimes under review and it is fascinating to hear [the youths'] comments on these. They are sometimes cautious in what they say, as it is now common knowledge that I have visited these clubs and am friendly with their leaders. This was met with darkest suspicion at first. I explained that I used to run a club and so was interested in what went on in local organizations. They seem to have accepted this with the somewhat cutting remark 'Yerse'. 'Yer look the type and yer sometimes sound like one.' On one occasion, they were discussing a new leader who had taken over the local boys' club. They agreed it would be fun to go and look him over because he would like to think he's got some bad ones in. 'What a lot of mugs.'[1]

There was evidence then that social workers – including youth leaders – are often regarded with suspicion and with the derision that sometimes surrounds those people who are the unwitting objects of sardonic amusement. It was also thought that an equally suspicious but even more hostile attitude prevailed against anyone who represented 'authority': the police, the probation officer, and perhaps the school teacher. Direct evidence of this was forthcoming from experience of similar work in the Hoxton area of London in the early 1950s.[2] Here, the research worker had secured employment on a fairground,

1. Ewen, Jean, *Report on the Chelsea Café Experiment*, July 1958.
2. Turner, M. L., and Spencer, J. C., 'Spontaneous Youth Groups and Gangs', in Kuenstler, P.H.K. (Ed.), *Spontaneous Youth Groups*, University of London Press, 1955, pp. 57–8.

knowing that at least two gangs congregated on it. He was not successful in making contact with them and a further attempt in a pin-table alley was frustrated by the rumour that he was a probation officer.

In the light of this it was decided that the workers should live in the neighbourhoods where it was hoped to investigate and contact the unattached, and that initially at least they would not be in any way attached to any of the local youth organizations. Further, with the exception of the local advisory groups, they would remain anonymous, revealing the true nature and purpose of their residence in the neighbourhood to as few as possible of the local adults and even fewer, if any, of the local youths. It was also felt the experimental nature of the project made their anonymity even more desirable, especially as any undue publicity might prejudice the experiment's success before it had even begun. An initial period for observation of the leisure-time haunts, habits, pursuits, and groupings of local unattached youth was planned, then the position of the worker in each area would be reviewed, and in the light of the facts that had been discovered the points of contact could then be explored.

It was decided to work on a number of basic assumptions and put them to the test. One was that there was no single 'correct' method of contacting the unattached. Contact might be achieved in a variety of ways, the correctness of each approach being determined by and dependent upon the local situation and, in particular, upon the characteristics of the local youth, rather than the method itself. A second basic assumption to be taken into account when making contact was the belief that one characteristic of unattached youth, whatever the locality, was a suspicion of anyone representing 'authority' or 'social work'. For this reason, any course of action which might cause the workers to be associated with these identities in the minds of local youth was initially to be avoided.

With this theoretical background the project began in each of the areas. The assignment for the first two or three months was for the workers to acquaint themselves as fully as possible with the local area: to discover its various districts, to attempt some assessment of the existing Youth Service facilities, and to find the coffee bars, dance halls, and other places obviously attractive to young people. It was recognized that opportunities might occur for making some contacts, but this was not the major task at this stage, since premature concentration on a few individuals could stunt the broader aim of investigating a wide variety of young people. Slowly, with the help of the local advisers, after interviews with officials of Local Education Authorities, the various public and social services, and the leaders of local youth clubs, and after spending a considerable amount of time in walking around as well as sometimes sitting passively in coffee bars, a picture was formed of three distinctly contrasting areas and types of young people.

Within periods of time varying from six weeks to five months, and by methods to be described shortly, the three workers successfully located, contacted, and developed relationships with 170 to 200 unattached youth mainly in the fourteen-to-twenty-one age group. In addition, information of varying kinds and depth was collected relating to approximately 300 other teenagers with whom the workers had had some form of casual contact, without the development, for a number of reasons, of any deeper relationship. The complete range of contacts together with the length of time taken to develop relationships is summarized below in Table 1.

TABLE 1

Approach	Type of Young Person Contacted	Number	Result
One SEAGATE			
1. Coffee-bar sitting	16–21-year-old middle-class boys and girls	30–40	Relationships established within 4 months and maintained with 30–40 outside coffee-bar
2. School teaching	14–15-year-old secondary modern pupils (boys)	30	Relationships established with 10 boys within 3 months but not maintained
	15–19-year-old day-release students, apprentices, etc.	100	13 relationships established outside place of contact within one year but not maintained

Approach	Type of Young Person Contacted	Number	Result
Two NORTHTOWN			
1. Café waitress	15–20-year-old working-class youths, boys and girls	40–50	Relationship established within 3 months and maintained with 40–50 outside café
2. Factory work	16–25-year-old working-class girls	20	Relationship established within 9 weeks and maintained with 2 girls outside factory
3. School teaching	14–15-year-old girls in a secondary modern school	40	Relationship established within 3 months and maintained with 20 outside school
Three MIDFORD			
1. Swimming instructor	15–25-year-old working-class boys and girls	20–30	Relationships established with 15 within 3 months and maintained outside baths
2. Dance-hall steward	16–25-year-old working-class boys and girls	200–300	No relationships established within one month; approach abandoned
3. Coffee bar	16–20-year-old middle-class boys and girls	15–20	Relationships established with 20 within 5 months and maintained outside coffee bar
4. School teaching	16–19-year-old farm workers	30	No relationships established outside place of contact within 6 months
	15–17-year-old day-release students	20	No relationships established outside place of contact within one month. Post terminated

Approach	Type of Young Person Contacted	Number	Result
5. Frequent visits to jazz clubs	15–25-year-old, male and female	60–70	Relationships established with 20–30 within 3 months and maintained outside place of contact
6. Individual casual contacts	15–25-year-old male and female, wide social class range	20–30	Relationship established with 20–30 within 3 months and maintained beyond place of contact

3 Varieties of Approach

The workers were successful in trying out at least six different ways of approaching the unattached and found, to their surprise, that contacting the unattached was not itself a major problem. By far the most difficult and demanding task was developing a superficial acquaintanceship into a deeper relationship and handling such a relationship once it had been established.

Getting to know the unattached can be broken down into three distinct stages: locating groups and individuals; contacting them; gaining their acceptance. Each stage has its own characteristics, but the final one may fairly be said to be the most important and the most difficult.

The favourite meeting grounds of youths could be discovered easily enough and anywhere. A coffee bar, jazz club, or swimming-pool which over two or three weeks seemed to attract the same faces was obviously the most likely place and therefore more thoroughly explored in order to single out the unattached. Later, when the work and school settings became the more prominent methods of making contact, the problem became one of persuading the school authorities or the prospective employer to employ the worker. But at most times, the cooperation of the local people was forthcoming; although occasionally given with a faint air of bewilderment, suspicion, or amusement.

No claims can be made to have located *all* the unattached in Northtown, Seagate, or Midford and then to have selected from amongst them the most 'typical' cases or those who would possibly benefit most from the workers' attention. In both Northtown and Seagate, the area was much too extensive for a single worker to hope to cover all of it. It might have been feasible if the aims of the project had been confined to investigation, but the terms of reference – apart from building up a general picture of the unattached – included helping them in whatever way seemed appropriate, and to do this it was necessary for the worker to be selective and to spend a great deal of time with the groups of young people to find out if they were in need of his attention or would benefit by it. To gain the confidence of these young people is a demanding, time-consuming process. But, unless their confidence is first assured, the very nature of their difficulties means that any information they offer is highly suspect. Instances could be quoted of escapades, achievements, and attitudes confided in early acquaintanceship which later proved to have been invented to impress the worker.

'Participant observation' was judged to be the most favourable method of collecting reliable information and leading to the establishment of friendly relationships. Obviously it could be practised with only a very limited number of young people at any given time. In Seagate it will be remembered the worker had some choice between concentrating on the group located in the Mardi Gras and the out-of-school discussion groups. In Northtown the worker had to choose between trying to develop further relationships with a café group or trying to contact two different groups – some girls in a factory and a school group of problem pupils who had been directed into her classes at the school. In Midford the worker often deliberately chose to spend more time with one group or individual than others on the basis of degree and kind of unattachment.

Once he had decided on suitable groups or individuals with whom to spend his time, the worker then tried to find ways of bringing himself to their attention without arousing too much mistrust or fear. The aim was that he should become a familiar part of the group surroundings and at the same time establish some form of communication, as distinct from merely sitting around and observing. In practice such communication, in the form of spontaneous conversations, was most often developed initially with fringe or marginal members of the various groups and only later extended to the leaders or the more popular members.

As Table 1 shows, seven different ways of making contact were tried. Six were successful: the one complete failure was the dance-hall stewardship, due to the risk that sooner or later the police would ask the worker to give evidence in Court and endanger his anonymity. Of the others, school teaching was productive in Northtown but not in the other two areas, where both the workers believed the failure to have been due to the artificial nature of the groups, the insufficient time for establishing contact when teaching a class for only a couple of hours a week, the size of the class, and the authoritarian atmosphere of various schools. The first and last reasons are the least plausible in view of the fact that the classes in Northtown were equally artificial and yet the worker did not feel it to be a hindrance. Similarly the secondary modern school in Northtown had basically an authoritarian atmosphere but the worker was soon able to exercise her own highly individual brand of discipline with her pupils. The real contrast is found however with both the length of time and the size of classes involved. The Northtown worker taught three days a week, her 'special' classes numbering only eight or ten pupils. All the evidence suggests that the two fundamentals to the success of using the teaching approach to make contact with the unattached are adequate time for the worker to become an accepted part of the school pattern, and small enough classes – ten pupils being ideal, but fifteen being the maximum. In addition, three other possible factors in the effectiveness of the school approach are the personality of the worker and the age and sex of the pupils. It is interesting to note that the Seagate worker recorded being irked by the authoritarian atmosphere at his school to a far greater extent than the other two in theirs, and it is obvious that a given means of contact is more likely to succeed if the worker feels comfortable in using it and his personality is taken into account when selecting means of making contact. It is also worth noting that most progress was made with a fourteen-to-fifteen-year-old group of girls although the evidence is in fact inconclusive about the age and sex of the pupils.

The second method of contact was 'hanging around', especially in coffee bars. This particular method has provoked the most discussion both amongst the workers and in the available literature.[1] For example, in *Spontaneous Youth Groups*, one contributor – M. Lloyd Turner – partially rejected it on the

1. See Suggestions for Further Reading, p. 227.

grounds that it would arouse too much suspicion. In examining possible approaches, he suggested,

a worker who sat in cafés and wandered aimlessly around the streets and who did not appear to have to work for his living would immediately arouse suspicion. For 'hanging around' as a method of making contacts has its limitations. To make a natural approach, the worker would have to live in the neighbourhood and possibly work in it.[1]

On the other hand the New York City Youth Board in its work with street-corner groups and gangs regards 'hanging around' as a practical and valuable means of making contact; but the whole approach is much more open and direct, and the New York worker tries consistently to make both groups and individuals aware of the reason for his interest in them. The following extract from a report of a New York street worker during the early stages of contacting a teenage gang in a drug store illustrates this point:

Big Al asked me if I liked the Billie Holiday recording. I told Big Al that I thought it was a good record although I thought Billie Holiday was kind of 'gone'. Big Al then wanted to know who paid me. I told him that I was paid by the City. He asked me then what did I do. I told him that my job was to work with a group of fellows and help them to do some of the things they like to do. I told him that sometimes I can help around jobs or other things. ... He then wanted to know what did I get paid for. For instance Al asked 'Do you get paid right now? For just standing here listening to this record?' I told him that any time I came down to the block and played the juke box or had a soda or stood on the corner talking, I was being paid. Al shook his head and said, 'Darn, that's a crazy job.' I said 'Well, as you understand it a little better, you will see I work.' Al then called over Tommy and there was a running conversation for about five or ten minutes. They made much to do about my taking the City's money for doing nothing.[2]

This directness contrasts strikingly with the extremely cautious approach adopted by the present project. It may seem even more surprising in view of the fact that the New York City youths

1. ibid., *Spontaneous Youth Groups*, p. 57.
2. *Reaching the Fighting Gang*, New York City Youth Board, 1960, p. 126.

were 'hard-core' and often violent delinquents, whereas few of the anti-social individuals contacted by our workers were hardened delinquents.

It would have been extremely difficult to apply to this project the same approach as the New York City Youth Board. The American method has been evolved over a number of years, has developed techniques suited to its prime purpose of combating juvenile delinquency, and offers its workers a comprehensive training programme. To apply the American method without a similar training programme here would have been demanding too much of the workers. It would also have been dangerous to assume that British and American youth would necessarily respond to identical techniques. New York workers are attached locally to a known youth organization. Their aims are understood and accepted by at least some other social work agencies in the community and even by some of the gangs themselves. For a New York worker to explain his job with a youth organization which is a recognized part of the neighbourhood is infinitely more practical and less anxiety-provoking than it would have been for our workers to have tried to explain why they had been sent from London to try to help the youth of Northtown, Seagate, and Midford. If a clear statement of identity and purpose is to be attempted and presented so that it makes sense to the local youth it would appear to be of great importance that the workers should be a part of the local community and sponsored by a local youth or welfare organization.

In view of the experimental nature of the project and the fact that the workers would be operating without any attachment to a local youth organization, a much more cautious approach was taken on the N.A.Y.C. project. This reached its extreme expression in the concealment of the workers' identity, which did not prevent the 'hanging-around' approach being attempted in Seagate and Midford to enable contact to be made with large numbers of the unattached, despite the workers' own doubts about its effectiveness. They frequently thought at the time that they were provoking undue suspicion. They also found the unnaturalness of the situation caused them considerable frustration. But there is ample evidence that it was not the 'hanging around' which discomfited them so much as the lack of a clear identity. Great stress was laid in their reports on the number of occasions on which they were asked by young people 'Who are you?' and 'What do you do?' The Seagate and Midford workers professed initially to be writers; the North-town worker avoided the problem by assuming the identity of a social science student working for practical experience first in a coffee bar and then a factory, and then again – later – assuming the identity of a school teacher. It was only when the Seagate worker became a part-time teacher and able to use this identity that he really felt comfortable 'hanging around' in a coffee bar; similarly with the Midford worker, when he took a job as a swimming instructor and began inquiries about school teaching. It seems that the 'hanging-around' approach only presents difficulties if the worker is unable or unwilling to give his reasons for doing so, or, if he lacks a recognizable identity in the local community. M. L. Turner's suggestion is that the worker should obtain a recognizable identity by living or taking a job in the neighbourhood. The possibility of the worker revealing his identity was never tried on this project and it seems to have been insufficiently experimented with in work of this kind in this country.

Working in a factory was the third method of making contact. This produced only two contacts in nine weeks. The length of time taken could only have been justified if the girls could not have been reached in any other and quicker way. The information gained about attitudes towards work was extremely valuable, but as a means of making contacts which could be maintained outside the factory setting this approach was found to have several limiting factors. One was the difficulty of obtaining suitable employment, especially if the job demanded a certain amount of training. Another was the physical arrangement of many factories, which did not permit the free and easy communication essential for this type of work. Then, some employers were understandably reluctant to risk having unknown social research workers disrupting the peace of the factory floor or the employee–management relationships. All this – with effort – could have been overcome, but there was a final and overwhelming disadvantage. Strong evidence has been amassed that many individuals prefer to spend their leisure time with people other than their workmates. Leisure-time and work groupings tend to be separate, the former being based on choice and centred around a certain street, coffee bar, or housing estate, the latter being determined mainly by the employer and a certain amount of chance. This is not a clear-cut distinction, and the two groupings are by no means always mutually exclusive, but as a generalization it was found to hold true for large numbers of youth contacted and it has important implications for work of this kind. The most obvious is that the unattached worker is unlikely to contact many ready-made friendship groups in the work setting; more likely are relationships with one or two individuals which will lead to introductions into the leisure-time groupings outside the place of work.

This brings the focus eventually back to the leisure-time group. The work approach is much the most time-consuming way of contacting the unattached as well as being unnecessarily devious and difficult. But a short spell in a local factory is an excellent way to get to understand the attitudes towards work of many youth, unattached or otherwise, and to gain insight into the colour and character of a neighbourhood.

Working in a coffee-bar, the last means of making contact, seemed to provide an almost ideal situation. Although suspicion of the worker still persisted, the question of identity was temporarily at rest and the worker enjoyed a casual but structured setting in which friendships could develop almost naturally and spontaneously. Opportunities to extend the work outside the coffee bar arose frequently, and while it seems doubtful if the enthusiasm of the local youth for the Northtown worker to join them at the pub would have been aroused quite so immediately or persistently if she had been a man, there is plenty of evidence that a male worker could have been successful in this setting.[1] Success is not automatically assured – the Chelsea Café Experiment has shown that this is by no means so and its limitations lie in the worker's knowing how to develop, extend and use relationships once contact has been established in such a setting.

The third stage in the process of getting to know the un-

1. See, for example, reports on the Heeley Teen Bar, Sheffield, 1958, and the Manhattan Club, Alloa, 1960, both available from the N.A.Y.C. See also the Y.W.C.A. project for work through a street coffee stall.

attached is gaining acceptance. The word 'acceptance' has so far been used to mean the approval and liking of the unattached for the worker. A prerequisite for the acceptance of the worker by the unattached is, of course, the worker's own acceptance of *them*. This implies that the worker is able to like and respect them as individuals or groups, as he finds them, without wishing immediately to impose change or express moral censure on their behaviour and attitudes. The ability to do this is largely dependent on the worker's own maturity. For most people it needs a certain amount of training and acquired skill as well. The initial attitudes of group members of all ages and types to an outsider is to regard him with suspicion and prejudice. This will not be unduly perturbing to a worker who has confidence in his abilities and in his knowledge of human behaviour. He knows that the outsider is at first disliked simply as an outsider, not as a person; and that the outsider will eventually be accepted by the group if and when it approves of his behaviour. The workers on the project were untrained (with the possible exception of the Northtown worker) and, unfortunately for their own peace of mind, were unaware of this, as the anxiety and fears in their reports show. It is a remarkable tribute to their sensitivity and stability that they could function as effectively as they did without more on-the-spot guidance and support to help them cope with their own feelings of frustration. This is particularly so since it has long been recognized that even the most mature and skilled of workers can lose their objectivity and become over-involved with the people or situation at hand. There is also the danger that a worker will be unconsciously influenced by his own feelings and attitudes and that, unless these are recognized and understood, they may affect and possibly control his attempts to develop relationships. The opportunity to discuss his feelings and attitudes with an objective outsider is one safeguard against this over-involvement on his part. The workers had some opportunity to do this, but in retrospect they all felt strongly that more frequent discussions with a supervisor on a regular bi-weekly basis would have improved their ability to be objective and lessened their feelings of anxiety and discomfort. There is a strong connexion between objectivity and self-confidence, and the ability to accept people as they are, and it is because the importance of this has been recognized that the feelings of the workers have been presented in such detail in this book.

It can be seen that all three workers for the most part were able to identify and control the feelings which the youth they were working with provoked in them. The notable exception to this was the Seagate worker and his reactions to the 'tough' type of youth with whom he felt he could never work because his personality and background would be so different from his own. Persistent encouragement by his advisory committees, both local and central, enabled him to increase his intellectual understanding of the reasons for his inability to contact this type of youth. However, since the problem was an emotional rather than an intellectual one, this was not much practical help, and even while sincerely agreeing in principle that he could and should try to work with the tougher type of youth he never in fact did so. When a minor opportunity for attempting it presented itself with the school group he deliberately avoided it. Even though he sincerely wanted to, he was unable to work with them, for emotional reasons which he could not fully allow himself to identify or admit. An objective outside observer who was able to help him work through these feelings on an emotional rather than an intellectual level would have been helpful to him at this stage.[1] As it was, he wisely recognized his own limitations and concentrated on the group with which he felt most at ease.

This experience of the Seagate worker, which is an extreme example of worker rejection, has been used only to demonstrate that it is necessary first for the worker to accept the group. Without his complete acceptance there is very little possibility of the group in their turn accepting him. Even when the group as a whole has been accepted by the worker, individuals within it may be rejected and disliked. This does not mean that the worker must be expected to have a personal liking for everyone with whom he works, but he must be aware of his own feelings and able to control them so that they interfere as little as possible with his relationship to individuals whom he may per-

1. This whole problem together with the value of supervision will be treated in greater detail in Chapter 6.

sonally dislike. With the exception of this one group in Seagate, the rest of this book offers many illustrations of the objective ways in which the workers reacted to their contacts and were prepared to go a long way to meet the unattached on their own terms and to withhold any expressions of conventional moral judgements. Only by doing this could the workers show their acceptance of groups and individuals. Without it, little more than superficial contact could have been developed. If the worker's actions as well as his words show he has accepted groups and individuals on their own terms the problem of their acceptance of him will be minimized.

In the early stages, all of the groups and individuals regarded the workers with suspicion. It is doubtful if this could have been removed by explanations by them about their identity or purpose. It disappeared as the young people began to realize from their actions and words that the workers were not trying to preach at them, or harm them, or to reform them but were prepared to listen to them, to try to understand them, and liked them enough to spend their time with them and to want to help them in any way that they would allow, by lending books, offering lifts, accompanying them to jazz clubs, and so on. The process was a slow one. Even then, almost as if they could not believe that anyone would be genuinely interested in them for their own sake, they set out to provoke the workers to test how genuine their attitude was. Thus the Northtown coffee-bar youths watched how the worker would react to obscene language or to being invited out for a drink and a date. They knew, or at least expected, that she would disapprove of their language and reject their invitation. They would probably have been disappointed with her if she had not, but what they wanted to learn was would she reject and disapprove of them as she did so? Skilfully she did not.

The Seagate coffee-bar youths constantly failed to keep their rendezvous with the worker, and waited to find out if he would reject them because of it. They attacked him and accused him of marital infidelity and watched to see if he would reject them as a result. Again he did not. Many other examples could be quoted of the workers withstanding and passing through this testing period to the satisfaction of the young people. As a result, certain indications began to appear that the group was being won over and their acceptance and confidence being earned. The worker began to receive spontaneous invitations to join the youths in the search for parties, or to accompany them to jazz clubs or the cinema. There was also a marked increase in their willingness to confide in him their personal problems: difficulties with parents or with work or with each other. It was only when these signs finally appeared, indicating that some of the unattached had come to accept and trust the worker, that he could set about trying to help them.[1]

This process can be clearly identified in each of the cases where the workers were successful in establishing a deeper relationship with the various groups, including contacts made through coffee bars and jazz clubs, through acting as a swimming instructor, and – most unexpected of all – school teaching. This latter raises doubts about the validity of the earlier belief that an attempt will fail where the contact is made through an identity which is representative of authority. The evidence of the project is that the suspicion and probable hostility of some of the unattached towards the worker is an occupational hazard. It is to be reckoned with irrespective of the identity which the worker may care to assume; it is impossible to prevent it from arising, but by skilful handling, which largely depends on the worker's self-confidence, insight, and maturity, it can be overcome.

TRYING TO HELP

The workers' next task was 'to try to help the unattached in whatever way seemed appropriate'; the second part of the terms of reference. To try to help them to change their standards of

1. The New York City Youth Board believes that even at this stage, full acceptance of the worker by the group cannot be said to have been gained. In their view, full acceptance is only achieved if the group maintains relationship with the worker *after* understanding who he is and what he is trying to do. Further, they believe that work of a meaningful nature with groups of this kind cannot legitimately be said to have begun unless acceptance as so defined has been achieved. In their experience the establishment of such a working relationship takes from three to seven months.

See *Reaching the Fighting Gang*, pp. 135–6, for a fuller discussion.

personal behaviour was one way. They would benefit if they could learn to take more responsibility for their own behaviour, to get on better with each other, to derive more satisfaction from less delinquent activities, to come to better terms with the local community, to feel less hostile towards adults – especially parents – and, in many cases, by managing to make a more satisfactory adjustment to school or working life. These pronouncements were easy enough to make. But how was this to be accomplished in reality? What methods could help the unattached to change their attitudes and behaviour? Even from the depths of an armchair these problems appeared formidable. It was more helpful in looking for answers to consider the problem in the light of what was happening to the unattached, rather than to think in terms of what they needed to do or become. Here were several groups of young people suffering from various forms of frustration and social *malaise* which, like anyone else, they set out to relieve. Unfortunately, the only ways in which this could be achieved for most of them were unacceptable to other members of the community. In turn this often made their problems greater. To enable them to understand what was happening to themselves would therefore be one way to help.

It would have to be done with extreme caution. Most of them, at the start, were not prepared to listen to the worker or any other adult. In a fleeting moment of confidence, or in times of acute distress, some may have admitted to disappointment, dissatisfaction, and even despair. A few might go on to confess that they did not know what to do about it. But, for the most part, any direct indication that the worker thought their way of life unsatisfying or in need of change would have been rejected – particularly in the early stages of their acquaintanceship – in spite of their friendship with him. In some cases, their reaction would have been one of disbelief, anger, or apathy in the form of 'So what?', and they would have avoided him thereafter. The workers' discovery of the unattached's inability to take adult criticism, no matter how well-meaning the intentions of those who offered it, made it abundantly clear that any direct attempt on these lines would be doomed to failure. In any case, parents, teachers, employers, and – in some cases – magistrates had all tried lecturing or criticizing them with complete lack of success.

So it can be seen that it would have meant the rejection of the workers by individuals and probably by whole groups if, in the initial stages, they had attempted to criticize the way of life of the unattached, to impose any suggestions for change, or have implied that the young people were not all that they might have been. They could never afford to ignore this any more than they could afford to forget that these young people had never asked for help. The worker was not a youth club leader whose members had chosen to join the club on agreed terms and who could therefore be thrown out for misbehaviour – even if the worker thought it helpful, he could not throw the unattached off a street corner or out of a coffee bar. Nor was he a probation officer, with the authority of the law behind him to insist that they meet him at regular intervals. The unattached had to be met and helped on their own terms. The only direction or control the worker could exert was that which the unattached chose to accept by virtue of *their* liking for his personal qualities, *their* identification with him, and *their* conviction that he was a friend.

Helping the unattached was, however, only one part of the job. It became clear during the preliminary investigation that some local communities, especially in Midford and Northtown, suffered such social and cultural deprivation that even rebellion was preferable to an apathetic acceptance of existing conditions. When the worker came across this state of affairs his first task, both with adults and young people, was to get them to react against this tacit assumption that because things had always been this way, they must necessarily always remain so. As a result, in practice as well as in theory, the worker found himself forced to tackle two problems simultaneously. The first was to try to strengthen the abilities of the unattached to come to terms with themselves, each other, and society – and in that order; the second was to aid the local community to a more tolerant understanding of the problem of the unattached and to enlist local support.

These two problems and facets of the work were necessarily interwoven, as these young people could not be considered in isolation from their local communities. Their difficulties were of a composite nature, interrelated, and having an effect not only on the use or misuse of their leisure time but on every aspect of their daily life. To have concentrated merely on the individuals themselves would have been to ignore the importance of parents and family, work or school, and the physical and social conditions of their immediate environment. Claims that workers were directly responsible for changes in any individual's way of life are made only very tentatively in this book. One reason for this is that it would be a dangerous over-simplification to assume that the worker was the only influence affecting these young people for good or ill. Changes for better or worse could equally have been sparked off by any number of other factors, such as a change in parental attitude, the acquisition of a steady boy/girl-friend, or a different job.

Because of this multiplicity of factors, the workers came to the conclusion that the problem of the unattached was, above all, the responsibility of the local community. Many of the young people – and in some cases their parents also – fell into what has aptly been termed 'the various bits of no-man's land which exist between the different fields of care for which the community makes itself responsible'. Some of the youth were sufficiently delinquent to be catered for by the probation or other corrective services; others were delinquent enough but they happened not to have been found out, while a smaller minority seemed in need of psychiatric or child guidance service. But the majority did not fall into any of these more extreme categories and it became appropriate to think less in terms of the unattached and more in terms of the uncatered for.

Much work with the local community was impossible on this particular project, apart from any that was specifically undertaken on behalf of the groups or individuals with whom the worker was directly concerned. But even from this limited experience it became clear that any detached worker on a continuous rather than on an experimental basis must regard the working with adults in the local community as of equal importance to working directly with the young people themselves.

In practice the workers were drawn into the community. It was often necessary to search the neighbourhood for facilities or equipment for the various activities. The hunt for rehearsal halls in Seagate, a meeting place in Northtown, and some means of transport in Midford are three simple examples of ways in which the unattached were brought into contact with local adults. When the workers departed in late 1963, it was hoped to transfer their groups to other social agencies or adults in the community. A considerable number of young people in each area was in need of the kind of help which the workers had been offering. Without the slightest difficulty they could have tripled the number of their unattached contacts within two or three months, had time or resources been available, and they were always on the look-out for ways of bringing these disturbing facts to the attention of local organizations.

But finding local agencies who would take on responsibility for the workers' existing groups, let alone for providing a continuous service to other unattached young people, seemed to be an insoluble problem.

4 Northtown

Northtown, with a population of 130,000, is a region of heavy industry in the north of England. The town is part of a mass of industrial and urban development which has sprung up over the past one hundred years. To the south of the city is a busy river and, beyond this, a dockside area known as Lymport (pop. 20,000), where the project was to take place.

A first impression of Northtown is of rows of mean, low, terraced houses running geometrically north–south, east–west, and hurriedly built to accommodate workers for a quickly expanding industrial area. This pattern is repeated again in Lymport and west of it in the neighbouring dockside area of Avonmore. The oldest part of the city, where the original town was founded, is between the present city centre and the river. As these houses decayed, the area became notorious for its violence and crime. Now, most of the terraces are empty or have been demolished, and new three-storey flats, already looking rather dilapidated, have been constructed. To the east are many more nineteenth-century terrace streets. This is the present problem area of the town, and the small coloured community also tends to be centred here.

Northwards from the town hall, an area of Victorian middle-class housing extends to Victoria Park. It is in decline, and large houses are increasingly being divided into flats and bed-sitting rooms. Up to fifteen years ago, Victoria Park used to divide the town socially: to the south were the small, quickly and cheaply built houses for the workers, together with facilities for work, trade, transport, administration, and entertainment; to the north the more spacious area of twentieth-century middle-class housing. This north–south division has been altered by post-war development. Now the main middle-class area lies well to the north, out of the city and into the country. The housing estates are to the west of the city. Some are pre-war, but most have been built since 1946 and many are pleasant, although their spaciousness may seem intimidating after overcrowded streets. Communal facilities are gradually being provided but so slowly that whole generations suffer before facilities are available and the task of creating community feeling and interest is made infinitely more difficult.

The middle and upper class are steadily moving out of the city, and Northtown is now largely an area of wage-earners dependent upon the heavy industry, the docks, and a few lighter industries of post-war origin. The town lacks social diversity. There is difficulty in attracting professional people and there is a shortage of teachers and social workers. A reliable post-war social survey noted a lack of balance between work and leisure in the town. To some extent, this is still true. Historically, the hard and physically demanding nature of the work and the deeply ingrained notion that 'muck' and money go together have resulted in a lack of imagination and of diversity in leisure-time facilities. It is thus a town dominated by industry, but this no longer has the power to pull the area together so that the general impression is one of an unintegrated mass of urbanization, lacking any sense of social cohesion. The area retains vivid memories of the 1930s. During the period of the project there was a recession in heavy industry coinciding with the bulge of school leavers, an unemployment level consistently more than twice the national average, and considerable short-time working.

Northtown has a greater than average proportion of young people per head of the population and the under-eighteen-year-olds are particularly affected by the general dearth of leisure-time facilities. During the project, cinemas became fewer, and one of the two dance halls gave way to Bingo. Youth organizations are distributed unevenly throughout the area and are insufficient. There is a boys' club at Avonmore which is thriving, but the corresponding girls' club at Lymport caters for a smaller number of girls in premises which have long awaited improvement. In 'down-town' Northtown there are several well-established boys' clubs and two well-known mixed clubs. The new housing estates lack adequate facilities for young people: anyone under eighteen is excluded from the community

centres now established on those estates built from 1945 on-
wards. Youth centres are planned for some of these estates, but
it will be a long time yet before they materialize. Meanwhile,
Northtown discourages the use of schools as meeting places for
youth organizations. Of the non-statutory authorities, the Roman
Catholics, by contrast, make extensive use of their schools and
other buildings. Young Catholic Workers groups function erratically at most of their churches, but those who attend are in-
clined to regard them as cheap dance halls. The non-conformist
churches run popular youth clubs but they limit their membership.

Lymport has even fewer facilities. Those which exist are provided mainly by the churches and the public houses. The girls'
club meets on three evenings a week and an open mixed club
run by the parish church twice a week. The Roman Catholic
church runs a social club and the Baptist church a youth club
for its own members. In addition, there is an excellent swimming pool, a recreation ground which is unfortunately even
farther away from the town than the pool, and a cinema. But to
have a choice of films, to go to a dance, to sit about in different
coffee bars, these young people must go into Northtown, a six-
penny bus ride, or to Sunport, a seaside resort a shilling bus
ride away. This undoubtedly detracts from any sense of identity
with Lymport as a community in its own right.

In December 1960 the young woman worker, holding an
Honours degree in social science and with a year's experience of
working in a probation hostel for girls, moved into a flat in
Lymport as part of this project. Casting about for ways to contact the unattached she soon found that the public house was the
main social institution. It was doubtful if it had any real established rival outside the home, although with the teenagers there
was some interchange between the public house and the coffee
bar during the course of an evening, particularly when money
was short. However, an attractive, educated young woman could
have scarcely sat around in pubs without creating an inordinate
amount of comment and suspicion. The coffee bars in Northtown seemed a far more likely solution. These were certainly
more accessible and, in the evenings at least, they attracted an
almost exclusively teenage clientele. She visited a variety and

found some far more popular than others with young people, although this probably bore little relation to financial success, as they bought very little.

One of these was the Phoenix on one of the main roads leading into the central shopping area of Northtown. It was run by a family of Italians and had a bar and an espresso machine downstairs and another room upstairs which boasted a juke box and was usually crowded in the evenings. The décor was constantly being improved with new wrought-iron lamp brackets, quilted leather panels, and exotic paintings of ice blue mountains and groves of heavily blossomed trees. The worker's report gives a good idea of the general atmosphere:

The Phoenix is primarily a meeting place for groups of young people. Its juke box is at least as popular as its coffee and there appears to be no pressure to buy anything. About once a week, a jazz group plays in the upstairs room and two shillings is charged for admission; these services are quite popular. The young people here are in general quite sophisticated for this area. . . . Many of the boys wear smart Italian suits and both boys and girls wear tight pointed shoes, some 'winkle-pickers'. The girls have neatly groomed bouffant hair and the usual short tight skirts. Many of these work in shops; the boys do a much wider variety of jobs.

Good features of the Phoenix are the occasional bit of general conversation which will arise and the good relationship between customers and staff. Thus the eldest brother shows off his new wall brackets before they are put up, and one of the boys explains to him in great detail how and where he could install heaters. On another occasion, this same boy came swaggering in with a copy of *Lady Chatterley's Lover* which he sat down in a corner to read, rather self-consciously but hoping to arouse some reactions. On the whole, this was treated with amusement; there were perhaps nine or ten other regulars in the coffee bar at the time.

Sitting around in coffee bars gave the worker a brief insight into some of the teenagers in the area but it wasn't a very effective way of gaining more than fleeting impressions. Superficial contact with the boys was easy enough but a major problem was how to make contact with the girls.

They sit there, attractive and bright faced, but will contribute nothing to a discussion or conversation, afraid to look silly while the boys are present. They seem not to want to show themselves as individuals in their own right. As girls never go about alone and rarely without some male accompaniment, this presents a considerable difficulty for me.

The other problem was how to transform a superficial and fleeting relationship with the boys into one of greater depth and permanency. By the end of the first month in Northtown, the worker had concluded, perhaps a little prematurely, that sitting in coffee bars would not achieve this deeper relationship. She decided there were two alternatives for overcoming the problem. Either she could make a more direct approach by asking more direct questions, giving some clearer definition of her position; or she could try to get a job through which she could assume some recognizable role. Fearing it might limit her later if she revealed too much of her purpose at this early stage, she opted for a job, and although it had been useful to cover quite a dispersed area initially, she decided it was now necessary to concentrate on a particular neighbourhood.

With the help of the local Advisory Committee the worker obtained a job in the only coffee bar in Lymport. It possessed the two essential pieces of equipment – a juke box and an espresso machine – but apart from these, it was ill-equipped, inefficiently organized, and badly run. The coffee bar was run solely by the manageress, whose responsibilities included cooking, serving, cleaning, and keeping order – the latter a considerable task since the clientele included the toughest element of the neighbourhood, many of whom came in because they had nowhere better to go or not enough money to go elsewhere. The manageress, however, excelled at this and seemed to be on very good terms with the toughest of the youths.

She was an extremely large woman and most of the customers were under the impression, probably mistaken, that because of her size she was stronger than they and her wishes ought therefore to be respected. Besides this, the police station was directly opposite.

The worker was employed in the coffee bar as someone who had studied social science and now wished to do some practical work. She later found it necessary to explain to her employers that she did some writing for some people in London; this covered the absence of her insurance card.

The coffee bar attracted in the main a group of youths aged sixteen to twenty. Some were out of work and some were on shift work. Most times of the day were useful for making contacts. Those who worked did a variety of jobs: two were welders, one was a plater, two others worked on coal delivery vans, several were more casually employed on building sites, two worked in a bakery, and one for an undertaker; another worked for an engineering firm, one was still at school, one did asphalting on roofs, and two worked at the local fairground. They all seemed to treat the coffee bar as a useful meeting place where few demands were made on them and which provided a convenient place for them to spend the day if they took one off from school or work. It was also a useful place to spend the evenings when money was short and there was nothing else to do.

Within a relatively short time the worker was able to build up a remarkably detailed and absorbing picture of the type. This was achieved gradually and casually. She was careful to avoid asking too many pointed questions, but anyway much of the most interesting and valuable information presented itself naturally and spontaneously through general conversation in which the worker was often included. By the end of six weeks the worker's reports of the youths' reactions to her and the intimate nature of the information she was obtaining (much of which was verified by subsequent knowledge of them) made it clear that more than a superficial contact had been made with a group of semi-delinquent youths. Her comments on her relationship with them, written at the time, highlight some of the difficulties and fears which are now believed to be an inherent part of the detached worker's job.

I would just like to add a brief assessment of their attitude to me. I think that I am accepted now as part of the coffee bar by many of the regular customers. They have accepted that I am rather peculiar in some ways – that when one of the youths comes in and suggests that I shut the shop and go for a drink with him, I do not go. I do not think that my presence makes any difference to the way they behave, the things they talk about. The language is well punctuated with the usual adjectives and some of the girls are as bad as the boys over this. Once or twice, someone has come out with a string of abuse and has then looked at me to see how I have taken it, but in general, their conversations are extremely straightforward and free.

My status as a student has been accepted quite satisfactorily. When pressed further about what I study I am as vague as possible as I do not want deliberately to mislead them too far. Usually, it is assumed that social science is a science, but if to the still inquisitive I have to elaborate, then sociology, economics, etc. They do not understand and so stop asking questions. Some of them clearly look upon me as a rather amusing curiosity and some greatly enjoy teasing me about the way I speak. This worried me at first. I could not get hold of the local dialect and colloquialisms at once and feared that this might prove a difficult barrier, although I felt it better to talk more or less naturally than to put on a phoney accent which they might at once distrust. However, I now find that several of the youths find this very amusing and like to imitate me. In fact this has come to be quite a useful, friendly gimmick which I sometimes play up to.

The two most important things for me in working in the coffee bar are: firstly, that I am no longer looked upon with suspicion by those with whom I am trying to make contact. In a friendly way, they may think that I am rather a curiosity, which is rather different and does not shake one's self-confidence in the same way. Secondly, having an immediate job to do and a role to play has been of considerable value in avoiding and overcoming problems of little-defined relationships with both boys and girls.

Working in a coffee bar was therefore undoubtedly successful in achieving the first aim of the project of discovering facts about a group of unattached youth. There remained the more difficult task of deepening the relationship so that the information gained could be used to help the youth concerned. To the worker's own surprise she found that a deeper relationship was easier to establish with the girls who used the coffee bar than with the boys. Once she had become friendly with the boys, she discovered that the girls followed suit and became more friendly too. Now they occasionally invited her on their frequent visits to the cinema. It obviously pleased the girls when she accepted, but this also brought a renewed spate of invitations from the youths to come for a drink which the worker refused because she felt her relationship with them remained too ambiguous to make it wise. Questions regarding who she was did not cease. The following extract from a report was written two months after the one just quoted:

There have been more questions as to who or what I am, provoked I feel certain by Mike O'Connor. He came into the coffee-bar situation from outside, being on leave from the Army. He was quite intelligent and perceptive enough to feel that I did not quite fit. This, in a way, was unfortunate because by this time most of the Lymport young people had come to take me for granted, as part of the coffee bar. However, this question kept Ben, Mike, and Terry talking in the coffee bar instead of drinking in the local public house for nearly an hour one Friday evening – a point on which they commented jovially at the time.

I was told that they could reach no satisfactory conclusion about me and I was careful to give them none. Mike told me that they had thought of three possible reasons to explain my presence in the coffee bar. These were: that I needed the money (but this was not satisfactory as they knew that the pay was low and thought that I could earn more elsewhere). The second idea was that I was studying them and the third that I was lonely and so took a job which would bring me in touch with lots of people. I managed to divert the conversation by discussing their first suggestion and we went off with another discussion on money. However, I was very interested in their ideas and while they showed considerable curiosity no one seemed perturbed that any of these possibilities might be near to the truth.

Unfortunately the coffee bar closed in March 1961, just three months after the worker had become a waitress. The relationship established with the older boys was still too ambiguous in its sexual aspects for the worker to suggest meeting them outside the coffee-bar setting. This did not apply to the girls. During the next two years over forty of them visited her Lymport flat, at least twenty regularly. They also brought with them younger siblings and relatives of both sexes. Partly because some of these younger ones were relatives, a casual contact was maintained in addition with the older coffee-bar youths. Many of them left Lymport either voluntarily to join the Army or with compulsion to the County gaol and, while it was not possible to work with them directly, their respective fortunes were followed and recorded very accurately. They often visited the worker on their brief returns to Lymport and some wrote to her while away.

The closing of the coffee bar, the only one of its kind in Lymport, meant that both a means and a place of contact had been removed. Some new means of approach was necessary, even though it was clear that relationships and friendships already established through the coffee bar could be continued. There was considerable discussion with the local and central Advisory Committees and a thorough exploration of the possibilities. A job in one of the local factories employing large numbers of young people was decided on. Such work was not easy to obtain. Many personnel officers were either unsympathetic and unenlightened or unable to help because the work available was too skilled and required periods of training of about six months. Eventually work was obtained in a factory making soda-water siphons on a trading estate in the north-east of Northtown. The worker explained her reasons for seeking employment to the two directors, who were considerably amused but agreed to employ her. No one else in the factory knew anything about the project, so the worker was able to make any necessary explanations herself. After they had handed her over to a female supervisor she had no further contact with the directors. There was no personnel department, two women supervisors being responsible for employing new girls.

About one hundred and fifty girls were employed at the factory, the majority being under twenty-five years old. The hours worked were eight a.m. to five-fifteen p.m. with mid-morning and lunch breaks. The noise of the factory machinery was quite considerable and made talking very difficult unless one was sitting very close to someone else. A conversation involving more than two people was virtually impossible, and in any case talking was discouraged by the supervisors who came and stood over girls who seemed to be talking too much.

The worker, with eight girls aged fifteen to twenty, was principally engaged in checking and packing siphons as the orders for them came in. It soon became obvious that the supervisor was making greater efforts to be friendly towards her than towards the other girls, but she managed to avoid any relationship developing, by minimizing contact. A further hindrance to making contacts with these girls was that production tended to be split up amongst them and the worker found that she was rarely with the same two or three girls for more than a day at a time. This was annoying as it so often interrupted her attempts to become friendly with particular girls. In spite of this she became on good enough terms with two of the girls to be invited into their homes. These invitations seemed to be made on the spur of the moment. Take for example Margaret W., a fifteen-year-old girl who had started at the factory immediately on leaving school a month earlier. The worker recorded:

I first went to Margaret's house after six weeks of factory work, when I was invited back to tea. We went straight from work. The house itself was untidy, as one might expect with three small children tearing in and out of the room. . . . I was made very welcome by the mother and got on very well with the other children. But the father, when he came in, barely noticed me and, having had his tea and washed, at once went out again.

Similarly, her first visit to Sheila D.'s home:

I was asked to Sheila's home on Sunday afternoon. It was a neat polished house with a television, record player, tape recorder, etc. I met Sheila's mother, a small, squarely plump, and compact person who clearly did not know how to react to me and found it difficult to talk at first, speaking to me through Sheila and referring to me as 'the lady'. I found this most disturbing but Sheila appeared not to notice and the atmosphere was more relaxed after tea.

Sheila was a friend of Margaret's, both girls having started at the factory at the same time and both being described by the worker as bored and listless at work and with leisure-time horizons limited to television and the cinema.

Thus the worker was able to make some contacts in the factory and to carry these over into a relationship outside the work setting. But this method proved so expensive in time that the worker terminated the attempt after nine weeks. The ban on talking and the arrangement whereby continuous daily association with the same girls was not possible placed very definite limitations on the value of this approach as a means of developing relationships. Nevertheless, it was a valuable means of gaining information, this time more particularly about unattached adolescent girls and their attitudes towards factory work.

After further discussion with the local Advisory Committee it was decided to investigate the possibility of making contact through a more formal setting. An approach was made to the Director of Education for Northtown and it was arranged that the worker should teach at a secondary modern school for girls. Underlying this decision was the aim that the worker should try to develop relationships with groups and individuals in the classroom and then extend these relationships, even after the girls left school at the age of fifteen. The school, for six hundred pupils, was one of three secondary modern schools serving a large area of new housing estates, a proportion of which rehoused families from slum-clearance areas.

The worker was to teach in the school three days a week, taking seven groups of final-year girls with eight to ten in each group. She was also to teach four groups of younger girls, thirteen- and fourteen-year-olds, to complete the timetable for three days. It was here, for the first time in the project, that the worker was able to select in any direct way the particular type of girl she wished to contact. With the help of the Headmistress's assessments, the worker's final-year classes were made up almost entirely of girls who were known to be difficult both in and out of school, those on probation, and those from poor or broken homes. The Headmistress felt that many of these difficult girls presented a social problem with which she had neither the time nor the staff to cope. In her opinion there was a genuine need for someone on the staff, some sort of social or welfare liaison worker, who could undertake work inside and outside the school with such girls and their families.

The school approach was found by the worker in many ways the easiest of the three methods so far tried. Her classes were held on a discussion basis. Teaching periods, lasting eighty-five to ninety minutes, were introduced to each group as an opportunity to express and sort out their own ideas, attitudes, and feelings, and a chance to examine suggestions of different ways of looking at some aspects of life. Girls were encouraged to introduce subjects in which they were interested or about which they wished to know more. In a report written after her first month in the school, the worker felt safe in judging:

I have been accepted relatively swiftly and easily by these girls. They did not in general seem surprised suddenly to be taken in groups for unusually informal and different lessons called 'discussions', although later some girls did question why they had been chosen and what these sessions were for. Most of the girls were soon talking freely about most subjects which interested and concerned them. It has become clear also that this is a relatively easy way of making friends with young people. Discussions on the amenities of the locality led to suggestions that I should go to some of the local dance halls with some of the girls. There was also a suggestion that I should go to the fair with some girls when this came to the area.

It is obvious from this that the worker was soon in an excellent position to extend her relationships with the girls outside the school. It was at this point, however, that the importance of chance in work of this kind was first demonstrated. It could not have occurred had the worker not also been living in the area where she was trying to contact the unattached. The report continues:

But the real link between in- and out-of-school relationships with the girls was initiated by Marion and Barbara, two of my coffee-bar acquaintances whose cousin is at the secondary modern school. As soon as they knew where I was teaching, Marion and Barbara brought the cousin and a friend round to my flat for an evening and this was the real beginning, within the first two weeks of term, of the extension of school relationships.

From the start the worker's relationship with the girls was a remarkably easy one but, as later developments were to show, it in no way lacked depth because of this. Some of the most successful work accomplished in Northtown was with the group of girls who were contacted in this way and who, having left school, continued to meet the worker. But in spite of the speed with which the worker came to be on easy terms with the girls, they were still suspicious. Even after four months, despite the acceptance shown in the previous quotation, she was still subjected to occasional cross-examination about her identity. In her report for January 1962 she writes:

More recently, some of the girls were alarmed to learn from another member of staff that I was not a 'proper' teacher. They thought I might have something to do with the 'Welfare' and were uneasy about this because 'we tell her all our secrets'. However they were quite quickly reassured about this when I told them that, like other members of staff, I was officially employed by the Education Committee for Northtown.

The girls were quick to notice too that unlike the other teachers the worker did not often discuss the things the girls told her in the staff room as soon as the lessons were over. There were always girls handing round tea or coffee in the staff room during break times in the morning and afternoons and conversations about pupils were carried on apparently oblivious to their presence. One girl actually remarked to the worker, 'You are the only one who doesn't go straight back to the other staff.' Occasionally during classes a girl would conclude with 'You won't have to tell the Head, will you?' The general reaction from the rest of the group was always 'Of course she won't!' and it came so swiftly that the worker hardly needed to reply for herself.

It was not only the girls who were suspicious of the worker. Some of the staff looked upon her as in some ways an outsider. At first a few people politely thought that the work must be interesting; one thought it must be utterly boring. Several others wondered whether the worker was studying them, which led to a certain awkwardness in some relationships in the staff room. In general those members of staff who had least sympathy with the girls tended also to extend this attitude to the worker or to think that she was being unnecessarily 'soft' with them.

By the summer of 1962 the acquaintances made through school, the coffee bar, and the factory totalled some sixty to seventy unattached young people, many of whom were in the habit of visiting the worker in her one-roomed flat. The school group was fortunately able to meet in a housecraft flat on the school premises but the rapidly increasing number of acquaintances, the time involved in regular meetings with all of them, and the total lack of any suitable meeting place in Lymport meant that no further experiments with making contact with the unattached youth of Northtown were possible or desirable. It was at this stage that the Central Advisory Committee decided that intensive work with one or two unattached groups would be most profitable in order to see what could be accomplished with them. The two groups selected from the Northtown area for this purpose were the school group and the Lymport coffee-bar youths, although the worker maintained a casual friendship with many of the others until she left Northtown. It could safely be concluded by now that all three methods of making contact which had been tried in Northtown had been highly successful in gaining information about the unattached and two approaches – the coffee bar and the school teaching – had provided practical means of developing relationships.

THE LYMPORT COFFEE-BAR YOUTHS

The account of these youths is necessarily briefer than that of the Seagate group because the worker spent less time with them. This was partly due to the coffee bar closing down before she had sufficient time to get to know them in such great detail, and partly because some of the youths left the area. However, the amount of information obtained gives a remarkable insight into the lives, attitudes, and behaviour of a group of older adolescent, delinquent youths.

In complete contrast to the Seagate group, the Lymport youths invariably came from economically poor homes located in mean streets of inadequate housing or on one of the more dreary post-war housing estates. The section of the community from which they were drawn showed many characteristics of a delinquent sub-culture. Pressures to conform to the standards and values of wider society did not seem to be strongly felt by many people in the area. There was little pressure on children to develop skills or improve themselves through education, and any discipline the child may have received seemed more a matter of parental convenience than of any belief that it was socially right or necessary. The police were regarded with ambivalence if not with resentment or suspicion even by adults, and certain forms of helping-oneself – such as shop-lifting – which elsewhere might be regarded as a crime were here often considered normal and justifiable.

Like the Seagate group, the youths who used the Lymport coffee bar showed many individual and sub-group differences which make generalizations dangerous. Three distinct groups were distinguishable: a main gang of five to ten members aged eighteen to twenty which epitomized the extreme of anti-social and unsettled behaviour; a larger group of seventeen- and eighteen-year-olds whose rebellion against society was more tempered by the demands of reality, not without the accompaniment of a certain amount of cynicism; and thirdly, a younger group of fourteen- to sixteen-year-old boys, who showed latent possibilities for developing the attitudes and habits of the older groups but at this age were more amenable to outside influence. There were in addition two or three different types of girls' groups, more individualistic and less cohesive, which displayed a similar gradation from the pleasant and fairly respectable to the one or two who were 'on the streets'. It would take a great deal of space to give full descriptions of all these various groups, and it is more fruitful to focus on the main and most extreme gang of youths. In most respects, however, the behaviour and attitudes of these youths will be compared, in passing, with the behaviour and attitudes of the less extreme youths of both their own and younger age groups.

The five central members of the main gang were Scotty, Ed, Bill, Ben, and Tiny. They were *habitués* of the coffee bar, where they appeared likeable, friendly, and humorous, being well endowed with local wit. There were several youths on the fringe of this nucleus who may have been involved in any delinquent activity. They were certainly on friendly terms with the leaders. The five central members had received a secondary-modern schooling, which had been abandoned at the earliest opportunity. For the most part they professed nothing but contempt for schools, but this attitude occasionally gave way to a feeling of inferiority with 'I only went to a secondary modern school'. The typical home background included one or a combination of the following: large families (Bill was the third of ten children; Scotty one of eight), broken homes, and parental behaviour characterized for example by heavy drinking or marital infidelity. Their leisure time was almost entirely free of parental demands, admonition, or expectation. Once a boy had left school he was generally regarded as a law unto himself so long as he worked fairly consistently and did not get into trouble with the police. If the latter occurred, the normal punishment, after a row, would be a threat to throw him out, and there the matter would rest.

It was the convictions for delinquency that finally dispersed this gang. Apart from frequent drunk and disorderly behaviour,

more serious delinquencies such as house breaking or shop lift-
ing were planned in detail. Some of these thefts, particularly of
foodstuffs, seemed attributable to hunger. Ben and Tiny, who
lived with Ben's family, were charged with such an offence.
Ben's family consisted of his mother and older brother aged
twenty-three, his father having left the home. The mother was
generally neglectful, and spent any money her sons or Tiny
gave her on cigarettes or in the pub. At one stage, Tiny was the
only member of the household earning regular money and the
rest of the family cheerfully lived off him. The general state of
the home is shown in the following brief extract from the
worker's report:

Towards the end of March [1961], Tiny was taken to hospital with
pneumonia. According to some of the girls, he had had nothing to
eat for the previous week and when the doctor came to him in the
middle of the night, they had to hunt for candles because the elec-
tricity supply to the house had been cut off.

However, even in this case, it was extremely doubtful if hunger
was the main reason for delinquency. Tiny, for example, worked
very consistently and was able to earn up to £17 per week. Ben's
most obvious failing, on the other hand, was his unwillingness
to work. He was described as quieter than most of the coffee-bar
youths and seemed rather more sensitive and shy.

A common pattern could be traced with the tougher and more
delinquent youths. Most had been in trouble in their early teens
so that by the time they left school they were familiar with probation officers, attendance centres, or the Juvenile Courts at
least. At work they appeared to settle down for a couple of years
and kept the one job. At about seventeen, boredom with work
seemed to have reached a peak. The advantages of a regular and
growing wage packet seemed insufficient compensation, and
unless there was some additional stimulus to carry them past
this crisis they left the job, the excuse being that they were tired
of shift work or some other aspect of the job or had become so
careless that they were sacked. At this point restlessness set in
and they moved from job to job and from employment to unemployment and were soon in trouble again with the police. By
the time they reached twenty-one, if they had managed to avoid

any serious trouble, they had begun to think of marriage. This involved them in the necessity of settling down into some more regular and consistent employment.

The worker, commenting on this pattern which she had observed, considered that:

This sense of being dissatisfied, bored, restless, is probably well founded and is more desirable than a mechanical acceptance of the problems and limitations of living and working in an area such as this, i.e. it seems to me better than the more apathetic acceptance of things as they are which seems typical of many of the girls. That these young people should have to work out their incoherent criticisms in this anti-social way seems to indicate the measure of the failure and inflexibility of existing channels in society and the waste of something potentially constructive in these young people. They enjoy being destructive because there seems no point in being constructive, and they follow the existing social pattern of escape from their problems in getting drunk, smashing windows, fighting – instead of coming to terms with them. Personal as well as social responsibility is involved here, but if we could find answers to some of the social problems the margin of personal failure and frustration should become more limited.

Even the more stable youths took the odd day off because they were fed up or could not be bothered to get up. The heavy drinking, which is part of a long-established social pattern in the area, was also characteristic of these youths. They seemed to enjoy getting drunk because they no longer controlled what they were doing; this was part of the fascination. Underlying this was the fact that getting drunk provided an escape from their boredom and from their lack of self-confidence. They were not unaware of this themselves. Some, including the more stable ones, attributed their heavy drinking to there being 'nowt else ter do'; others explained that they would not dare to go dancing without a few drinks first; another, aged sixteen, who worked as a scaffolder, said he only felt safe on the job after he had had a couple of drinks. The following type of report was frequently written by the worker:

Another drinking mishap concerned George. He works for an undertaker and is a real 'Teddy boy' with sideboards which come down to his chin and a long jacket which almost reaches his knees. In behaviour he is fairly sensible, working regularly and able to make his money last throughout the week so that he can drink every night.

George was sitting in the coffee bar when I came in one afternoon. His arm was swathed in heavy bandages and in sling. He looked very pale and told me he had just come out of hospital. He had been in a fight in a pub the previous Saturday and had fallen on to some broken glass. His arm was badly cut and he had severed an artery. He said he was drunk at the time 'paralytic, man' and that he felt nothing before he passed out. He expects to be off work for six months. He also expected a summons, but was let off.

At the end of March, Ted was 'run in' on a drunk and disorderly charge. He had just been turned out of a pub at ten o'clock with his mate Bob when Bob ('ever such a quiet chap') had jumped from behind on to a policeman and had started fighting him. Ted had joined in and there was a general scuffle as two more policemen came to help their colleague. Ted and Bob spent a sobering night in the cells. They were let out and a summons was served at five thirty the following morning. As he dared not go home, Ted went straight to work, arriving two hours early. He was later fined and bound over to keep the peace for one year. This seems to have had a slightly subduing effect on him.

The youths enjoyed telling the worker of their drunkenness, not in any particularly boastful way, although they doubtless regarded it as an indication of their manhood, but principally because the only dividing line between having a drink and getting drunk was the financial one. This again was as true for the more reliable and stable youths. In the area as a whole no one, it seemed, took much notice of age and the serving of drinks in public houses. The police periodically descended on various public houses, but these youths generally knew where it was safe to go, even with their fourteen- or fifteen-year-old girl-friends.

Over the past few years drinking amongst the girls had been increasing. On a Friday evening it was usual for girls as young as fourteen or fifteen to go into the pubs, but not in the immediate neighbourhood ones because their parents would know. They went in groups or with a boy and seemed to pride themselves on not getting drunk, though this was not unknown and there was occasional talk of drinking nine or more half pints of beer in an evening.

The general attitude of the youths towards girls lacked respect, although many of them seemed strongly attached to their mothers: 'the old woman'. All the girls were called 'tarts' by the boys but the girl that a boy was courting (which merely meant that they had been out together more than once) was referred to as 'my woman'. The worker gathered from their conversations that sexual intercourse was accepted as a matter of course quite early on in any relationship. Despite this general attitude they were normally indignant about prostitutes and about the girls who went down to the docks to spend the night on the boats. One evening, for instance, two girls came into the coffee bar looking for some foreign sailors. After they had gone there was an outcry of disgust, abuse, and contempt both from the boys and the girls. Apart from four girls who were the steady girl-friends of individuals from the boys' groups, three other types of girl used the coffee bar. There was a group of five girls, two sets of friends, who met in the coffee bar before going to dances at Sunport. These were pleasant, fairly respectable girls, friendly and helpful to the worker. They often complained of nothing to do but seemed more stable than many others. A second type consisted of girls who came singly or in twos or threes. Some were very unstable and unhappy at home. They seemed determined to have 'a good time', and were careless of the consequences. Many looked poor and pathetic, worn beyond their years. They were resentful of authority and official sources of help but seemed unequipped against undesirable influences or exploitation. For example, they were prepared to be picked up by passing cars. The third type of girl was the older one. These girls were more able to take care of themselves and tended to be hard and materialistic in outlook. They looked forward to at least one night a week for drinking.

Although the girls who worked probably earned only half as much as the boys, in general they were frequently expected to pay for the boys who took them out, as well as lend them money. Many of the youths were capable of earning extremely good wages; nevertheless money was a perpetual problem for most, particularly with the older boys and those who worked only spasmodically.

The worker recorded:

Money is a frequently recurring topic in the coffee bar. This reaches a crisis after the week-end when many of them are broke after three days of unrestricted spending. Wednesday is generally the leanest night, when demands for loans, for a cup of coffee, a glass of orange 'on tick' or 'on the cuff' reach their peak. Most pathetic of all is the plea for twopence to make up threepence for the juke box. Many of them borrow money during the week from their mothers or older brothers. Also they lend money between themselves, usually small sums to make up enough money to go to the pictures or a dance, or for three pints. By Thursday, money is beginning to be more plentiful again, although there is a certain unwillingness to reveal the fact that they are loaded; this is perhaps the problem in part of avoiding paying back last week's loans, and in part an avoidance of being pestered for loans by those not yet paid. I have lent a few small sums – sixpence or less – and have always been paid back so far.

The pawnshop was frequented. The main gang of youths in particular seemed to use the pawnshop as a 'paying wardrobe', the only clothes they possessed outside it being the ones they wore. Clothes were almost communally owned by this group and they were for ever swopping around between themselves. Money was sometimes raised by selling clothes amongst themselves, not without a great deal of bargaining. The amount of money they paid for their keep varied considerably. Those serving apprenticeships and the girls usually handed over their complete wage packets to their mothers and received in return their food, most of their clothes, and some pocket money. The older youths, however, gave their mothers a set amount each week, usually £2 to £2 10s., and spent the remainder as they pleased. Theoretically they bought their own clothes. In practice they more often paid the first instalment and then conveniently forgot about the rest, leaving their mothers to pay it off.

For at least a considerable section of these Lymport youths, money was the all powerful god. 'They say that money isn't everything, but what can you do without it? Nowt?' – with the implication that with money one can do anything, everything. This philosophy was equally shared by those who worked hard and put in extra shifts in order to earn as much as possible and those like Ben and Scotty, who were irresponsible and work shy.

Ben told the worker that he would do anything for money – except, it seemed, actually work. Asked what he would do if he had money, he replied he would open a chain of betting shops: 'It's obvious they *must* make money.' The ideal was to get money and then use it to make more. This was accompanied by a certain resentment against those who already had it. There was a sneering suspicion that anyone to do with the police must inevitably be well loaded. There was also a feeling of contempt amongst some of these youths for those who had money and were tight with it.

It has been very difficult to assess the significance of this praise of money as an end in itself. Probably it was not as powerful as many of the youths pretended. Ben and his friends carried out a series of somewhat unprofitable burglaries. If they dreamed that these would bring them a large fortune they were mistaken, but in fact it seems very doubtful that they had any such belief. Despite all their talk, it was the worker's impression that money was more important to those who worked consistently than it was to the layabouts. A common pattern for the latter was to have saved one or two hundred pounds between leaving school and the age of seventeen, when a period of extreme instability began to set in. They would then spend these savings in a matter of weeks or months.

Their attitude towards prisons is worth recording. To hear many of them talk one would imagine that even the idea of the County gaol left them unperturbed. To what extent this was bravado is again difficult to assess, but in the coffee bar the idea of earning a few shillings sewing mailbags – 'workin' for the post office really' and occasionally 'catching sight of a fag' seemed very amusing. Ed, one of the most experienced in such matters, was particularly light-hearted, describing the gaol as a 'proper 'ome from 'ome'. Ben and Tiny, however, were sobered by the experience of a week in police custody after their breaking-and-entering offences. Conversely Bill, aged twenty, whose most recent term of imprisonment had been for stealing a motor-cycle and driving it without a licence, claimed to enjoy being 'inside' so much that he found it difficult to settle when he came out and at Approved School, where he had been quite content, he had been miserable when he had to go home for the holidays.

His mother told him that he should join the army if he liked that sort of life.

The youths spent a fair amount of time in the coffee bar, which they used almost as combined social centre and meeting place. A lot of time was also spent in the pub, and the main gang must have spent at least some time planning and carrying out the various delinquent escapades. Many were also interested in swimming, football, and boxing. A very good swimming pool, within easy reach, was used in the afternoon by small groups who met first in the coffee bar. Some of them enjoyed watching football and supported the Northtown team and occasionally hitch-hiked to watch away matches. Only Ed actually played football. In addition, a number of boys had at some time belonged to the Avonmore Boys' Club, where the attraction was boxing. Scotty and Ben were particularly enthusiastic and they often talked in the coffee bar of matches they had seen and taken part in. Several times, they discussed whether to go to the Club for boxing, but each time enthusiasm waned. Despite the most scathing and disparaging remarks from the boys, one or two of the coffee-bar girls were 'fringe' members of the Lymport Girls' Club. However they weren't particularly involved. One explained, almost apologetically, that she went just to sit by the fire. It was noticeable amongst these youths that the group pressures against going to the Girls' Club were much stronger than those against going to the Boys' Club.

The shortage of other leisure-time facilities in Lymport meant that for most of the time many of the youths were bored and aimless. Not surprisingly, the worker wrote:

A perpetual mid-week moan in the coffee bar is that there is 'nowt ter do'. The terraced houses of Lymport are small and the rooms are small and it is evident that they are overcrowded and that there is little privacy for any member of the family. The teenagers do not stay in on these cold evenings to watch television because the rest of the family are there; it is not television they object to, but to having the rest of the family – younger brothers and sisters – all around and over them. Thus, on an icy cold Sunday afternoon, I went down to open the coffee bar at three o'clock, which was later than usual for a Sunday. As I came towards the coffee bar, walking down the main road, I could see, standing in twos or threes in shop doorways, groups of our regular customers. About fourteen of them followed me into the coffee bar; they had nowhere else to go and had been waiting for it to open.

When the coffee bar closed, the worker feared that contact with these young people would be lost. In fact, she found that it was almost impossible to 'lose' some of them no matter how tactfully she tried. During the first six months of 1962, almost a year after the coffee bar had closed, forty-three of the group called on her at least once at her flat. Half were boys, including five or six of the older youths, who generally came in twos or threes or occasionally alone. They came to talk. By this time Ben and an older brother were in Borstal and prison respectively, having finally been caught and sentenced for their house-breaking offences. Tiny was reported to have become engaged to one of the coffee-bar girls and Scotty appeared to be drinking as heavily as ever and only working spasmodically. Bill, who had been involved in the house breaking with Ben but had been discharged, was toying with the idea of joining the Army. He called several times to discuss the idea with the worker:

He talked sensibly and in some detail about the advantages and disadvantages of joining the army. He was sick of Lymport and its limitations. But he also doubted whether he would be able to stick Army life and was afraid that he might 'desert or something'.

A week later he called to tell me he had decided to join up and we discussed how long he should enlist for. ... He said he had been rather sickened by his parents' attitude. His father had called him 'all the names' and his mother had reacted similarly. He felt: 'Yer don't know where yer are. Some say it's a good thing and some call yer all these names.' He promised to write if he goes away and wants to lend me his Tarzan books to read, although he will want them back when he returns.

Bill joined the army and so did two or three of the older youths later on. At first Bill was pleased with the new life. Soon he became very depressed and discontented. He was posted abroad but it was clear that after the initial novelty of using guns and learning to drive had worn thin he found the discipline irksome and the lack of activity boring. When on leave he often procured a doctor's note and returned a week or more late.

All of these youths, including Ben when he was released from Borstal, continued to visit the worker and sometimes spent an evening with any other groups which happened to be at the flat. Of these one was composed of nine or ten older girls aged sixteen to eighteen. They had originally been contacted in the coffee bar. Alone or with a friend they came principally to talk, but they also enjoyed listening to records and occasionally dancing. Another group of twelve younger girls aged thirteen to fifteen also came regularly to talk and to listen to records. Finally, there was a group of fifteen younger boys aged twelve to sixteen, who had been introduced to the worker by their relatives and friends after the coffee bar had closed.

Any or all of these groups might arrive without warning at the worker's flat. At times, they became thoroughly interwoven, particularly the groups of younger boys and girls. They grew quite enthusiastic about various games such as charades, miming, quizzes, which had begun quite casually but gradually became popular and a regular part of an evening in the worker's room. Even 'tough' lads became completely absorbed in such 'tame' activities, attracted by the opportunity it gave for simple self-expression.

Even from this brief picture of the characteristics and problems of the Lymport youth, it can be seen that many of their attitudes arose directly out of their social, cultural, and domestic environments rather than because of any personal maladjustment. In some cases, individuals had adjusted only too well to their environment, accepting with apathy and indifference the idea that there was nothing that could be done to improve things. For example, the boys' reaction to the closure of the coffee bar was 'It's us layabouts that's done it. Never make money with us about, do yer?' And the girls felt even more strongly that it was 'no good having owt good down here because the boys do not appreciate it. They'd wreck anything. No wonder there's nowt to do. And then people moan about lads and lasses going to the pubs – but where else is there down here?' It can't be denied that there were some individuals who suffered from personal and emotional conflicts. Nevertheless much of the criticism directed against society by the less apathetic of these youths was intelligent, and the spirit of rebellion was justified. This is by no means an attempt to blame the condition of these youths on the social and cultural poverty in which they lived, thereby relieving them of personal responsibility and effort, but it is clear that work with the unattached must go considerably beyond contacting and directly helping them to a process which involves the whole community. This need will be seen again in the following description of younger girls, contacted through a Northtown secondary modern school.

THE NORTHTOWN SCHOOL GROUP

The worker taught in a secondary modern school in Northtown in the hope of establishing contact with fourteen- to fifteen-year-old girls who would soon be leaving school, and she got to know some seventy girls in class. Most came from post-war housing estates, and they tended, with few exceptions, to be less tough than their Lymport contemporaries. They often had more money, and were more sophisticated both in manner and appearance. But, as informal class discussions soon showed, their leisure-time pursuits were almost as limited in both variety and depth. Nineteen of the girls attended some sort of youth club. Amongst the others, dances, coffee bars, hanging around street corners, and baby sitting were the customary ways of spending free time. The girls who attended the youth clubs did not seem to differ particularly from the others; girls on the 'delinquent fringe', for example, were to be found in both groups. Ten of the girls who did not go to youth clubs had had no first-hand experience of youth organizations, but thought that they were probably boring, and in any case, they 'could not be bothered' to go out in the evening, preferring to watch television. These appeared to be the most apathetic and least articulate girls in the school discussion groups. Some ten other girls who were generally lively and enthusiastic in the school group preferred cheaper and – to them – better commercial entertainments to the local youth clubs because there was 'nowt doing at youth clubs'. They probably would have joined a youth club which offered more to them. The remaining thirty girls said they preferred dances, cinemas, and other commercial entertainments to youth organizations because they were opposed to any type of commitment and did not want to be tied down in any way nor to be 'guided' or 'helped' by an 'interfering' adult. When asked what kind of an adult would be acceptable to them in a youth club, they instanced someone who was a businessman rather than a social worker, someone who would not interfere with them as long as they behaved reasonably well and who would ensure the smooth running of the club.

The general attitude of most of the girls towards their teachers is interesting. Although a feeling of resentment towards authority as such was apparent, the real focus of dislike was the teachers' 'poshness', which the girls felt was often assumed in order to demonstrate that a social gap existed between teacher and pupil; they felt especially strongly against younger members of staff on the grounds that not merely did younger teachers not understand the girls, but that they did not want to understand them. It was easier to accept that someone of forty or fifty could not understand what it was like to be a teenager in the 1960s than it was to accept that someone in their twenties would not try to understand them. While some girls thought that only middle-aged people could effectively keep order amongst a mixed group of teenagers, they felt that only younger adults could understand them, if they cared to make the effort.

From these seventy girls, the worker was able to select twenty who were known to be difficult both in and out of school and concentrate her attention on them. Within six months, these twenty had come to accept the worker sufficiently to want to meet her outside school hours and continue to see her even after they had left school, twelve of them seeing her consistently. Five of these had been caught shop-lifting or found guilty of larceny, and one had been fined for riding a motor-cycle without insurance or licence. None of these offences carried any social stigma within the group, they were widely accepted as normal behaviour. A sense of insecurity or inadequacy was common to most of them, as they showed by their extreme self-conscious-ness, their diffidence away from their own group, and their socially gauche and fearful reactions to new social situations, such as visiting a youth club for the first time. Some awareness of social inferiority was partly compensated by a forceful de-nunciation of anything 'posh'. As usual, they were oversensitive to the criticisms of adults irrespective of whether or not the criticism was justified. There was also general resentment of the authority of parents, school teachers, and employers, coupled with a widespread feeling of not being understood or liked, and hence a further retreat into the limited teenage group. They tended to believe that parents, if they showed concern at all, only did so as their daughters became wage earners. This was merely one aspect of their insecurity at home, where most of them seemed unhappy. They were experiencing difficulties with one or both parents, feeling that they were unable to talk to them. To their fathers they were often resentful, defiant or fearful. Five of the twelve girls had come from homes broken up by death or divorce; two of them had a mother who was an invalid or mentally unstable. Only three seemed to have reasonably good relationships at home. The following descriptions outline the characteristics of some of the girls and their families.

Yvonne P., aged fifteen, was the youngest of five children, having two older married sisters and two older brothers. One brother, aged twenty-three, was unmarried and living at home with his 'girl-friend' and the children of her marriage. Both of the married sisters had large families and severe marital problems, including infidelity, desertion, and cruelty. Since Yvonne's birth Mrs P. had been a chronic invalid. Both parents were in their late fifties. Mr P. had long appeared indifferent to the behaviour of his family. He sometimes blamed Yvonne for her mother's illness, and drank heavily – a state in which Yvonne preferred him because he was then at his most affable. Yvonne's relationship with her brothers and sisters varied. The eldest brother, who lived away from Northtown, seemed very protective towards her. Yvonne was fond also of the youngest brother but not of his 'girl-friend', who tended to be very offhand with Yvonne, refusing to prepare meals for her and occasionally criticizing her for rudeness and insolence. There was intense friction between the two. Yvonne was very affectionate towards her mother.

In her last year at school Yvonne was charged with larceny, including shop-lifting. She seemed to have led two or three other girls astray in doing so. The Headmistress's report severely criticized Yvonne and suggested that she had no desirable characteristics whatsoever. Yvonne disliked school and was often absent. When she started work in a factory she disliked it even more, complaining that she was frequently picked on by the supervisor. She took odd days off, but held the job – which seemed a promising achievement. She was very conscious that she was only a factory worker, but seemed afraid of being associated with anything 'posh'. She liked to be the centre of attention but could accept no form of overt criticism, and either wanted to fight or sulk when it occurred. Her relationships with girl-friends were short-lived. Her boy-friends also were constantly changing and she was probably promiscuous. She had every opportunity to be so when she left home to live with a sister. Although she had a likeable personality, her sense of right and wrong seemed inadequately developed. In view of the home background this was hardly surprising.

Joan H. was the eldest daughter of 'solidly respectable working-class' parents. She generally dressed with care. There was a younger sister aged eight, and the home seemed fairly stable. Joan was fond of both parents but had some difficulty in discussing personal problems with them. Mr H. was the disciplinarian. At school she did not excel but her conduct was good. Towards the end of her school career, however, friendship with Yvonne and another girl led to trouble. Joan was charged with larceny. The Headmistress wrote a favourable report and she was conditionally discharged. Major rows at home resulted from her escapade and she was forbidden to associate with Yvonne. The episode made a considerable impression, and nearly two years later Joan still felt a sense of shame and disgrace. Nor could she tell her parents that she had started associating with Yvonne again. Her adjustment to factory life was good, with only occasional complaints. Although lacking in self-confidence and tending to be very reserved emotionally, she seemed in many ways to be the most stable of the girls.

Marilyn K. was the third eldest child in a family of nine, aged from two to twenty. Mr K. was the dominant personality in the home. He was consistently unemployed, believing that it was not his responsibility to provide for his family. He ruled younger and older children alike by a lavish and fierce use of the belt. This resulted in considerable collusion amongst the family to conceal misdemeanours from him. He was deeply suspicious of outsiders and allowed no visitors in the home whilst he was there. It seemed probable that Mr K. was at least mentally unbalanced. Mrs K. seemed completely dominated by her husband. She occasionally went to the N.S.P.C.C. but later withdrew any evidence.

Marilyn's fear of her father was apparent and she wanted to leave home. Her relationship with her mother was weak and they seemed to find talking to each other extraordinarily difficult. At school she was more cooperative than most of her friends, who regarded her as too quiet and submissive to the staff. Although a friendship with Joan H. was established, she tended to be apart from her contemporaries. She had few friends and was openly regarded as odd because of her prudish attitude to sex and her avoidance of boys. She found the idea of marriage repulsive and impossible. Marilyn acknowledged any references to her attitude with a slightly embarrassed shrug but made no effort to change. She was also criticized occasionally for her near-hysterical reactions which upset anyone who happened to be with her. Adjustment to factory life was good and she clearly derived some sort of satisfaction from it. Money seemed abnormally important to her, perhaps as a proof of ability or as a means of independence. She was unlikely to risk being without a job, because of this.

Brenda V., aged fifteen, appeared very thin and under-developed. She was very self-conscious about her appearance and seemed most at ease dressed in old jeans and long sweater, which she wore perpetually. Her parents were divorced, and Brenda remembered her father with resentment. Mrs V., who had a history of mental instability, had remarried and Brenda disliked her stepfather, who attempted to impose discipline on her. She seemed very fond of her mother. In addition to Brenda there was an older married sister and a brother of eighteen of whom Brenda was fond. Another, younger, brother of twelve seemed severely maladjusted.

At school Brenda produced inadequate work and often played truant. She had a lively imagination and enjoyed writing stories in her spare time, although her spelling and grammar were poor. She disliked school, resenting its discipline and finding concentration difficult. With another girl she was a peripheral member of a large and quite notorious group of youth, led by a sixteen-year-old boy and involved in anti-social activities. On leaving school, with a poor school record, she had difficulty finding work, but eventually went to the siphon factory. This she found unpleasant and exhausting. She became very depressed and anaemic-looking, and when she took a day off work for illness, she was sacked. After two months' unemployment and considerable pressure and unpleasantness from her stepfather she found work in another factory. Here she seemed more stable.

In general she had a pattern of erratic enthusiasms for people and activities. Two youth clubs had not been able to cope with her, and most of her friendships were transient. Friendships with boys with motor-cycles led to a fine for riding a motorcycle without licence and insurance. She enjoyed being the centre of attention and had unrealistic dreams of becoming a great entertainer and writer. She was more demonstrative than most girls, and bestowed affection generously on anyone to whom she felt grateful. She still seemed very amenable to influence, good or bad, but with a mother who had not the ability to be really concerned and a stepfather who was so resented, the prospects were not good.

On leaving school, ten of the twelve girls worked in factories and most did not like their work. Considerable hostility built up against what was felt to be the restrictive atmosphere of work as well as boredom and, in some cases, fatigue. Some of the girls gradually learned to compensate for these frustrations through such means as acceptance into a work-friendship group. The money tended to encourage stability, and although many repeatedly expressed dissatisfaction with their jobs, only two girls were sacked or had to seek work elsewhere within the first year of having left school. The mere fact of having and holding a job boosted the ego of one of the most erratic girls.

The worker's own experiences of factory employment had given her insight into the conditions to which these school leavers now had to adjust. Some went to the same factory in which she had taken a job. It was fairly typical of many in the same area, and the worker's first-hand impressions of factory life are therefore valuable, offering an objective, adult view to support what might have been the emotionally distorted impressions of some anti-social teenagers. She wrote:

No one at the factory to whom I spoke appeared to like her job, or the factory, or the firm. I was not surprised by this as I found the work extremely monotonous. At times I found myself looking at the clock at least every ten minutes and often more frequently. The conditions were often unpleasant with too much noise and heat. Some of the girls who worked at soldering fainted or complained of feeling giddy quite often. This seemed to be a matter of course to those in charge, although there was an undercurrent of complaint and resentment amongst the girls. This became most explicit and outspoken in the toilets. Nor were there adequate compensations for these conditions. Wages were not very high, and apart from the possibility of a bonus at Christmas (depending on length of service) and the possible deduction of one penny per hour for bad time-keeping, there seems to be little incentive in this wage system.

In relation to their work, these girls were bored, apathetic, uninterested, sometimes critical, more often resentful for some reason or for no specific reason. Complaints of boredom were frequent . . . and of the slow passing of time. . . . The degree of one's boredom and irritation varied greatly with time of day and depended also in part upon whom one was working with. Mostly we worked in groups of three, and in order to get jobs done efficiently cooperation between those working together was essential. Often this was completely lacking and there would be an atmosphere of rivalry which wasted considerable amounts of nervous energy as well as time. Jane, for example, would be checking siphons while Sheila and Margaret packed them, but she would not give them the siphons as they were tested. Instead, she would hoard them until she had filled about two packing cases. This meant that the others had nothing to do for some time but had to look as if they were fully occupied, and then suddenly had more work than they could possibly cope with. In this way, Jane was able to establish a sense of superiority over the younger girls which was both irritating and frustrating. This sense of competition rather than cooperation was often prevalent. . . . Thus tempers often became edgy and arguments would occur. This often ended by girls 'calling' each other, spreading around scandalous stories about each other and their families which might lead to threats to fight it out after work. This behaviour was observable only among the younger girls; the older ones were content with a few malicious words or a refusal to speak.

Life at the factory appeared to be most difficult for the younger girls. They had to take the blame for many of the mistakes made; often the fault was not theirs, and sometimes they made mistakes because they had not been shown how to do a job properly. Both the supervisor and the other girls on the line tended to use the two fifteen-year-olds as scapegoats on whom to vent their irritation and bad temper, although at times the supervisor was pleasant to them, as were the other girls.

I asked the younger girls whether they preferred school or work, but their replies were uncertain. They had been trouble-makers at school and they disliked the restricted atmosphere of the factory and the often unfair way in which they were treated. Against this, however, they enjoyed the status of being wage earners. I think it would be most accurate to say that, while at work, they thought nostalgically of the fun and freedom of school, but once outside the factory, they were pleased to be wage earners and no longer school-girls. . . .

Thus briefly to summarize, the general attitude of work tended to be critical and resentful. Sometimes this seemed justifiable, sometimes unnecessary, I thought. A sense of boredom was repeatedly expressed, but apathy or inertia or fear seemed to override most desires to improve conditions or to find more pleasant work.

These extracts from the worker's reports may seem to have deliberately emphasized the worst aspects of work conditions, but there was in fact very little that seemed commendable in them.

It was against a setting of working conditions such as these and against the home and cultural backgrounds described earlier that the unattached school-girls had to be seen and understood. Only when these circumstances had come to light could the worker claim to know the unattached and, on the basis of such knowledge, try to help them.

WORK WITH THE SCHOOL-GIRLS

There was a notable contrast between the fourteen- and fifteen-year-old girls of Northtown who lived on housing estates and attended secondary modern schools and the sophisticated, older youths of Seagate. Yet in working with either kind of adolescent the qualities demanded of the worker, the type of relationship that needed to be developed, and the method of working with groups and individuals were virtually identical. The details naturally varied. The Northtown worker was not particularly interested in jazz or drama, but neither were the girls, and her work as a result was centred on other activities. This did not, however, mean a change in method. The fundamental problems for the Seagate and Northtown workers were the same – that of helping young people to come to terms with themselves and each other.

When the Northtown worker had begun teaching in the secondary modern school her long-term goal was to develop so strong a relationship with the girls that they would want to meet her outside school. Obviously they would only want to do this if the worker could show that she had something to offer them. So the worker's immediate goal in the classroom was to make her teaching sessions as enjoyable as possible, prove her friendliness, and show her willingness and ability to help with any individual problems the girls might bring her.

The first lessons were generally spent in encouraging the girls to talk factually about themselves, especially about their homes and families, to establish a relaxed, informal atmosphere. The girls were then asked to draw up lists of subjects in which they were interested and which they wished to discuss. These included: living on housing estates, facilities for recreation in Northtown, the chances of a nuclear war and its possible effects, the dangers of fallout from nuclear testing, the Eichmann trial and its implications, Hitler, jobs, the Youth Employment Service, relationships with parents and parental discipline, sex, the facts of life, what and when to tell children, moral aspects, television viewing, cinema, advertising, attitudes to death, the colour bar and problems of mixing different nationalities, experiences of youth clubs and attitudes towards them.

This is not an exhaustive list as it only approximately covers the topics suggested by the girls themselves. The initial compilation was useful to the worker, in revealing the level of sophistication and experience of the girls. It doubtless also made them more interested in the discussion sessions which followed and which provided a renewed opportunity for the worker to discuss personal and social values in a non-judgemental manner. While such sessions in no way 'cured' any of the more seriously

maladjusted girls they were useful to that broader band of
pupils who, by their fourth year, did not feel themselves to have
been successful at school and who did not always get the support and consideration they needed at home.

It is suggested, however, that more important than any advice
or knowledge the worker could give these girls through the
discussion sessions was the friendship she offered them. It was
not easy to communicate such friendship in the classroom
setting and in an atmosphere of predetermined hostility towards
school teachers. An overtly authoritarian approach would have
been ill-advised, and despite the teacher–pupil relationship the
worker could in no way afford to make the girls feel inferior
to herself. Nevertheless a certain order and discipline had to be
maintained in group discussions. The worker could not allow
the class to take advantage of her friendliness by becoming disorderly, as this would lead only to a loss of respect for the
worker. A certain firmness of approach was therefore demanded,
but it had to be a firmness in which the girls could feel comfortable rather than one against which they felt a constant need
to rebel.

The fact that the girls wanted to meet the worker after school
hours showed her success in coping with this problem. But just
as the Seagate worker had found that he could not mix the
two divergent groups of school and coffee bar so did the Northtown worker who wrote:

One evening, the number of people who came and stayed for the
evening rose to fifteen. These included a group from school, some of
the younger girls from Lymport and one of the coffee-bar youths
and his girl-friend. Some of the girls from school had arranged to
come, others had just called to see me. My room is not large enough
even for everyone to sit down, though, somehow, one couple con-
trived to bop in a corner. There was a certain amount of edginess
and little interchange between the groups. The girls from school said
that they had felt that some of the others had been talking about
them. . . . The regular Lymport group of girls tend to be resentful of
my friendship with the other girls.

Having found an adult who was warmly interested in them,
none of these young people could bear to feel that her interest in
them was not exclusive, so they suffered pangs of jealousy. It

was very similar to sibling rivalry for parental affection; the incident was yet another indication of the insecurity of the unattached and their almost child-like need for attention and affection. This suggests that the number of young people a detached worker can help successfully over a given period of time must necessarily be small.

Because of this need for exclusiveness and because of over-crowding in her one-roomed flat the worker gained permission in January 1962 to use the school housecraft flat for evening meetings with the school-girls. The flat contained a lounge and kitchen and provided a well furnished informal setting in which ten to twelve girls could meet weekly. The worker had become friendly with about seventy girls in school discussion groups but it was impossible to admit them all to the evening sessions so the worker selected fifteen or twenty girls who would benefit most, mainly on the basis of need. This selection had to be done indirectly, by special encouragement of some girls and tactful discouragement of others lest membership of the evening group should make the girls feel too obviously ear-marked and self-conscious. In practice, once it had become apparent what sort of girl this group was intended for, girls who considered themselves and were considered by the school and others to be socially and morally outside it tended to attend the evening meetings less frequently. This was reinforced in September 1962, when, after the summer holidays and all the girls had left school, the worker made an effort to remind the more unstable about the evening meetings.

The pattern of the evening meetings developed slowly. The worker concentrated throughout on keeping the atmosphere personal and informal. At first evenings were spent in talking, making coffee, listening to records, dancing, and tidying the flat. Later, other activities were tried such as cooking, entertaining the members of staff, talks, and demonstrations on make-up and fashion; visits were organized to youth clubs, cinemas, and swimming baths. There were outings to the coast and a week-end at a youth centre in the country. However the main purpose and value of these meetings, both in the flat and outside it, lay not in the activities but in the informal talks and personal relationships which were developed. The girls themselves also valued these more than the incidental activities. This became particularly noticeable after September when all of the girls had left school. Individual attendances became more regular, which showed both the need the girls had for a group experience of this kind and the worker's success in creating and maintaining an atmosphere which could satisfy it.

Something of the general character of these evening meetings can best be gauged from one of the worker's reports, written in July 1962:

Despite torrential rain Janet, Wendy, Doreen, Brenda, Betty, and Nancy came to the flat, all more or less drenched. Betty had brought her brother's record player. We rolled the carpet back and the early part of the evening was spent in dancing.

I mentioned that Miss Jones, another member of the staff, was still at school, staying late to mark books. [Miss Jones was a history graduate in her mid-twenties and just about to leave the school staff.] Brenda at once suggested that we should invite her up to the flat. I pointed out that she was marking books but it was agreed that she should be invited for coffee. Brenda and Janet went to deliver the invitation. Doreen followed me into the kitchen and we talked mainly about school while preparing coffee.

Entertaining Miss Jones proved difficult, and both she and the girls seemed relieved when she could make an excuse to leave. I think that the cause of this was Miss Jones's apparently somewhat inflexible attitude towards the girls and the possible un-school-like atmosphere of the flat. Her manner appeared to them superior and abrupt. I think that she honestly did not know how to behave with these girls in any role but that of school teacher. Although she did try to talk to them, asking what they had been doing and about the selection of records, she succeeded only in talking down at them. The girls responded by becoming more self-conscious and by giggling uncontrollably. Brenda, Nancy, and Janet frantically passed biscuits around. Their manner towards me became temporarily more formal and I was repeatedly addressed as 'Miss —'. The situation did not improve when Miss Jones took out a cigarette and smoked it in front of them. (If they are not allowed to smoke in the flat, why should anyone else?)

Miss Jones did not stay long and when she had gone no comments were made, but the others resumed their dancing while Janet and Brenda washed up. Doreen was content to sit in one of the arm-chairs talking to me or Betty. As the other girls noted afterwards,

Nancy took no notice of Doreen, although she had first introduced her to the flat. Some attempts were made to improve hairstyles. We tried to suggest a new hairstyle for Brenda, whose long fringe flops down over her eyes so that she always seems to be peering timidly at the world around her. Brenda wants to 'look like a beatnik' and studies her appearance with some care in order to achieve this. To emphasize the point, she performed a jerky 'beatnik dance' and followed this by a tap dance. Although extremely self-conscious, she enjoys showing off but she seems terrified that she may not get a sympathetic audience, and, although she first suggested these dances, she immediately seemed incapable of performing them and had to be persuaded and cajoled into doing so.

There was a good deal of anxious talk about jobs. The end of term was only two weeks away and no one had any job to go to. With the shortage of jobs in the area, the prospects were gloomy. Brenda and Janet are certain to have bad reports. Janet said she didn't care and would enjoy staying at home. Brenda said her stepfather would throw her out if she didn't find work. . . . After this rather gloomy discussion, we began to tidy up ready to leave. . . . We finally went out into the pouring rain. Wendy and I had to wait for buses and Janet and Brenda insisted on waiting at the bus stop with us although there was no shelter and they afterwards had to walk about three quarters of a mile home.

Many of the evening meetings were like this but this example is useful because it points the differences in method and attitude of the worker and those of the more orthodox school teacher. The girls for their part were ill-at-ease with Miss Jones who, in turn, either did not want to, or could not, alter the formal teacher–pupil relationship which she had established with the girls inside school hours. Miss Jones later remarked to the worker 'it may be all right for you, but I remembered that I have to meet that Wendy in class twice more before I leave'. The implication was that if Miss Jones ventured beyond the role of a school teacher outside the classroom, even for half an hour, she would have difficulty in returning to it or in maintaining discipline when in class.

In an informal setting as relaxed as this the worker was able to offer help and guidance. Sometimes it was merely a matter of helping individuals with problems of health, since parental neglect was quite common. In addition some of the girls had used ill-health as an excuse to stay away from school so often that when they really were sick they were afraid to complain. There was also a shortage of jobs in the area and they were sometimes afraid to stay home ill for fear of losing them. Under such conditions the worker's help was of an essentially practical kind, to encourage the girls to get appropriate treatment.

More frequently the problems were less easily solved. For example, during one evening meeting the worker recorded:

Yvonne and Joan had disappeared for a while and I later went and found them talking very seriously together in the kitchen. There was silence when I entered. Then Yvonne said – 'I've left home.' She went on to explain that, after another row, she had carried out her frequently repeated threat to pack her bags. She had gone to an older sister in Northtown who had five children, the youngest less than five months old, whose husband had recently left her. Trouble has long been apparent in Yvonne's household. . . . On the whole, Yvonne did not seem to regret the decision and was convinced the family would miss her before she missed them. 'Good riddance they said last night, but come pay day they'll notice the difference.' Only one remark showed concern – 'Our mam [seriously ill] will never get any better with a family like us.' Yvonne clearly has some real attachment to her mother, but I think she has little feeling for the rest of the household, although she badly wanted them to miss her.

In this instance, the worker talked with Yvonne about the whole situation and it was decided that it was best for Yvonne to stay with her sister, where she was at least wanted and could be of some help. Beyond this, the worker tried to show Yvonne that she had some responsibility towards her mother, and suggested that she might try to visit her mother sometimes when the others were out. The most the worker could realistically hope for at this time was that Yvonne and her parents could be on speaking terms, and there seemed little point in urging Yvonne back home, since the problems would only recur. She did return home months later when other members of the household had left. Family rows and problems of this type were fairly frequent amongst the girls and while the worker could never provide any easy answer to the girls who confided in her there were several instances of the worker preventing some rash behaviour which they might later have regretted.

The need to make the atmosphere as relaxed and informal as possible has been stressed. So have the worker's attempts to encourage the girls to confide in her. This does not imply that the worker was afraid to exert any kind of discipline. It had become obvious that if some of these girls were ever to change they would need help in controlling their anti-social tendencies. Sometimes their behaviour demanded a stern reaction. They would have been surprised, even bewildered, had it not been forthcoming. Unfortunately most of their experiences of adult discipline, particularly that of parents and teachers, had been of a nagging, punitive type, devoid of much real affection. It was, therefore, particularly important that the worker, in applying discipline, should not reject the girls, even when she was forced to disapprove openly of their behaviour. Initially, this usually meant that the worker, while not condoning anti-social behaviour, did not condemn it in any moral sense but was prepared merely to point out the inevitable consequences. Later the girls became more assured of her genuine friendliness and a more forceful reaction was possible. This was particularly necessary if the misdemeanours were of the kind which the girls themselves acknowledged to be inexcusable, such as fighting in the school flat. They had had many discussions about this and in theory they all accepted the futility of fighting as a means of settling disputes. If they found the urge to fight uncontrollable they tried to wait until they were well away from the school. There were exceptions of course and one evening the worker had been talking to one of the girls when a fight broke out. The worker's account continues:

Those who had supposedly been making tea in the kitchen returned to the sitting-room followed by an irate caretaker, who tried simultaneously to shout at the girls and to tell me what had happened. The fight had been between Yvonne and Mavis, over Yvonne spreading rumours about Mavis's friend, Maureen. The others had heard some of this and had gone to watch. . . . The caretaker wanted to hold a cross-examination. I suggested that I could deal with the situation and saw him out of the flat, which he left muttering bad-temperedly about what had occurred.

I returned, showed my annoyance, and said roughly the following: you all agree that fighting settles nothing and yet behave like this. You know the trouble we had to persuade the Education people to let us use the flat and that we have to keep on the right side of the night school and of the caretaker to remain and yet you stand in the middle of the school screaming abuse at one another. Is it impossible for you to stop and think before you behave like this? Can you have no consideration for other people? Do you not realize that you let yourselves down when you behave like this and justify all the criticisms against you? Etc. Finally, I suggested that someone should make the tea and that all should behave in a more sensible way. There was a deathly silence! I went out to see if there was anyone else who had been involved. Brenda and Lynne started making the tea. There was a general atmosphere of unease. Lynne was particularly worried about possible repercussions. Yvonne came out to the kitchen to me and talked briefly. She was reasonable and apologetic, saying she had not intended this to happen but that the others had come out and had wanted her to 'go for her'. . . .

The remainder of the evening was spent in talking and dancing and the atmosphere gradually returned to normal. When the time came to clear up and leave most of them wanted to stay longer. Lynne and Brenda came with me to the bus stop and said they thought something would have to be done to reorganize the group. They were anxious lest I should get into trouble.

Two points seem of interest from this record. There is the question of timing. This incident occurred after about a year of meetings in the flat and it is probable that, had the worker reacted in this manner before she had gained the girls' friendship and respect and they had become convinced that she was really concerned about them, then they would have dismissed her as merely another hostile and nagging adult. The language and style of her reprimand must have seemed like a hundred others levelled by parents or teachers and to which their accustomed reactions had been to answer back, become temporarily deaf until it was over, or to listen in apparent obedience and then continue as if nothing had happened. This time, however, they apologized. Some even began to see a need to reorganize themselves. A second point is that the worker only *appeared* to be extremely annoyed. She was in fact in full control both of herself and the situation. She consciously chose to react in this way rather than in any number of other possible ways – such as ignoring the incident, trying to initiate a calm and rational discussion of what had happened, or asking the culprits to own up. It was a shock tactic used in a similar way to the Seagate worker's outburst when he 'blew his top' because the drama rehearsals were being held up by the members. It had the same salutary effect. Generally, however, showing anger was not the best method, and the group would have soon disintegrated had it been used continuously. The worker was still able to influence the girls' behaviour in milder ways as, for example, when she took some of them out for a day in the country during school holidays.

Having arrived at a village, everyone crowded into the small general store. In the crush, Barbara managed to place herself beside the refrigerator and calmly, almost I think unconsciously, took a packet of wooden spoons from it and some sweets from the shelf. She was about to put them in her bag and seemed surprised and slightly hurt when I quietly suggested that they were not hers and that she should perhaps replace them. Of the others, only Joyce reacted to this at all and decided that she would see that Barbara put them back.

Sufficient examples have been given from both Northtown and Seagate to show that although the workers had to be extremely cautious and sensitive in their methods of guidance and of control, they did it *in such a way that some young people who had hitherto been noted for their rejection of adult guidance and discipline were able now to accept both.* Similarly, although the workers were careful to avoid passing moral judgements on behaviour this did not mean that they abrogated their own values and standards. In Seagate, for example, the worker once refused to falsify a reference for Howard even at the risk of losing his friendship. It was equally important for the worker to make her own values clear to the less sophisticated girls of Northtown, especially since the school discussion groups had revealed that many were unclear about their own standards and values, and seemed to be looking to the worker for guidance. So in numerous ways, such as setting standards for behaviour in the flat, the worker made clear what she expected of them and they even began making a few rules for themselves, such as regular weekly payments for refreshments. When the worker took four girls to a youth centre for a week-end she was careful to prepare them for the fact that they would be expected to do some domestic chores. Yet, when it was their turn to wash up the girls assumed that the worker would be as eager as them to try to slide out of it. They were amazed by the worker's refusal. One girl became sulky and awkward and dashed off to put her hair in curlers. The others went to the kitchen with the worker and tackled the job energetically and merely complained about the quantity of washing-up.

The question of the worker's values also became explicit over the issue of relationships between the girls and the way in which they treated each other. In particular it was often necessary to protect some of the weaker members from the hostility of the more aggressive girls. It was clear from their inability to sustain deep friendships for any length of time that all these girls needed help over personal relationships. Even within the small group who used the flat this week's inseparable friend frequently became next week's enemy. Sometimes their liking for the worker seemed the only factor the girls had in common or could reach agreement over. In this maelstrom of relationships it was important that the worker should have indicated clearly that though individuals might be rejected or ostracized by the others nevertheless she still continued to value them. This did not mean that they were never allowed to criticize each other; sometimes they were able to accept hard truths more readily from each other than they could from an adult; but it did mean that the worker refused to allow an excessive expression of hostility. Where possible the worker also tried to interpret the deeper reasons underlying their behaviour. For example, in March 1963, the worker recorded:

After coffee, dancing resumed in the sitting-room. No one wanted to wash up, but Joan and Yvonne followed me out into the kitchen because they wanted to talk to me again. After some persuasion, they washed up. They were talking about Marilyn, with whom Joan had fallen out. This does not surprise me as they have little in common, with Marilyn's dislike of dancing and boys, both of which interest Joan considerably. Joan complained that 'she shows you up so'. They had been out together and had seen a dog run over. Marilyn had gone into hysterics and Joan had felt very ashamed of her and

avoided her ever since. Both went on to enumerate other faults in
Marilyn – that she made such a fuss over everything. Tonight, for
example, she had been worried because her new dress was too long
when all she wanted was to be admired in it. 'Why can't she just say,
don't you like my dress?' They distrusted her motives over wanting
a flat to live in: 'It's just for the lads', 'She says she doesn't like
anything like that but our mam says the quiet ones are the worst',
etc. I countered their more unreasonable remarks by revealing their
lack of evidence. Over the last remark, I pointed out that Marilyn
had wanted to leave home for a long time because she was not happy;
that they had no evidence that she was 'like that', even if her sister
was a prostitute. They found this unconvincing, but over the earlier
point, I did succeed in making them admit that Marilyn lacked self-
confidence when she was with more than one or two people, so that
while – like anyone else – she wanted her clothes to be admired, she
found it difficult to express this directly. I also implied that if they
were more prepared to help Marilyn, her attitude towards other
things might gradually become more normal and acceptable to them.
But Joan and Yvonne felt there was no reason for them to bother
with her; to avoid her was preferable. They accepted that I did not
agree, but we had no time to continue this further, nor do I think I
could profitably have continued at that moment.

They needed help to enable them to become more tolerant
of each other and to enable them to understand what was
happening to themselves in their adjustment or lack of it to
work and in their relationships with boys. Nor was the worker
trying to offer help with these difficulties in a vacuum. She was
working against a background of the various activities which
interested the girls, and she was careful to maintain a balance
between introspection and attempts to influence behaviour and
keeping the meetings lively and enjoyable.

If she had not done this, she might have been left without any
girls to influence. Activities were extremely important and provided an opportunity for the girls to develop self-confidence or
a sense of achievement, both of which they desperately needed.
New hair styles and dress sense visibly added poise to some
girls. Dancing and practising dance steps in the flat supplied
sufficient confidence to persuade some to go to a dance. When
four girls did finally agree to go away to a youth centre for a
week-end, they returned almost boastful of the experience,

having made friends amongst youth-club members after their first nervous reaction and initial aloofness.

It is very difficult to assess the effectiveness and usefulness of this work with the girls. Undoubtedly the worker was successful in attracting and holding some of the more unstable of the unattached girls, which is all the more noteworthy since girls so often tend to be the inactive or overlooked members of youth clubs and fewer of them are 'attached' at all. But it is impossible to measure the extent to which any of the girls improved because of the experience, or the extent to which any of them might have deteriorated in the absence of such an experience. To the worker, the main justification and value of her work was the provision of a stable and neutral environment in which problems, frustrations, and experiences could be discussed and where some of the tensions could be resolved, or at least where individuals could be reassured that their problem was not unique. Thus, although some girls continued their delinquent activities others showed signs of increasing stability, particularly in relation to work. For some, the relationship which had been established in school with the worker gave support and reassurance while they adjusted themselves to the differences in the demands and atmosphere between school and work. Even those whose behaviour showed no appreciable change, such as Yvonne, seemed to have received satisfaction from the evening meetings. In part perhaps this satisfaction was derived from a friendly, consistent relationship which they were unable to find elsewhere. Whatever the reason all of the girls became more articulate in the sense that they could now talk about some of their personal problems and difficulties, whereas previously few would have acknowledged or even have been aware that there was anything to discuss.

Some other tangible changes could be seen in the gradual development of self-confidence and self-reliance and, in a few cases, of increased tolerance towards one another. In one case, the advent of a regular and approved boy-friend apparently transformed the relationship between a girl and her parents. For most of the girls, however, home life continued to be chaotic. A more established worker would have been able to cooperate more closely with parents. However, with financial independence, some girls were ready to leave home and take a flat or find some other accommodation. This in itself constituted an improvement for a few of the worst affected, but for others it would doubtless create new temptations and problems of uncontrolled behaviour.

THE NORTHTOWN WORKER AND THE LOCAL COMMUNITY

In Northtown the shortage of suitable meeting places was a major problem which soon brought the worker into contact with the local community. There was, of course, the school house-craft flat which she was fortunate in being able to use for the school group but, in spite of exhaustive efforts, other suitable accommodation – leaving aside her own flat – was never found for the Lymport groups, either during or after the project.

This shortage of leisure-time amenities of all kinds would have been serious in any town, but in Lymport it was tragic. In the face of cramped and inadequate housing and frequently inadequate parents, the normal adolescent desire to get away from parents, home, television, and younger siblings became positively urgent. Yet apart from the public house, there were few congenial meeting places. On top of this many had to face problems of adjusting to working conditions like those in the siphon factory or to schools where there was often a shortage of interested teachers who could conceivably have offset some of the effects of poor home backgrounds.

The most a single worker could expect to achieve was to draw attention to the size and nature of these problems, which un-doubtedly affected far more than the fifty or sixty young people with whom she was in contact. Even with this relatively small number, there seemed no hope of finding any local organization which would be prepared to continue the kind of work which she had successfully shown to be possible and valuable. This lack of any follow-up was particularly unfortunate in view of the heavier dependency of the Northtown young people on the worker, than, for example, the drama group's dependency on the Seagate worker where, by the end of the project, many of the group were ready and able to leave the area to work or study in London. In Northtown, the former school-girls were still comparatively young and very much in need of the understanding and support which the worker had given them.

A couple of attempts were made to integrate some of the school-girls into local youth clubs – more because these represented the only youth facilities available than because they were thought to be the ideal solution. One attempt arose out of a week-end which four of the girls and the worker had spent at a youth centre and where they had met some other young people from the Lymport Girls' Club who happened also to be there. On their return to Lymport, one of the school-girls became a regular member of the Girls' Club, while the three others visited it frequently. Two of them then spent another week-end at the youth centre but unfortunately they became friendly with a group of the older and more difficult club members and all went off with some local youths on motor-cycles to spend an evening in a near-by pub, to return late in a rebellious and un-cooperative mood. This escapade marred the week-end. After this, their visits to the Girls' Clubs became infrequent and eventually the leader chose to discourage their going. The other girl, Brenda, finally went to the club only if she heard that something special such as a dance or an outing had been arranged and was told that this was not good enough and that, if she wished to enjoy such outings and activities, she must attend the club more regularly. Because of their behaviour on the previous occasion and because they had hardly been to the club since, the two other girls were likewise refused permission to attend a further week-end at the youth centre. Both were immediately bitter and resentful and had some harsh things to say about the leader, with whom neither had established a very satisfactory relationship. Nor had they developed any sense of loyalty to the club itself, where they made friends with the older club members (nineteen-year-olds), who though good-hearted tended to be rather irresponsible, so that they seemed mutually bad for each other. Thus it was perhaps as well that the girls' link with the club ended. Not however in Brenda's case. She was badly in need of a stabilizing influence, and for this very reason her attendance at the club was irregular and unpredict-

able. At one point, she seemed to be developing quite a satisfactory relationship with the club leader but the latter finally
became exasperated by Brenda's unreliability and considered
her to be a disturbing influence in the club.

An attempt to introduce the entire school group to a youth
club was made in April 1963. A new youth centre had recently
been opened on a near-by housing estate. It was arranged that
the worker would take the school group to visit the centre on
one of the evenings when, because of school holidays, the housecraft flat was not available. The idea was not enthusiastically
received by the girls, but about seven of them agreed to go.
The worker's account continues:

As we came in sight of the centre, everyone regretted coming and
did not want to go in – wasn't it 'posh', 'everyone is staring at us',
etc. However we got inside and were ushered into the leader's office,
where the leader welcomed us, apologized for there being nothing
special on tonight, and gave us the run of the club.

We went to the ladies' cloakroom and into a further room – a
girls' sitting-room/retiring-room, with armchairs, full-length mirrors,
etc. We spent an eternity here. Self-confidence had gone, self-con-
sciousness, uncertainty in unfamiliar surroundings were shared by
all. The retreat was to mirrors to comb and re-comb already tidy
hair, to scrutinize make-up and general appearance. Certainly the
attitude of the other girls was unhelpful – they stared, looked us up
and down, and demanded to know if we were members. Lynne was
in a panic, pushing her hair (which looked perfectly all right) this
way and that, saying that it looked dreadful and that she would stay
in the cloakroom for the evening. The others, although less truly
upset, reacted similarly. Eventually, after much reassurance from me
about how nice they looked, we emerged.

The leader showed us the lounge and coffee-bar section and left
us. We found chairs in a corner and sat down, a small group on the
defensive. Although still wishing that they had not come, some admission of how pleasant the surroundings were had to be made. It
was noted also that there were more boys than girls; that everyone
was still staring and that the place was wasted on 'this lot'. We discussed who paid for it. Janet and Lynne began to dance but others
would not. They were very reluctant to move away from the corner
and it was only when I walked across the open space of the dance
floor that they would follow. We moved into the table-tennis room
and this seemed to be the turning point. Two girls began to play and

one of the boys tried to persuade the others to join in but they refused – too many people watching, etc.

We returned to the coffee bar and were joined by the leader. All were enjoying themselves now and were more relaxed. . . . We left just before ten thirty, and everyone wanted to know if they could come again. This had been a fairly successful evening, except that there had been so little interaction with the club members.

Unfortunately, it was not possible for the school group to join this centre because it was already full. However Brenda managed to become a member, and with such enthusiasm that she served on the members' committee. Typically, however, the leader found her influence difficult to cope with and after a few weeks she ceased to attend. She was eventually dropped from the committee and deemed no longer to be a member of the club.

These two experiences with the Lymport Girls' Club and the youth centre showed that, even with the provision of more youth clubs, girls of Brenda's kind would not necessarily be easy to attach, assuming it to be desirable that they should be. In Northtown, it would have been easy to conclude that the lack of facilities was the main cause of unattachment, but these two incidents served as sharp reminders that even with new youth centres the problem of girls such as Brenda still remains and is beyond the scope of the average club leader, if only because of the amount of time, attention, and patience their behaviour demands.

In order to integrate these girls into the life of the club, the worker might have to go with them at the start, perhaps meeting with them as a separate group. With the worker's support and help, their urge to be disruptive would gradually diminish and they would be ready to become more involved in the general affairs of the club. It was disappointing that the worker did not have the opportunity to attempt this integration, but the insecurity of the girls shown in this extract from the worker's report makes it clear that integration would have had to be brought about very gradually and would have taken months rather than weeks to accomplish. It would also have demanded considerable tolerance of the resident club leader.

The worker consulted the local Advisory Committee in her efforts to find other ways of continuing work with the school group after her departure from Northtown. It was suggested as a first step, that the worker should submit a written report to the Director of Education for Northtown, outlining the work she had been attempting in the school setting and assessing its value. The Advisers were strongly in favour of the continuation of the school work, but such a development clearly depended upon the support of the Local Education Authority and head teachers. Certain head teachers in the Northtown area who already had been approached informally were ready to support the idea of appointing teachers on a similar basis to the worker's appointment. In May 1963, the worker submitted a report on her work to the Director of Education which, at the time of writing, is being studied by the Local Education Authority.

The appointment of more school staff with an assignment similar to that of the Northtown worker would be a valuable long-term development of the project. A more immediate outcome was a change in attitude which had occurred amongst some of the teachers in the school. Initially many had been rather sceptical of, or uninterested in the project. However, a few came to grasp and appreciate what the worker was trying to do, though not to the extent of trying to emulate her. Assuming the staff of the Northtown school was typical of other secondary modern schools and that a school is an important social as well as educational institution, then two other points emerge forcibly from the Northtown worker's experience. Both have considerable bearing on the problem of the unattached. First, take the attitude of some of the staff towards the pupils:

There seems to be a bland assumption that a middle-class upbringing is 'normal', that middle-class values are right, and a serious failure to understand or appreciate the very difficult backgrounds of almost all their pupils. It is apparent and perhaps to some extent fair that the teacher's attitude to a class is very different from my own – and I have many advantages in dealing only with small groups. However, one or two of the members of staff do succeed in breaking down these barriers, while others, by contrast, seem to take pride in finding the gulf too wide to be bridged. . . .

I thought it significant that when the Marriage Guidance Council organized a lecture and discussion on the social and personal needs of young people and the teacher's role in this, only one member of staff (a part-time housecraft teacher) thought it relevant and important in such a school to have more understanding of this. . . . Amongst some there is a tendency to despise or look down on the pupils as socially or mentally inferior beings and, in a few teachers, this goes very deep. . . . I think, also that there is almost no appreciation at all of the school as a social institution or of its place or role in our society.

It must be explained that since the worker had most contact with members of staff under thirty years of age her observations were limited to them. These younger members represented two thirds of the total staff, and it is probable that a more enlightened attitude on the part of some of them would be valuable in alleviating some of the problems of the unattached.

Another point was the apparent waste of the school teachers' knowledge of their pupils, which could be more widely used in preventive work. In the Northtown school it seemed generally agreed that, with a class of about thirty pupils, most teachers could identify the 'problem children' – the misfits, the antisocial, the trouble-makers and potential trouble-makers in and out of the school. The Headmistress remarked to the worker many times that she was able to tell even during their first year which pupils would cause trouble in or out of school as they grew older, and though she could foresee this when the girls were only eleven years old, she felt powerless to do anything about it. The Head's resigned attitude and subsequent manner created the danger that in some cases her diagnoses would act as self-fulfilling prophecies, but, whether or not this was so, the Head and some of her staff had very considerable insight into the different personalities of the pupils, even those who might not be noticeably troublesome in class. It was unfortunate that this ability to identify potential trouble-makers could not be related to helping the children concerned either in or outside the school.

Some interesting material on the possibility and usefulness of contacting the unattached at an earlier age was also provided by some of the younger Lymport groups, aged between eight and thirteen years. While these groups were outside the age range of both the project and the Youth Service, some brief facts are included because it seems futile to assume that children who have run wild for so long can become suddenly or miraculously transformed and led into 'worth-while' activity at the age of fourteen.

The younger children who became friendly with the worker derived from two 'sources'. Some were younger brothers, sisters, and cousins of the older teenagers who had been visiting the worker in her flat for some time. Others were brought by Sandra K., aged ten, who used to come into the coffee bar every day, usually alone. When it closed she became a very frequent visitor to the flat and brought other young friends with her. The worker tried to discourage these young visitors, not only because they did not come within the terms of reference of the project but also because they did not always mix amicably with their elders. Sandra was outstanding in that she continued to come frequently (often about five times a week), despite the discouragement and frequent hostility of the older girls, which sometimes led to fights, and the fact that the younger ones continued to brave such hostility and the worker's own discouragement is a strong indication of their need for the friendship of an older person. In Lymport, there were no recreational facilities for them except those provided by Brownies, Cubs, and the local churches.

Besides roaming round the streets (the boys generally in gangs, the girls in smaller, less cohesive groups), a piece of waste land near the docks is a favourite playground. Old pots and pans and other metal objects extracted from a near-by scrapyard help to furnish the site as an ideal place for wonderful, if occasionally dangerous, games of the imagination. A café (later closed by the police) attracts many of the younger boys during the earlier hours of the evening (i.e. five to nine thirty). On one occasion I saw them running wild in here, puffing at stumps of cigarettes with great seriousness, dashing from one side of the room to the other and fighting. Their strength and energy were almost terrifying. Needless to say, most are already in trouble with the police. . . . Many of their families are notorious for their delinquency. In such families there is a shortage of room and a lack of interest at home. This seems to mean that, out of school, their time and activities are entirely unsupervised. An adventure playground might be interesting.

Sandra is one who has this unchained and brute freedom to excess. There are no restrictions on the time she should be home at night, meals are rarely cooked affairs, and times are very erratic. Invariably when I ask her if it is not time she went home (because it is late/dark/dinner-time/her mother will wonder where she has been for the past four/six hours) she replies that her 'mother won't mind'. This appears to be the truth. I knew the mother quite well, a friendly but hopeless woman, thin, pale, and tired-looking, who seems to have given up trying to impose her will on anyone. The family is large; the father works erratically and drinks heavily. . . .

Sandra wanders around Lymport, Avonmore, and sometimes to Northtown, often alone or sometimes with a friend. Friendships with children of her own age seem to last only a short time, but she has brought an odd assortment to the flat including an educationally sub-normal boy who throws bricks through windows whenever annoyed. . . . It seems quite certain that she is delinquent and has been for some time. She was recently caught shop-lifting but the case was not taken to court. . . .

When Sandra, her friends, and the gang of boys visited the worker's flat, they often amused themselves drawing, writing, playing draughts, or other games. Occasionally the worker took them walking in the country. There is little doubt that more facilities could be used to benefit both the children and the community considerably.

But gravely disturbed family backgrounds of many of these younger children, of the older groups in Lymport, and of most of the girls in the worker's school groups undoubtedly explained much of their anti-social behaviour and attitudes. As in Seagate, the worker had only a casual contact with parents and could not attempt much direct work with them. The size of the problems in the worst affected families required social services – possibly of a combined casework, group-work, and psychiatric nature – to a degree which was beyond the scope of any existing welfare agency in Lymport. In Seagate, many of the parents had been sufficiently concerned about their sons and daughters to make the suggestion of a family-counselling service a reasonable one. However in Lymport such a suggestion was inappropriate: delinquency was regarded as normal and few parents considered their children's behaviour worrying or wrong. Any attempt to work with these young people could scarcely be fully effective while nothing was done about their families and their home situation remained unchanged or even worsened.

This long-term assessment of the situation applied to the more extreme cases. In the meantime, the worker was left with the recurrent and immediate problem of finding an alternative meeting place and another adult to take over some of the Lymport groups when the project ended. With the help of the Local Advisory Committee a meeting was held attended by interested people in and around Northtown, including two local Councillors, an industrial chaplain, two youth workers, and two representatives of the Roman Catholic Church. They agreed that there was little hope of finding any immediate replacement for the worker, but that they should try to provide some meeting place, such as a coffee bar, for young people in Lymport. Then, if a suitable worker could be found, another project for the unattached could be centred around it. The group was optimistic that once a definite project had been formulated a direct appeal could be made to local industrialists for financial support.

Despite this favourable start and further meetings of the group, the idea of a coffee-bar project was eventually abandoned. In retrospect, this seemed due both to the over-ambitious nature of the project and because the group had failed to become fully convinced that any clear cut results would be forthcoming from such a project. The Northtown worker had been unable to point to any unattached young people having been integrated into existing youth clubs in Lymport nor could she produce case-studies which could show that there had been a change in attitude or outlook in any of the adolescents who had been contacted. This was a disappointing outcome although the idea of a follow-up in Northtown does not seem to have been completely rejected. Current efforts in the area are being directed towards finding a peripatetic worker who would be attached very loosely to a youth club and at the same time who would make contact with the unattached on the street corners and in the public houses. A final hopeful sign is that several local authorities in and around Northtown are now at least considering similar appointments to their normal Youth Service staffs.

5 Midford

Midford is a country town in the east of England with a population of over 18,000. It is a business centre for a wide area, where the major industries are agriculture and dependent trades; some light industry including brewing and malting and a variety of retail trades. Unemployment is low, but the choice of occupations is very limited and the chances of advancement are small. Most young people seem at least to consider moving away at some stage, and the drift from the area, for employment reasons, is substantial.

The town has a good shopping centre, and several buildings of historic interest attract a few tourists. The town centre is pleasant, clean, and compact, but at busy times the narrow streets are congested with traffic. A large and thriving cattle market is a source of civic pride. Roughly, the plan of the town is that the larger buildings are in the centre with terraces of small houses on the outskirts. Most of the old, small property lacks indoor lavatories and bathrooms. New buildings have sprung up between one and five miles from the town centre. A large and expanding council estate lies to the south where there is also some private building of the two-to-three-thousand-pound type of house. There is another estate on the eastern side of the town which will eventually join the other, the whole being designed to accommodate the London overspill which has been allocated to Midford. A new upper-middle-class estate (£5,000 and over) is developing to the north of the town.

There are several large towns with populations of as much as 100,000 in this county. Near by there are several villages, such as Hartford and Brockway, where commercial entertainment facilities are few. Those with a population of 6,000 may have no cinema. For recreational purposes, there is considerable movement between town and town, village and town, and village and village, but the bus and rail services are poor and this effectively isolates those members of rural communities who have no other means of transport. The lack of evening bus services hits the young people in the villages particularly hard.

In Midford the social amenities are what one would expect for a town of its size – two cinemas; two dance halls with weekly dances, and two other places where dances are held occasionally; a greyhound stadium; an outdoor swimming pool; the usual public houses and coffee bars. Partly because of the poor public transport, Midford is not so lively as these amenities would suggest. The social services of the area, including Midford, are limited. The education service had no educational psychologist or youth organizer until 1962 and it was not till that year that the statutory authority began to assume any real responsibility for provision of a youth service. It is not possible to give any accurate picture of the existing youth organizations in Midford and district, the variety, quality, and membership of each being so erratic that any simple numerical statement of the youth clubs in the area would be grossly misleading. But the youth-service provision is widely accepted by both statutory and voluntary organizations as being inadequate.

Work in Midford began in 1961 and the initial pattern was much the same as in the other two areas. The male worker, aged twenty-eight and married, spent the first few weeks feeling his way around the town and surrounding villages. Unlike his other two colleagues, the Midford worker almost immediately made contact with individual young people. He at once got to know Robin, aged eighteen, to whom he was introduced when seeking a flat. He was already living in the same house and, having moved in, the worker chatted to him several times in the court-yard. After about a month, the boy formed the habit of dropping in regularly at the worker's flat for a talk. He also became friendly with a fifteen-year-old girl, Susan, who lived in another flat in the building and had struck up a friendship with the storeman of a garage store and warehouse to the rear. In a very short time the worker managed to become friendly both with Susan and the storeman. After a few weeks Susan was confiding in the worker such things as family rows over jobs. Soon she began visiting the worker's flat, and this continued until her family moved to a new housing estate. Even then she still came back to visit the worker's flat, being particularly drawn to his wife.

These two initial contacts were fortuitous. Equally fortuitous was the fact that both Robin and Susan were unattached and in personal difficulties. Robin was mentally affected by a road accident which occurred when he had borrowed his father's car without permission. Also he had recently been obliged to marry a local girl. Susan, while exhibiting less extreme behaviour, came from a home with severe marital problems.

The worker began looking for places where young people congregated. One of the most useful proved to be the local swimming pool, where casual contact was quickly made with most of the youths who used it regularly. In June 1961, the worker recorded:

There is one group of about seven who seem to have accepted me quite happily and call me 'mate'. They are mildly curious about me, but the relationship seems on a fairly sound, if very casual basis. This group consists of all secondary modern school pupils, of about fifteen years of age. They are all obviously of a working-class background. In addition, there is a fringe group of a further four or five with whom I have some contact through the first group.

So fruitful was this setting that the worker took a post as a part-time swimming instructor at Hartford, an expanding township of seven to eight thousand people about fifteen miles from Midford. He taught swimming some nine hours a week to classes from local schools. In addition, he gradually became associated with the Hartford Swimming Club, which he described as 'virtually a gossip shop', many young people dropping in for a chat.

Partly as a result of having met many young people at the swimming pool, the worker found them less suspicious when he began frequenting the four coffee bars most popular with the younger element in Midford. The Roundabout proved to be the one providing the most contacts. This had no juke box and was frequented chiefly by students of the local college of further education, older secondary modern school pupils, apprentices, service people with local friends, and the hangers-on of any of these groups. Some used the coffee bar as many as six evenings a week, arriving at five, going home later for a meal, and then returning for the evening until about nine p.m., when the Round-about closed. Through such ordinary incidents as lending a boy a pencil or offering another a lift he was able to establish many superficial acquaintances within a week or two. As public trans-port was so infrequent, hitch-hiking to see friends and relatives or to attend social events was a common-place in Midford and district. Offering lifts provided the worker with many opportun-ities for meeting people. At the end of the first month he recorded:

The number of young people who acknowledge me when we meet in the street is small but encouraging. These are chiefly people I have been able to speak to casually at the swimming bath, dances, motor scrambles, in coffee bars and public houses. I feel at this stage that to be known, no matter how vaguely, by as many people as possible is helpful. I am making no effort to push any relationship, as I think it would be most unwise. As yet, I have no real lead to what one might call the hard core of the area's tougher element. I think this will in any case be an extremely difficult problem, but I hope that by casting as wide a net as possible I shall eventually find some solu-tion to it.

The swimming pool at Hartford also led to interesting de-velopments:

One group of girls from Hartford Secondary Modern School are popularly supposed by their teachers, neighbours, and contempor-aries to be rather wild. One girl in the group (Mavis) has had some psychiatric treatment, is beyond parental control, and has been involved with a great many local boys. Jean (a member of the swim-ming club) talked to some of this group recently and told them of the dangers of leading this sort of life. They bluntly told her she didn't know what she was missing. I met this gang one evening as I returned from the swimming club at about nine thirty. They were outside the public lavatory, where I had seen some of them four hours earlier. They told me that they had nowhere else to go. From what I know of Hartford this seems likely enough.

Exploratory work in other neighbouring villages and towns continued, and in August the worker noticed an advertisement for musicians in the local Press by a jazz group in Brockway, which he persuaded Robin to follow up. Robin joined the group, of which he soon became a leading light. They played once a week in a room above a coffee bar. Average attendance was thirty or forty of whom the majority were teenagers, although a number of visitors were usually present also. The whole atmosphere was very relaxed and casual, with a great deal of coming and going during the course of an evening – everyone diving into a near-by pub for a drink when the band took half an hour's break. By going regularly the worker soon came to know the majority of the members. The club attracted people of all types and no particular social class predominated. Ages ranged from fourteen to thirty, and although one or two of the younger girls were still at school nearly all the members had jobs.

The group had been organized originally by a jazz-loving lawyer who was also interested in young people. Relationships between the lawyer and the members were particularly strained at the time of the worker's introduction into the group. Improving this relationship and helping the group to reorganize itself was seen by the worker as being a necessary job and one well within his terms of reference, especially as the jazz club was an ideal place in which to contact many of those uncommitted to any more formal youth organization. Work with the jazz group continued throughout the project.

In the autumn of 1961 the worker began part-time work at the Farm Institute, which provided a practical agricultural education for the sons of farm workers. Thirty students were enrolled each year and the course ran for two consecutive winters, from October until Easter. A certificate was awarded on successful completion of the course, but the educational standards of most of the students were low, the majority coming from B and C streams of the secondary modern schools. Most of the students were in fact farmers' sons and sons of farming families where the father did not himself farm. The age of entry into the Institute was normally sixteen, and students usually had at least one year's working experience before admission, so that the age range was sixteen to nineteen. The Institute was residential and students were allowed home at the very most for one week-end a month.

The worker arranged to visit the Institute two afternoons a week to help teach soccer. It was compulsory for all the students to attend. Half the students returned to work immediately following the games period, but the other half were free for an hour afterwards and the worker hoped to use this time to get to know the boys better.

Simultaneously with this appointment at the Farm Institute the worker took a temporary part-time teaching job at the college of further education for one hour a week, teaching English to a class of twenty boys on day release who were taking a course in engineering. The age range was fifteen to seventeen, and the educational standard roughly equivalent to that of the Farm Institute boys.

The reaction of the worker in both cases was that the jobs gained him information about the students but did not prove a very fruitful opportunity for the development of relationships with them. In particular, of the class at the Farm Institute, he wrote:

This is an artificial group. Through the Institute it is possible to contact young people who, because of the demanding nature of their work and the remoteness of their dwellings, would be difficult to contact in any other way. . . . The majority of the boys are members of the local Young Farmers' Club but this is encouraged by the Institute and, as it provides an evening out away from a residential Institute, it is hardly surprising that a high proportion avail themselves of the opportunity.

The appointment at the further education college ended after a month, but the worker continued at the Farm Institute until March 1962 because of the interesting information he was obtaining about the boys.

In October 1961, he started going to the local Midford Saturday-night dances. There were three dance halls in Midford: the Memorial Hall, which offered jiving during the winter; the Town Hall, which was open throughout the year, offering sometimes jiving and sometimes ballroom dancing, depending on the tastes of the sponsors for the particular evening; the Merchants' Hall, where there were occasional Saturday-night dances, mainly jiving. The price of admission to each was approximately five shillings, but only the Town Hall had a bar. The Town Hall dance was held in a roomy and elegant Hall in Regency style, but the Merchants' and the Memorial Hall were both rather bare-looking with an iron hand-rail running around the dance floor. The Town Hall dances were fairly respectable, and public disturbances, while not unknown, were infrequent. At the Memorial Hall on average there were twice as many males as females and, while there was no bar, the worker estimated that at least half of the males had usually consumed enough alcohol before entering to make it probable that they would be rowdy. Their average age was about twenty; the girls were somewhat younger. A small minority of the men, whose ring-leaders were in their middle or late thirties, seemed to take a pride in their rowdiness and regarded causing or watching a disturbance as one of the entertainments of a Saturday night. Most of the incidents were minor ones, such as deliberately blocking a gangway and allowing no one to pass until forcibly required to do so. Fights were also common but they involved individuals rather than groups and often no one, even the individuals concerned, quite knew how they started.

The worker became interested in the Memorial Hall and, seeing it as a possible means of getting to know some older teenagers, he next took a part-time job as a steward there. His duties were threefold: to break up fights, to exclude undesirables, to protect visiting celebrities. The 'undesirables' were usually known trouble-makers who had been thrown out on previous occasions. To the worker's dismay he found that, including himself, there were only four stewards on duty and the plan of the building was such that major disturbances were extremely difficult to control. Shortly after taking the job he was involved in a considerable brawl:

At about eleven p.m. the chief steward was removing a man for some reason when he was set upon by a gang. They succeeded in getting him on to the ground and were intent on beating him up. As the chief steward is the man who is mainly responsible for keeping order, he has a good many enemies – and in a few seconds a crowd of between one and two hundred had gathered. As I was involved in all this I have very little idea what happened at this stage, except that there was general fighting involving a great many people. The police arrived, but order was not fully restored until the Hall was cleared at eleven forty-five. One girl was kicked in the stomach, but was able to walk home after treatment. Two men were taken to hospital, and the police made some arrests. The chief steward, who is six foot six and weighs twenty-two stone, escaped with minor cuts and bruises.

The worker had failed to foresee that in the event of trouble he would be one of the first people the police would be likely to ask to be a witness. He narrowly escaped being so involved after the incident just quoted and so left the job after one month. In spite of its brief duration the post did enable him to see first-hand what went on in a 'rough' local dance hall, as well as providing a rapid introduction to the tougher element of the area.

While acting as a swimming instructor, a bouncer, and teaching in two colleges, the worker still went regularly to the coffee bars, in particular, to the Roundabout. His relationship with the young people here had been growing steadily throughout his first summer in Midford, but he still felt himself to be under suspicion. However, in the same way that a single episode in the Seagate worker's experience marked the turning point in his acceptance by a group, so in Midford the worker quite suddenly – and to his own surprise – found that he was 'in'. In October 1961 he wrote:

My relationship with the patrons of the Roundabout coffee bar has been improving steadily. For some months, I have known individuals who use the coffee bar but I was not accepted by any of the groups. When I talked to people there, they either moved places in order to speak to me or talked directly to me in a way that excluded me from contact with their group. There seemed nothing I could do about this without endangering the fingerhold I had gained. This situation changed quite suddenly towards the end of September, when I became someone it was all right to know. I probably trebled my number of acquaintances with this section of the community in a matter of days. While this change is very gratifying, I am at present unable to account for it. The two possibilities which occur to me are, firstly, acceptance came as a result of the time I spent in the Roundabout. I have visited the place four or five times a week and sometimes much more frequently. Secondly, I have been accepted by somebody, possibly Jack, who has a strong influence over the rest of the group.

The patrons of the Roundabout are predominantly middle class. The younger group are still at school: secondary modern, grammar, or private. The group seems to be unified by home background, not by the type of schools attended. The older patrons came, I imagine, from the same sort of home background and maintain close ties with the younger section.

This group is barred as a whole by their parents, by their social aspirations, by the condemnation of their friends, or by their own prejudices from attending many of the public entertainments in the town. They do not attend the Memorial Hall or Town Hall. Some rely on small private parties, and somebody has a party nearly every week-end. Many of them seem to go to the cinema at least twice weekly. A majority would seem to be desperately bored for much of their free time.

As a whole, this group has a strong prejudice against the 'Teds'. They tend to regard the coffee bar across the road (Mack's) as a cage full of wild and potentially dangerous animals. To a large extent, this division is a very artificial one. Many of the patrons of Mack's have interests, intelligence, and educational attainment comparable with that of the patrons of the Roundabout. Many of the Round-about boys wear the jeans, black jackets, and winkle-pickers that is the uniform of the boys from Mack's.

The worker kept contact with this group for the remainder of his stay. Meanwhile, apart from methods so far described, he was quite successful with more unorthodox approaches – for example, in June 1961 he saw a local Press report that Steve, aged eighteen, had been on an Outward Bound course. He called at his house, left his own address with an uncle and a message that he would like to talk to Steve about the course. A few days later Steve visited the worker. It was obvious, after a brief con-versation, that Steve was the kind of person the project was interested in. He had been sent on the Outward Bound course by his firm – he was an electrical apprentice – but he felt that the firm had sent him on the course for their benefit not his own : it gave them good publicity. However, he had enjoyed it and was ready to be interested in similar activities. The worker maintained contact with Steve for the rest of his stay in Midford, got him to join in many activities, including camping trips, and through him came to know many of his friends who were even less connected than Steve to any kind of youth organization.

Several other individual contacts of this kind were slowly built up into fairly intensive relationships with isolated groups and individuals. By January 1962, the type of contact had become so varied that a re-assessment of the Midford situation was necessary. One of the major criteria for selecting groups and individuals for the project was that they should have rejected the opportunity to attach themselves to a youth organization. But in many of the towns and villages around Midford there was no youth club and therefore no one had even the opportunity for attachment. In others, where a youth club existed, everyone tended to belong to it just as any social function in a village attracted the whole village and people from miles around. The worker therefore concluded on considerable evidence that youth service provision in the rural area of the county was insufficiently available to consider the unattached simply as those who had rejected the provision. In these more rural areas he came to see his function more in terms of trying to provide facilities and activities where few at present existed and less in terms of trying to attach individuals to youth organizations or of trying to discover causes of unattachment. In Midford, on the other hand, and particularly in the coffee-bar groups, the clientele was more in keeping with the definition of unattached.

Midford itself had one open youth club, administered by the Local Education Authority. It met two nights a week in a large room in an old civic building. Another L.E.A. youth centre existed in Brockway. In addition, there were numerous youth clubs sponsored by voluntary organizations, usually religious or distinguished by a uniform such as the Boys' Brigade and tending to cater more for younger people, teenagers of sixteen years or more making little use of them. Exact figures of youth-club membership were hard to come by, but in 1960 and again in 1963 an official though approximate estimate of the proportion of attached to unattached young people (aged fifteen to twenty-one) in Midford and district was one to six.

The quality of clubs varied considerably. Village clubs operated under difficult and unenviable circumstances. The greatest problem was to find skilled or at least enthusiastic leadership. With the exception of the youth centre in Brockway all youth clubs were run by voluntary leaders, who were scarce and reluctant to take part in any training schemes, partly a result of the difficulties of rural travel. Most clubs were closed from mid May to September, especially if the club leader happened to work in agriculture or any of its dependent industries, for which summer was the busiest time of the year. An extract from the worker's report illustrates this:

I spoke recently to a village youth leader who said he was already, with his club commitments, working a seventy-hour week and that he would have to close the club soon for this, if for no other reason. Also, it is likely that the rural club leader gardens for food on a scale unknown in the town and he must do this work some time. This last seems a trifling reason until one has spoken to someone who annually lifts a ton and a half of potatoes from his back garden and regards the success of his crops as a matter of some seriousness.

In towns such as Midford, Brockway, and Hartford, the provision for youth was a little less dependent on the seasons, but the reactions of the town as well as the rural youth left little doubt as to how inadequate they felt the youth service to be. There was a certain amount of grousing in the local Press, a recurrent theme being 'there's nothing to do'. When one local adult tentatively inquired through the Press why so many youths spent so much time in coffee bars he was informed, amongst other things, that it was because 'they do not like to mix with the screaming thirteen-year-olds down at the youth club'. A sixteen-year-old acquaintance of the worker who was training to be a secretary told him that some evenings she sat in the Roundabout coffee bar in Midford until nine o'clock, and added, 'But what do you do then? You can't go home at nine o'clock.' She was a member of a church youth club and had been to four others in the town at various times. She thought none of them any good. There were a number of reasons. Many were dirty (by this she meant both poverty-stricken in appearance and actually physically dirty). The proportion of thirteen-year-olds was too high. The premises were unsuitable ('You have to dance round the table-tennis table and you're always likely to have a dart stuck in your leg'). The activities usually were ping-pong and darts, with the very occasional opportunity of an excursion. Finally, she objected to the religious services at the end of the evening, which lasted half an hour. Many members tried to leave beforehand but she usually stayed and endured it, because of good manners rather than religious conviction.

The worker himself visited many clubs in the area and found them remarkably similar to this description. His conclusion was:

To some extent, these clubs seemed to me to attract the sort of members they deserved, but all might profit from something better. It would be false to assume that clubs of this kind would ever interest more than a small minority. I could never recommend such a club to the attention of my present unattached contacts.

Although this picture of the local youth facilities is depressing and negative, it must be seen in the light of the difficulties of organizing a service in a rural area. Nevertheless, for the worker the paucity of the youth-service provision was an acknowledged fact and while he could predict that five out of every six young people he was likely to meet would be unattached, he could also assume that many would be so because there was nothing to which they could usefully attach themselves. He thus had the perplexing task of trying to pick out those who seemed unlikely to have been attached had a better service existed. This selection was inevitably speculative, uncertain, and arbitrary. In practice, the worker found he was sought out by those who needed his help most and often found himself working with individuals more than with groups. For this reason it has been even more difficult to generalize about unattached youth in the Midford area than it was in Northtown and Seagate.

Perhaps the most striking characteristic of young people in and around Midford was the remarkable way in which they were prepared to travel in search of entertainment: the thirty Midford youths who were known to attend parties twenty miles away, the Midford group which travelled forty miles each way to a dance, Ann, a fourteen-year-old girl from Brockway regularly hitch-hiking twenty miles to Midford on Sundays throughout the summer to meet not so much a specific boy as boys in general in Mack's coffee bar, the jazz band which practised twice weekly and attracted members from a radius of twenty miles, Steve, who talked with the worker about the pubs he visited which were at least twenty miles apart. The means of transport varied as the public provision was so inadequate. Motor-cycles were fairly popular, but old second-hand cars were cheaper, more suitable for courting, and, to a certain extent, could be made to pay their way in an area like this where there were always a number of people wanting lifts. The social activities were likely to be meagre indeed for those young people who lived in villages barely touched by a bus service and whose parents were disinclined to allow them to hitch-hike long distances, to ride on the back of motor-cycles, or to go out with beer-drinking young men in ramshackle cars. This section of the community was one with which the worker had no contact.

The great distances separating young people meant that large friendship groups were difficult to maintain. From observation of such gatherings of young people as in the Kon Tiki Jazz Club in Brockway or in the Roundabout coffee bar, the worker found that basic groups were no more than two or three friends with a strong relationship between them. Larger groups tended to be loose, casual, and constantly changing. Gang life as such was virtually non-existent. A good example of a typical pattern was the Kon Tiki Jazz Club, which met in a room above the coffee bar. It had a membership of about a hundred, between twenty-five and forty of whom attended on an average evening. Ages ranged from fourteen to thirty, with a majority aged between eighteen and twenty. Occupations included unskilled labourers, typists, a hairdresser, farm workers, a window dresser, and a carpenter. None of the members belonged to any of the local youth clubs. The tougher 'Ted' type youth was not normally attracted to the Kon Tiki and on the few occasions when a few ventured in they met a mixed reception. They were recognized but received no great welcome by those who knew them; the attitude of the rest was mildly antagonistic. The general feeling was 'We just don't have anything to do with that sort; sooner or later they bring trouble.'

The club was generally free of violence, destructiveness, and rowdyism. The worker thought this may have been because jazz clubs did not attract the trouble-makers or that these behaved themselves in the particular environment of the club. This may have been due to the small membership and premises, both of which increased the chances of members getting to know each other, thus either controlling each other's behaviour to a greater degree or reducing the need of some members to behave antisocially, or both. With no restrictions and nobody in authority there was nothing against which to hit out, and this may also have been important. It is also worth noting that although during its history jazz has at various times been associated with dope, prostitution, and other evils, it has normally been depicted in a romantic rather than a sordid setting. Attending a jazz club may have fulfilled an emotional need in some of the young people: they could play at being depraved with very little chance of being hurt in the process. Certainly the make-up and dress of some of the girls supported such a suggestion.

Many members of the Kon Tiki were seemingly quite 'normal' young people whose individual and group behaviour gave small cause for alarm. Many were satisfied with their jobs, had a good relationship with their parents, were able to give and take in social relationships, and had values and standards which were in keeping with those of the rest of the community. There were however the exceptions.

Loretta was one. She was aged eighteen and employed as a typist in a lawyer's office, where she had been threatened with the sack for poor work on a number of occasions. When the worker first met Loretta she was sixteen and described as 'shy, quiet, and retiring'. Her hobby was classical music and she was quite a good pianist. Her friends, if she had any, were not in evidence but she soon formed a relationship with a girl called Judy. They 'darlinged' each other incessantly but each was spitefully catty when the other was absent. Loretta's relationship with her boy-friend seemed very healthy but finished when she was seventeen and he moved from the area. At this time Loretta began to frequent Brockway coffee bars and pubs more and more and to be a regular visitor to a Sunday-night jazz club which met in a pub. Among the membership was a group of hard-bitten young men to whom Loretta, being socially inexperienced, was particularly vulnerable. She began to drink considerable quantities of spirits and became adept at cadging drinks. Her clothes and behaviour became increasingly exhibitionist. Several times she stayed out all night. She had also been thrown out of pubs in Brockway for being abusive to the landladies.

Loretta was born in a village near Brockway and attended the local high school until she was sixteen. Materially her home conditions were good. Her father was a small businessman. His discipline was weak and ineffective until he was pushed too far, when he became violent. Loretta feared him. Little was known of her mother, who had been ill for some time. There were two younger sisters, of sixteen and fourteen, both of whom seemed more collected and self-controlled than Loretta. The older one worried about Loretta and tried to cover up for her. Loretta claimed to be 'making a hole in the fence of family restrictions through which her sisters could crawl after her'. The sisters saw it in this light too, though they disapproved of much that Loretta did.

Loretta became very unpopular at the Kon Tiki. They found her behaviour too outrageous; in particular they disliked her rather loud public-house conversations about whether or not she felt like sexual intercourse that night. This was not that the girls were necessarily offended by the morality involved, though some probably were. To be labelled sluttish in a society as small as this was damaging to one's marriage prospects. The boys disliked Loretta because of her unceasing cadging of drinks and lifts. Possibly this was also a sour grapes reaction when an individual found that she did not provide an adequate return for an expensive investment. But in spite of being generally disliked Loretta was rarely alone and quite able to force herself on groups that did not want her company.

Parental discipline was ineffective, though one particular sequence of events – a road accident in which Loretta was unhurt but her sister broke an arm, followed by Loretta being thrown out of a public house – caused her parents to keep her home for a time. One of Loretta's cousins, also a member of the Kon Tiki, who went away at this time to have an illegitimate baby also possibly influenced their decision. This show of parental authority appeared to subdue Loretta for a short while.

Judy N. lived in Brockway and was fifteen when the worker first met her. She had just left school. Physically she was a strong, well-built girl with good features and figure, yet her actual appearance varied enormously. At times she was attractive and quite striking; at others, slovenly, grey-faced, and red-eyed. On closer examination she seemed to have the rather dazed appearance of someone to whom overmuch had happened too quickly. Her home background was chaotic. Her mother and father, both in their late forties, had recently separated and both had been previously married. There were two younger children aged eight and eleven. Before the parents' separation, when custody of the children had been given to Mrs N., the family had lived in Bristol. Mrs N. had then moved back to Midford, her home town. Many of her relatives lived in the area but, owing to the frequency of divorce, exact relationships were confused. Mrs N., who worked as a shop assistant, was poor and Judy was always short of money.

During the two and a half years the worker knew Judy, she lived variously with her mother, a half-sister, her maternal grandmother, and an aunt. She ran away from her mother to the half-sister, where she was allowed to lead a wild life, stay out all night, and stay away for week-ends. Her mother took her way from the half-sister, and the whole family went to live with Mrs N.'s mother. Judy ran away, returned, and was later evicted by the grandmother for staying out late at night. She went next to an aunt. The latter, if not a prostitute, was certainly co-habiting with a number of men, and there was ample proof that Judy was in moral danger. Mrs N. from time to time exerted control over Judy. This was prompted by the occasional visits of Mr N., who seemed anxious to prove that his children were being neglected. Little was known of Mr N. except that Mrs N. alleged mental cruelty. During these two years Judy's personal standards deteriorated considerably, culminating in a 'beatnik' phase. At first she had been an active member of the Kon Tiki club. She had regularly helped on the door and cleaned the room every week for five shillings, walking four miles in order to do so. But her relationships here gradually deteriorated. She borrowed money from friends and failed to return it. She was accused, probably correctly, of stealing door money, and she cadged lifts, money, and invitations from other members, especially the boys, to such an extent that she became disliked. Meanwhile she changed her job three times and was finally asked to leave the local technical college where she had become a full-time student taking G.C.E. 'O' levels.

A less severe case was Ann R., aged fourteen and a half but

looking much older. Physically, she was a very attractive and vital girl with excellent features. Her family, while not well off, maintained a reasonable standard of living and were very prudent in money matters. Both parents were in their late forties and there were two other daughters: one, aged nineteen, with whom Ann had a very close relationship, and another who was married and living in Canada. Mrs R., Ann's mother, had been on a protracted visit to Canada for most of the time the worker knew Ann and there may have been some friction between the parents. Mr R. seemed liberal-minded and understanding but the relationship between father and daughters worsened to the point where he finally lost control of them.

Ann had been to a grammar school, made good progress, and was within months of taking her G.C.E. 'O' levels when she decided that the school atmosphere was intolerably repressive and left. She was often in trouble at school and Mr R. attributed her leaving to a particular incident with one teacher. Other girls, however, remembered Ann as being unmanageable. After leaving school, she became more unsettled and kept changing jobs. She finally left home to live in a caravan with her sister shortly after her sixteenth birthday when she had been recorded by the worker as 'drunk and incapable after a quarrel with the current boy-friend'. Socially, Ann had no real difficulties in relationships with her peers, and she was very active in the Kon Tiki club, serving usefully on the committee. It was her violent reaction to authority that worried the worker; first against school, then against her father, and then against her employers. There was also her susceptibility to sexual promiscuity; the sexual danger seemed considerable and the worker recorded several incidents of rescuing Ann from compromising situations with local boys.

Other cases could be quoted of youth faced with similar problems and all obviously in need of some adult support and guidance. This the worker tried to give by his presence at the Kon Tiki jazz club. Apart from the need to help individuals such as Loretta, Judy, and Ann, the worker found one other major problem in the jazz club when he first arrived on the scene. This was the antagonism which had developed between the chairman and founder of the club, John Andrews, and the young people who used it. The situation had deteriorated to such an extent that many people, including the most able, were unwilling to serve on the club committee. The worker's report elaborates the attitude of the Kon Tiki membership towards the chairman:

A number of young people have voiced to me their opinions of Andrews. He is generally not liked and a few actively dislike him. The reasons for this attitude would appear to be:

1. He does not make any obvious practical contribution towards getting things done. On one occasion, a group of young people spent two evenings decorating a hall for a dance. Andrews looked in for five minutes on one evening and made some suggestions. At the event, he received the compliments of visitors on the result. A number of young people have never forgiven him for this and have avoided all direct contact with him since.

2. He talks too much, and a number of young people dread getting into conversation with him because of the difficulty of getting away from him. He repeats himself frequently.

3. He is completely insensitive to other people when he is talking to them. I recently heard him enthusiastically expounding on the wonderful solidarity of the railway strike to a young man whose father had just lost money because of it and who held the opposite view on the value of strikes.

4. He is unreliable. On one occasion the ordering of a bus was the only item of organizing a dance that was entrusted to him. This he neglected to do and a number of people involved in sorting out the resultant chaos have not since associated with him.

Many people have given me accounts of their dealings with Andrews and many people have warned me about him. A number have expressed their willingness to help me, provided that I do not ask them to have any contact with him.

This reasoned attitude of dislike for an adult has been described in full because it offers a striking contrast to the unreasoned hostility which much of the Seagate youth held for adults in general. One sign of the 'normality' of many of the unattached youth in the Kon Tiki was this ability to recognize, treat, and accept or reject adults as individuals and not simply to dismiss them all out-of-hand merely because they were adults, as many of the Seagate youth tended to do.

The Kon Tiki jazz club in Brockway provided the largest group of young people with whom the worker had contact during the project, but he came also to know many individuals, particularly in Midford. With some he spent a great deal of time because they were in need of help.

One of these was Phil T., who had gone to the local probation officer to ask for assistance for a camping expedition he was planning with a friend and had been referred to the worker. Phil was aged seventeen, very tall, untidy in appearance, and with a clumsy manner. He came from a rather poor family and had a younger brother aged fourteen. Mr T., a caretaker at a local factory, seemed neither very intelligent nor very able. Mrs T. was much more alert but housebound. The social life of the parents was confined to a weekly visit to the maternal grandparents. Family holidays usually consisted of a day at the seaside. Phil had left a secondary modern school when he was fifteen and, being keen to work outdoors, became a farm worker. When the worker met him, he had only a few friends and was violently against any kind of authority. He was described as selfish, subject to temper tantrums, and occasional outbursts of violent behaviour so pronounced as to make it difficult for him to form normal relationships. He was socially very ill-at-ease, particularly with girls, which troubled him to such an extent that he was afraid he might be abnormal. In his leisure time Phil was on the fringe of the Youth Service and associated with a small camping, 'ban-the-bomb', 'abolish-hanging' group. This met weekly in Midford, held informal discussions, and organized walks and trips. Phil was one of the older members of this group and often made appeals to various branches of the youth service for assistance of one sort or another, but financial assistance was not possible because the group had no experienced leader over the age of twenty-five. As a result Phil received very little if any help but he was militant on this point, wishing to be neither organized nor led, and seemed to derive satisfaction from conducting a one-man war against the authorities.

This 'ban-the-bomb' group consisted of a number of small groups with a total membership of about twenty people, aged from fourteen to twenty-five, of whom at least seven were teenagers. Two sections were dominant, a Youth Hostel Association group and a Campaign for Nuclear Disarmament group. The Y.H.A. group had been formed by a young married couple in their early twenties, Peter and Margaret S. They had been married for about a year – Peter was a member of the local Communist Party and a strong C.N.D. supporter. He kept an open house for people who were out of work and for those of similar political persuasions to his own. Another young member of the group, Tony, lived there for some months, but he left taking Peter's wife with him. Another out-of-work member living with Peter was Lefty. He was aged twenty-two, constantly in and out of a variety of jobs and a heavy drinker. He had also experimented with marijuana, but found little satisfaction from it. Lefty's views were more extreme than Peter's and he could express himself with great vigour and skill. He was also an atheist and believed in free love. He was capable of behaving in a very responsible manner on occasions and both he and Peter could be stimulating through their wide interests. However many young people found Lefty too overpowering to enjoy his company for long. Peter, on the other hand, exercised considerable influence over some of the group. There were few direct attempts at political indoctrination and the worker believed Peter to be a good man rather than a good Communist. The activities of the group were by no means confined to political discussions, but included debates on many subjects, camping trips, midnight hikes, parties, and barbecues. In the event the worker spent considerable time with this group.

Another isolated individual in Midford was Nigel, aged eighteen, introduced to the worker through an acquaintance at the Kon Tiki. He had been to the same local grammar school as Phil and had left when he was fifteen. He was apprenticed at a factory in Hartford, and by the time he was eighteen had become a highly skilled mechanic. Nigel came from a comfortable and happy home. He had a brother of fifteen and a sister of fourteen. All three children had developed wide interests and hobbies with every help and support from the parents.

Nigel, for example, was competent at photography, amateur radio, cycling, and collecting various things. He once gave the worker a radio he had assembled at odd moments when he had nothing better to do. Despite all this Nigel was lonely to a degree which caused him considerable suffering. While not at the extreme stage of no longer trying to form human relationships, he had reached a stage where he was unable to give or to respond to normal human affection. The origin of his trouble was partly physical: he suffered from a badly overshot lower jaw which, besides marring his appearance, produced a noticeable speech defect. As a result he seemed to have developed a form of self-sufficiency as a defence against rebuffs; he was frequently curt and dogmatic in manner and often rejected friendly overtures from peers in a way that must have been very hurtful to them. It was not that he was insensitive to other people's feelings; rather it was as if he had been hurt badly enough in the past to make him want to hit out blindly on occasion. Certainly he was using his technical abilities and hobbies to compensate for his lack of social ability and sometimes as a bludgeon to establish his superiority. Consequently he was tolerated but not liked by most and some, including Phil, actively disliked him.

Nigel was at least fortunate in coming from a happy home background. In this respect he differed from the majority of young people whom the worker tried to help. Some sixty per cent of the worker's contacts who were having difficulty in forming satisfactory social relationships came from homes which had experienced some degree of disturbance, such as the death of a parent or a divorce. What percentage of the remainder came from outwardly whole but emotionally broken homes is not known.

The list and descriptions of individuals such as Nigel and Phil could be added to indefinitely, but a few brief generalizations about the attitudes of young people in the area may be more helpful if it is remembered in reading them that the less stable of the unattached such as Judy, Loretta, and Phil represent the extremes.

The much greater readiness of the Kon Tiki youth to accept adults on their merits when compared with the Seagate or Northtown youth has already been noted. Even Phil felt free to approach the Youth Service for assistance, albeit in a belligerent fashion. In many ways, especially in Midford itself, it was the adult suspicion of the young that was the more striking characteristic, although in the rural areas young people and adults mixed more easily. The worker offered one explanation of this:

Some sense of belonging to the 'young' is beginning to emerge in Midford, but in the villages this is generally absent and the question of being 'a square' or not 'with it' does not arise. Between certain groups, feeling in terms of money, class, politics, etc., may be strong, but specific prejudice which is related to age alone is very rare.

One probable reason for this is that the ages are forced to mix far more in rural than in urban communities. This mixing occurs at work, where if there is going to be any conversation at all youth has to talk to age, and during leisure hours, where one pub and fish and chip shop provide the meeting ground for the whole community. One result of an easier age mixing may be to make some adults more liberal in their attitudes towards young people and to make young people themselves rather more conservative.

The rather more suspicious attitudes towards adults that pertains in Midford is possibly the trade mark of an urban community. In Midford too, there would seem to be more of an adult attitude towards young people than there is a young people's attitude towards adults. . . . It is surprising that the general prejudice against young people has not produced a stronger opposing camp than it has.

It is perhaps worth noting also that the number of adults who meet young people socially may be very small whereas there are very few young people who have no social contacts with the adult world.

Similarly the worker judged it was one of the assets of the area that there was no general feeling against the Youth Service as such. Where feelings were expressed they tended to be apathetic rather than antagonistic. In casual conversation some young people affected to dismiss youth clubs as beneath their notice, but such an attitude usually seemed related to a particular club or organization and the feeling behind it was seldom strong. Prejudice against the Youth Service did not seem to go any deeper than this and the overwhelming tendency was for young people to consider youth clubs individually and on their merits.

The attitude towards sexual morality was perhaps the only consistent feature among the Midford, Seagate, and Northtown youth. Of the members of the Kon Tiki the worker wrote:

My opinion with regard to the girls of this group is that a fair number of them have had sexual experience. This is not a subject on which the girls themselves are particularly forthcoming. There is little talk of sex in mixed groups and little by way of provocative behaviour. My impression is that with the majority of these girls, sex is not a novelty. I find them more reticent than similar groups of girls I have met elsewhere and believe that this may be accounted for by the fact that many realize that they will probably marry local boys. . . . The youths talk about sex in much the same way that most young male groups do. It is extremely difficult to sift fact from fiction: fiction created not necessarily out of a sense of bravado so much as an unwillingness to let too close an adherence to the truth spoil a good story. In spite of reservations concerning the truth of a good deal of what I am told, my general impression is that promiscuous sexual intercourse is fairly common in the group.

These comments on the Kon Tiki group held true for many other young people in the Midford area and numerous instances of promiscuous behaviour could be quoted.

Of these the worker knew it was the more unstable of the unattached, girls such as Judy, Loretta, and Ann, who were most promiscuous. As in Seagate, much of the freedom in sexual behaviour had its focus in parties, although in Midford the bacchanalian character was less pronounced. There were three kinds of parties. There was the small party of a dozen or so, held in someone's home where everyone was conscious of the existence of the parents even though they were not taking part. Drink, music, dancing, and some degree of sexual activity were characteristic. Then there was the all-night party which occasionally extended over a whole week-end held at someone's home while the parents were away for the week-end, or on holiday, and were possibly unaware of what was going on. There were unlikely to be more than twenty there and activities were the same as at the smaller party with greater emphasis on drink and sex. It usually resulted in damage to property and strained relationships with the neighbours. Finally, there was the large party of a general 'everybody welcome; bring your own beer' nature for a hundred or more young people which was frequently held in a barn or a shed. The local publican sometimes ran an unofficial but lucrative bar from the back of his car and a band was usually hired for the evening. Jiving was the main activity, and although a common part of the scenery were couples sprawling all over the floor, real sexual activity was reserved for the journey home. So far as the boys were concerned one of the objects for going to such parties was to find a girl.

Complaints about work were frequent, but to nothing like the extent to which the factory workers in Northtown complained or the drama group in Seagate. Criticisms of wages, conditions of employment, hardness of work and length of hours were now and then voiced but by far the most common grievance was boredom, which meant either that the work itself was monotonous or that there was not enough to do. There seemed to be a definite discrimination against young people from rural areas. A boy or girl from the town was often chosen in preference to one from the country even when the latter was better qualified and more capable. The reason for this was that the town boy or girl was more likely to be punctual and less likely to be off work in periods of bad weather. As a result many young people in rural areas were working well below their capabilities and boredom was common. Resentment of the employer's authority by unstable young people accompanied by a boring job resulted in frequent job changes. Working conditions which proved frustrating to normal young people often proved to be the breaking point for the more unstable.

A final general point about Midford, which is of particular relevance in trying to understand the attitudes of the more unstable of the unattached, is that boredom was not limited to work. Even the most stable of the young people constantly complained that there was 'nothing to do'. One reason was the lack of entertainment and recreational facilities, particularly in the rural areas. Some were cut off also by lack of transport and by real or imagined social barriers.

Perhaps even more important, the real problems of the young, as the worker saw it, arose out of apathy, ignorance, and fear : apathy towards almost everything, with underlying feelings of helplessness; ignorance of their own potential, of the experiences life could offer, and – at a practical, mundane level – of what was happening in their own locality; fear of most things new, of failure, of rebuffal, and of launching out into unknown relationships. In part, such fear is characteristic of all young people, but in and around Midford it was to be found to an unusual degree. A history of failure seemed to dog most new ventures. For example the most frequent comment when a new jazz club was attempted in Midford was, 'It won't last long; nothing ever does around here' – an attitude strikingly reminiscent of the Northtown youths when the coffee bar closed. And over all, perhaps as a cause, perhaps as an effect, but certainly as a proof of the inadequate life, there was the steady movement of young people away from the Midford area.

TRYING TO HELP

Whereas in Seagate and Northtown the project had become concentrated on one or two groups, a much less coherent pattern of work emerged in Midford. Nevertheless the project was equally intensive, particularly in its concern for individuals. The worker also spent considerable time on two other major problems : the reorganization of the Kon Tiki jazz club in Brockway and effecting better Youth Service provision, not only for those with whom he was currently working, but also from the long-term point of view, as an example of the kind of youth service which young people in the sixteen-to-twenty-one age group might find more attractive.

The reorganization of the Kon Tiki was accomplished gradually over two years. By then a new chairman had been elected, the club had been reconstituted, the membership had more than doubled, and the jazz activities of the club had been widely extended. The worker's justification for taking such trouble over the Kon Tiki was that it housed one of the largest leisure-time gatherings of young people in Brockway as well as youths from Midford, and he found it more and more useful as a core into which he could integrate such unattached young people as Phil, Nigel, and the many others who were so desperately in need of friendship and acceptance by their peers.

The unsatisfactory state of affairs in the Kon Tiki when the worker arrived was due to ill-feeling between the members and the chairman of the club, John Andrews, and to haphazard organization. Less was being taken at the door than was needed to cover expenses, almost £50 had been paid out for damages to property which the club had hired for outside functions, and a recent treasurer had absconded with £80, most of which was subsequently recovered.

The worker spent the autumn of 1961 visiting the club, carefully assessing the situation. He came to be accepted both by Andrews and the members as a friendly, interested person who was prepared to help. In January 1962, the treasurer resigned and the worker was co-opted in his place to the committee, which consisted of six members and the chairman. The latter had overreached himself to such an extent that he was regarded as a dictator and the most able of the young people had refused to serve under him.

The worker soon discovered that his first task was to change this attitude of mind. In the hope of revitalizing the committee, he invited Bob, a young farmer, and his girl-friend to serve on it. They were apologetic but quite firm. Although both had worked hard for the club, they shied away from being closely involved with Andrews. Many others in the locality had the same attitude: while most were prepared to help up to a point, none would accept an official position. There was a risk they would be involved in difficult relationships with friends, neighbours, and employers because of the way Andrews set about things. They also felt they could not control him. No one else had succeeded in doing so, therefore the best thing was to withdraw. These feelings were particularly strong in those who had worked for the club at some stage and received no recognition for it; the commonest criticism against Andrews being that he was seeking self-glorification. Despite this, the worker knew that Andrews worked hard, albeit inefficiently, for the club which he had founded.

The intensity of these personal feelings meant the worker could only move slowly. By helping to organize the club more efficiently and by his influence on the committee as treasurer he gradually demonstrated to the members that a greater degree of self-government was possible and to Andrews that it was desirable. At a committee meeting in August 1962, three important points were decided on: the drafting of a constitution, none having existed before; a general meeting of the members; the open election of a committee. As a result the powers of the chairman were defined and thereby limited. Members who had previously refused to serve on the committee agreed to stand for election, which demonstrates the extent of the worker's influence. During the following year most of the committee members actually volunteered to accept individual responsibilities, which gave some indication of the progress that had been made.

The worker also gained a small grant from the local Association of Youth Clubs to improve the Kon Tiki premises. One of the conditions was that members of the club should carry out the alterations themselves and although there was some difficulty in preventing Andrews from hiring a building contractor, the members did eventually complete the work. Meanwhile activities expanded rapidly. Successful dances were sponsored in Midford. The annual County Jazz Festivals organized by the club attracted increased audiences and numbers of performers, and the Kon Tiki was represented at various Trade Fairs and at a nationally known Arts Festival. In addition a 'rock' club was started for younger teenagers. Attendance had to be limited to sixty because of the limited space. The popularity of the club was so great that anyone arriving less than half an hour before opening time was unlikely to get in.

Much of this new activity was organized by the committee, which was becoming increasingly confident. Attendance was high at the Annual General Meeting in August 1963. John Andrews was elected unanimously to the newly created office of president of the club, a position in which he could still be very active and useful; the vacant chairmanship was filled by Bob, whom the worker considered an ideal choice. The worker himself resigned as treasurer in anticipation of leaving Midford.

In just over two years, the responsibility for the club had been transferred from a dictatorial chairman to a young adult committee. More than the mere mechanical reorganization of a club structure, it had necessitated the building up in members of an attitude of mind that recognized that change was a real possibility. The worker, in assessing his role, saw himself as a catalyst, enabling the group to act in a way that it had not previously been free to do; his neutral, uncommitted position was undoubtedly an asset, because he was considered detached and objective enough to be accepted by both sides. He was thus in a favourable position to unite the warring factions.

The work with the Kon Tiki committee was a valuable but minor part of the worker's task and he was, at the same time, very much concerned with helping individual members of the club such as Loretta, Judy, and Ann, and many other young people in and around Midford. An idea of the general pattern of the project and the way in which the worker used his time can be seen from Tables 2 and 3. These show the meetings with individuals and groups over a typical two-month period when the project was in full swing.

One or two points should be noted. A number of groups in Table 3 had some members in common but formed recognizably different groups when new members were added and the circumstances or purposes of the meetings changed. The two 'worker's groups' consisted of those who would not have met as groups without the worker's intervention. Neither table in-

TABLE 2

Meetings with Individuals over Two-month Period

Name	Number of Meetings	Time
Phil	7	5 hours
Robin	12	5¼ hours
Steve	8	5½ hours
Lefty	1	2 hours
Ted	1	40 minutes
June	1	40 minutes
Ben	2	2 hours
Neville	1	15 minutes
Arthur	1	20 minutes
Sandy	1	20 minutes
Geoff	1	40 minutes
Judy	3	2 hours
Reg	2	20 minutes
Rita	2	15 minutes
14	43	25 hours 5 minutes

TABLE 3

Meetings with Groups over same Two-month Period

Name	Number of Meetings	Total Duration
Worker's Group 1	12	18 hours
Worker's Group 2	12	16 hours
C.N.D. Group 1	5	11 hours
Hartford Group 1	2	1 hour
Midford Jazz Group	2	1 hour
Kon Tiki Group 1	7	6½ hours
Hartford Group 2	15	9 hours
Roundabout Group 1	6	6 hours
Hartford Group 3	5	7½ hours
C.N.D. Group 2	2	2 hours
Kon Tiki Group 2	3	1 hour
Kon Tiki Group 3	4	7½ hours
Roundabout Group 2	2	2 hours
Roundabout Group 3	1	1 hour
Roundabout Group 4	1	1 hour
Kon Tiki Group 4 (Committee)	2	6 hours
Kon Tiki Group 5	1	1 hour
Ben's Group 1	4	6 hours
18	86	103½ hours

cludes meetings with courting couples, although these were frequent. In addition the tables give no indication of the other routine duties of the worker such as writing reports, business matters relating to the Kon Tiki club, meetings with individuals such as the Probation Officer, Children's Officer, Youth Organizer, Education Officer, organization relating to camping and other projects, correspondence, and London staff meetings.

In many cases individuals and groups met with the worker purely to talk. Sometimes they called at his flat; at others he met them casually or by arrangement in the jazz club, coffee bars, or public houses. For example, he met regularly with a group in a pub every Saturday lunch-time. He was also made welcome in most of their homes.

Once again an essential part of the job was to involve people in activities. He did this by infecting others with his own enthusiasms, by picking the moment when sufficient interest had been aroused to make suggestions, and by taking advantage to launch the contacts on any ideas which came from themselves. The variety of activities which this developed is too broad for detailed account, but included visits to places of interest in the country, slide shows, regular Sunday walks, trips to theatres, and folk-song concerts in towns thirty miles away. In addition, a series of camping trips grew from a week-end trip when Steve decided to accompany the worker, enjoyed himself, and reported favourably to his friends. With some encouragement, but without pressure, these friends joined the group for the next week-end. Within a year the members were sharing the responsibility for the organization and planning of a ten-day camping trip, although few of them had ever camped before and for one it was the first time away from home.

Transport difficulties in the Midford area were largely solved when the worker secured the use of a mini-bus. Initially the idea was rejected by the local Association of Youth Clubs on the grounds that there would be insufficient use for it. However, at a second meeting it was decided to purchase a vehicle which the worker could borrow. In the event not only did the worker use the mini-bus extensively for his own projects, but several local youth organizations also began to use it frequently.

People came to see the worker at all hours and, in an attempt to establish some routine, he decided to fix Tuesday evenings as an 'at home'. As it happened this made little difference to the frequency of visits, but the Tuesday-evening sessions took on a special character. Three people were regular attenders – Phil, Nigel, and Moira – and while the others varied, there were rarely less than seven. Sometimes as many as twenty were present. It was meant to be very informal and light-hearted but even at the beginning there was a tendency, which the worker fostered and encouraged, for serious discussion. This was led so as to allow members to get from the evening whatever they wanted. Nigel and Phil came to set the world to rights, Steve and Tom to discuss practical things such as cars and their jobs, Moira social chit-chat, others personal problems, and so on. There was no question of anyone being forced to take part, so it was important to keep the social atmosphere such that people could opt out of any particular discussion. If the girls were bored by a political argument, they could separate and talk about clothes. A code of social behaviour was evolved where anyone who did not want to take part in a discussion did so in such a way that people who were taking part were not disturbed. This freedom to opt out was very important to the worker, as he usually had one or two members he was coaxing into social conversation or serious discussion and it was vital that they should not feel coerced.

What was so crucial to the success or failure of these meetings was the worker's attitude and method. Since some of the more orthodox youth leaders seem to find this approach alien and difficult and because the whole tenor of the discussions and the worker's part in them provides such a concise illustration of the general non-judgemental attitude upon which so much stress has been placed, it is worth quoting the worker's account at length:

Almost anything can happen on a Tuesday evening, but as I am particularly interested in two possibilities, there are two items which occur with increasing frequency. One is discussion which is either intellectually stimulating or slanted towards some aspect of social training. The second is a mild form of group therapy. As I have a nucleus who talk fairly freely I can usually keep track of where the discussion is going and look after the refereeing at the same time. This is a matter of rewarding X for making her first contribution ever, stopping B and C ganging up on A and cutting him to pieces, remembering to smile at M, who gets nervous if looked at too intently, and so on.

The therapy sessions are rarer but very rewarding. What usually happens here is that someone presents a problem and others indicate that they have the same or a similar problem which is then fully discussed. Some aspect of not getting on with parents is a common example. In this work I have numerous functions. First, it is necessary to get all the cards on the table, but at the same time it is sometimes necessary to protect a member from himself to stop him stripping his soul bare in such a way that would be acutely embarrassing to him later. It is usually necessary to present the problem in a number of different ways and to invent a great many possible solutions, not as solutions, but as aids to the investigation of the problem. Often, it is necessary to get down to the business of interpreting people to themselves in a fairly direct manner. However, most of the work is done by the group itself and the session can be very searching and valuable.

For this aspect of my job, I pick my group in the sense that I do not embark on this sort of work unless most of those present are ready to respond to the demands it makes on them. The odd 'outsider' tends to be drawn into the group, but the process demands total participation, and distraction is unthinkable. For this reason too, it is necessary to give some thought to the physical circumstances – for example, people arriving or having to leave – and to adjust these as far as possible.

It is very difficult to assess the value of these sessions, but even the statement of the problem has a certain cathartic value in cases where it is something that has been bottled up for a long time. The discovery that a problem is not unique is immensely comforting and reassuring and a discussion of the problem often enables it to be understood. I would not say that this process solves the problem, but it does enable the problem to be solved. In many cases, there is no solution, but a lot of emotional pain is alleviated when the problem is understood and seen in its correct perspective. . . .

My role in this is very clearly understood. One evening we were discussing, in a very light-hearted way, each other's hobby horses, and had decided that our agnostic was obsessed by religion, that another member was 'against people who gave orders', another was obsessed by his pacifism, and so on. Eventually, someone turned to me and said, 'And I know what your hobby horse is – well it's not a hobby horse exactly, more what you like doing. You like drawing people out.' I was happy enough to admit to this, and was further pleased to learn that some members realized that when I was being provocative I was not necessarily expressing my own point of view.

Looking at Tuesday nights generally, I would claim that at their best they have been exciting and unusual. I am not alone in being impressed, and outsiders who have seen a little of what is happening have been surprised by the type of topic discussed and level of discussion. However, my favourite testimonial came from a very intelligent and socially active twenty-year-old (a boy whose chaotic family circumstances currently demand that he live in the slums of Glasgow with his father's mistress) who said simply that he had not enjoyed himself so much for a long time and that he had never before heard people talk as these people talked.

Of course Tuesday night is not only a discussion group. Plenty of things happen – whether it is listening to music, eating fish and chips, or gossip. The point is that serious discussion is one of the things that does occur.

What young people seemed to value most was the availability of a sympathetic adult who was prepared to listen to their problems and offer advice when asked. After many months of this, the worker began to notice a few changes in individuals, some which were doubtless due to the natural processes of growing up but others which may not have been. Phil with his poorly developed social abilities and aggressive reactions to authority came frequently to the worker for help and, through the support and encouragement he received, started to risk himself more in social relationships. He went on camping trips with the worker and became active in the affairs of the Kon Tiki jazz club. As he ventured into new and, to him, often alarming situations, he passed through a stage of heavy dependence on the worker which reached its height in the winter of 1962/3. During this period, the worker spent a great deal of time with Phil, talking about human relationships:

Our little sessions usually took place late at night in my flat or in the car after we had left the others. He got into the habit of presenting me with problems – anything from 'one's relationship with one's boss' to 'sex before marriage' – and, quite obviously, he had given a lot of thought to the subject for tonight before he threw it at me. These were intelligent and reasonable discussions quite unlike anything that would have been possible with Phil twelve months before.

This increased ability to discuss his problems was accompanied by a marked improvement in Phil's attitude towards authority. His difficulties with girls remained, but he had one or two short-lived affairs and could see the whole thing in perspective, which made it much less distressing to him. The most tangible difference was that Phil could now talk and think coherently, whereas before he could not. He had gained confidence, and a certain persistence had replaced the previous spasmodic enthusiasms. Phil himself was aware of this change and once said in a moment of honesty rather than conceit: 'People can sort themselves out if they make the effort; I know because I have done it.'

Superficially, Phil's problems were very similar to Nigel's in so far as both were 'friendless'. But whereas helping Phil to develop his social abilities triggered the release of other latent abilities, in Nigel's case, it was the reverse; the other abilities had already been developed and were being used to compensate for a lack of social ability. Nigel never missed the Tuesday-evening sessions and through the worker's support he developed more confidence. As he did so his need to be cruel gradually diminished. The worker also introduced Nigel to the Kon Tiki. Unfortunately he was slow to make any real friends; after ten months of very intensive work with Nigel, partial acceptance by peers was the most he seemed able to achieve. During this time his speech defect almost vanished, showing that its cause was nervous rather than physical. At first he had been uncommunicative, especially at the Tuesday sessions, but now he began to talk more freely and was able to accept and make 'personal' jokes. Outside this group, however, he remained a very lonely person.

Moira, aged seventeen, was introduced to the Tuesday-evening sessions by Phil; she was another who had frequent recourse to the worker, although relatively stable compared with many of the worker's contacts. She had a strained relationship with her father and resisted authority: she could sometimes be persuaded but never told to do things. She was unsettled in her job as a typist and, much to her concern, very 'cold' in her relationships with other people. In any group she was attention-seeking and mildly disruptive. Her behaviour was directed mainly at boys, but rarely at any particular one. On camping trips there were always incidents involving Moira. If to attract attention it was necessary for her to fall down and hurt herself then she fell down and hurt herself. She left things, lost things, fell into, out of, and over things, was attacked by wild animals and followed by strange men, all very ingeniously, her ruses rarely being spotted. Progress with Moira was slow but, particularly through the Tuesday-evening sessions, she began to develop more honest relationships and her attention-seeking behaviour began to ease up. Meanwhile, she decided to change her job and become a children's nurse. The fact that her father and one or two other adults had sensibly but roundly condemned the idea only stiffened her resolution. Faced with this situation where to change her mind would have meant losing face, the worker saw his main task as one of protecting Moira from undue frustration. He knew she would take a job as a children's nurse; he could only hope to make the experience more tolerable.

The majority of jobs advertised were in remote rural areas but Moira, entertaining glamorous ideas of farms and horse-riding, was completely unequipped for social isolation. I felt that the working experience might be valuable to her but did not consider that a period of undiluted misery was going to be of much use to anyone. In our frequent discussions, I tried to set her imagination working by getting her to think what her working day would be like, what the place would look like, how long it would take her to get home, and what it would cost. I think this may have helped her to consider jobs in rather more realistic terms. Eventually, she found a temporary job that was less unsuitable than most. . . . My wife supplied a testimonial, and we corresponded while she was away. She was hard-worked but stuck the job well. On her return, two months later, she was convinced she had had enough.

The next idea was hairdressing. . . .

Many other examples could be quoted to show the ways in which the worker tried to help individuals and groups. In some cases changes for the better were noticeable and possibly due to the worker's influence. But there were others who proved hard to reach, including Judy, Loretta, and Ann. Although the worker had become a trusted friend to all three and probably had as much influence over them as anyone, he felt that he was only applying first aid or, at the very best, nibbling at the edges of what were probably considerable problems. He felt that a woman worker would have been able to achieve far more with these three girls.

The degree to which the worker had become accepted by the local community can be gauged from the fact that, within twelve to sixteen months of being in Midford, people whom he had never even met felt free to seek his advice. These included parents as well as young people. Thus, in spite of his ill-defined identity, he had become a recognized source of help in the community.

Indeed, to a much greater extent than in either Northtown or Seagate, the Midford worker was able to involve himself in the affairs of the local community and thereby give an interesting demonstration of some of the liaison aspects of the detached worker's job. He was enabled to do this by the rather more open recognition afforded him compared with the other two workers. This arose in part from the conditions of rural life in and around Midford where it was clearly impossible for a youth worker to operate incognito or meet with one group unbeknown to another. Moreover, the Midford worker came into contact with a much wider range of groups and individuals drawn from a radius of twenty to thirty miles, and to provide facilities, equipment, and adult goodwill for such a broad scatter of young people inevitably meant approaching a greater number of local individuals or organizations than would have been necessary or possible if the Midford worker had centred his work on one small area of a large town such as Seagate or Northtown.

As a result, by the final year the worker's interest in youth work was widely known. So were his connexions with various youth officers, the probation officer, and the children's officer. Some of these people were members of the local Advisory Committee. The fact that the worker was leaving the area in order to take a youth job was well accepted; no one had as much as mentioned his writing activities for months and a local youth officer was becoming a regular visitor to the Tuesday-evening discussion sessions. The worker's open association with the Youth Service in retrospect seems to have been both inevitable and unavoidable for reasons which have already been explained and because one of the most effective ways of helping the unattached had been to work with the adult community to provide more facilities. Once the worker had recognized this and had become acknowledged by the neighbourhood as a person who was both interested and skilled in youth work, the way was open to a more community-focused approach than had been possible in either Northtown or Seagate.

The manner in which the Midford worker discussed the project and various young people with local social workers, educationalists, and a psychiatrist is a good example. On a small scale, an attempt was made at the kind of two-way traffic which, in a non-experimental service to the unattached, should be an essential part of the job. Thus, occasionally, the probation officer or children's officer directly referred young people to the worker in the belief that friendship with him and possibly acceptance in one of his groups would be helpful to them. Conversely, the worker sometimes aided young people to get help from local social services. The worker and local social workers were also often able to exchange useful information about young people.

For example, some local youths known to the worker were involved as receivers of stolen confectionery. No charge was brought against them, although one could have been. They tended to treat the matter very lightly and the probation officer suggested that if they could be warned that the case against them for receiving was still technically open this might be an inducement to future good behaviour. And in fact the worker was able to get them to take the matter much more seriously. In another case, also involving stolen confectionery, he persuaded a local adult as well as some young people not to be so foolish as to receive stolen goods and risk prosecution.

The worker found himself acting as a link between young people and the adult community, and it has raised in some minds the interesting question; if not the worker, then who in the local community is responsible for this kind of liaison work? The small grant which was obtained for the Kon Tiki jazz club and the loan of a mini-bus have both already been mentioned. Prior to this the worker had on occasion borrowed a bus from the local Round Table organization. He was also able to arrange a grant from the Children's Office in order that a boy under care could accompany him on a camping trip. Such forms of help were of course neither new or even unusual.

The worker was also responsible for bringing about a closer link between some of his contacts and the Youth Service. In the minds of most young people an important distinction existed between the youth club as such and courses organized by the statutory Youth Service. The two branches were attracting different young people. Attendance at one was not necessarily related to attendance at the other. As a result local clubs failed to receive any stimulus from the courses while non-club members attending the courses were left without further provision once the course had finished, and ended up by being disappointed in that there was no follow-up to an interest that had been aroused. A film-appreciation week-end was a typical example of this. A few weeks beforehand the worker armed himself with leaflets and application forms; his position may have debarred him from acting too obviously as a publicity officer for a Youth Service course, but he was ready to try to stimulate interest. Nevertheless a little dubious, he felt he ought to play safe in approaching only those of the unattached who could withstand the disappointment of the course proving a failure. With these reservations in mind, the worker chatted about the course to several people in the Kon Tiki, including some who would not dream of entering a youth club. He talked enthusiastically about it, describing its probable content and the kind of week-end it was likely to be. Eventually five people, including Phil, decided to attend. They were interested rather than keen when they set off but all enjoyed the course and were more enthusiastic in retrospect than they had been in anticipation.

There was however no follow-up. The worker regarded this as a missed opportunity. It might have been quite feasible to form specialist groups as a result of a week-end such as this although such a development would obviously have needed a large measure of quite specific assistance. But it seemed worth the effort. One of the major problems in organizing a rural youth service was the insufficient numbers of young people in any one village to support a youth club; a reliable local report stated there were under ten seventeen-to-twenty-one-year-olds in most villages, while many had just two or three. It was clear that under these conditions much youth work, if it were to be effective, would have to be done on an area basis, particularly so with specialist activities.

The statutory Youth Service was concerning itself at this time with building new youth centres in Midford and Hartford and regarded its function as being to provide a service which would attract young people to it, rather than one which reached out to them. It was hoped that the centres would provide activities unavailable in clubs, such as small specialist groups or an opportunity for training. The difficulty which the worker foresaw in all this was that unless someone went out to stir up attendance amongst the unattached the demand for such a service would not exist; the fact that so few of the young people who attended the Youth Service courses belonged to any youth club seemed to support his point. Ideally, it would be the function of a youth tutor to provide such stimulation, but the worker considered :

Since he is also running the centre, teaching, and educating adults, it seems unlikely that he is going to do much of this at ground level unless he is very determined to do so. I am not afraid that the centres will be empty, but I think there is a danger that they may become glorified night schools, not really related to anything outside their own walls.

It remains to be seen if this danger will materialize.

During the project the worker had initially asked his local Advisory Committee if anyone knew of a barn or similar building which he could hire for winter camping week-ends. He saw that there was a need for some kind of residential accommodation which could be used by his own groups of young people, particularly by those who were developing an interest in camping and outdoor projects of various descriptions. Eventually the idea of renovating an old building was put to the Committee of the local Association of Youth Clubs which then offered financial support for the scheme if a building could be found. The plan which the worker detailed to the Committee is outlined here because it shows the type of facilities and activities which the worker believed would attract some of the unattached in the sixteen-to-twenty age range.

Main Aim

To make available to young people an unstaffed centre offering residential accommodation of a simple kind similar to that found in un-wardened Youth Hostels.

Uses

1. A camp site including a tent site for summer camps, affording under-cover facilities for eating and cooking and a safe harbour in the event of very bad weather. As an in-county centre this may provide the opportunity of camping for clubs not at present undertaking this activity. It would have the advantages of being cheap, safe, and easily accessible. It would also be used as a week-end camp-

ing site to provide training facilities for groups before they go away on more ambitious trips and also for groups unable to get away for longer periods.

2. A hostel which would provide the winter equivalent of camping; a foretaste of what hostelling is like and a training centre from which to run the Duke of Edinburgh Award Scheme or similar projects. It would also cater especially for those young people who would welcome and benefit from the 'communal-living' aspects of youth hostelling but who either have no desire to walk or cycle, or who need leading towards these pursuits.

3. An open-country pursuits centre where an opportunity to learn camping, walking, cycling, and canoeing could be provided.

4. A centre for specialist groups.

Finally, the renovation of a building would itself be a long-term project undertaken by young people.

Unfortunately, in spite of an intensive search by the worker and other local adults, no suitable building could be found. All the same it could at least be said that some adults both within and outside the Youth Service had become aware and were not unsympathetic to the need for a residential centre of this kind.

A further disappointment was the difficulty in Midford, as in Northtown and Seagate, of finding local organizations which were prepared to take on responsibility for any of his groups when the project ended. In particular, it seemed essential that two of the groups should receive further support – the Kon Tiki jazz club in Brockway and the Tuesday-evening discussion group in Midford.

The local Advisory Committee was again consulted. It was suggested that the Kon Tiki could possibly become affiliated to the local Association of Youth Clubs. While this could have been of some value, the worker did not consider it to be an appropriate step at that time. He wrote:

It seems that an organization like the Kon Tiki, which in its own peculiar fashion is one of the biggest and most active Youth organizations in the county, is worth a little time and attention from the Youth Service. I would like to see a link forged between the club and the Youth Service so that the club committee has someone to turn to in the event of its ever needing the sort of help a Youth Service person would be able to give them, for example, advice on legal and financial matters and on organization and committee procedure. As the club runs two of the best dance bands in the county, one can imagine circumstances under which a little help could also flow in the opposite direction. This sort of link has to be made at a personal level and could be achieved by my introducing someone to some of the club and committee members. It is also a link which could be made quite independently of me, but I think that anyone I introduced would go in with certain advantages and would gain more rapid acceptance.

The worker made no progress in providing a contact of this kind for the Kon Tiki. The County Youth Organizer rejected the suggestion that this link could be made from Midford. He felt it was too far away. The worker disagreed, in view of the natural links between Midford and Brockway, and would have pursued the question further if the youth officer in Midford, who would have been responsible for the contact, had been keen on the idea. But he was not, feeling strongly that he was not the jazz type. However the worker had not been the type either, originally, and so felt justified in writing:

This is an irrelevant objection, but if the Youth Officer still feels this after I have made the project look as attractive as possible then it is clear that this aspect of the work is not for him. Any success here can only be gained if I can overcome the fears of the people who are actually going to form the contacts, and the degree of informality to which I have become accustomed is obviously quite frightening to some people.

The worker was more fortunate over the Tuesday-evening discussion groups. A youth tutor, Mr Price, was attracted to the idea and ready to work to keep the group alive.

There was a period of two or three weeks when the presence of a stranger seemed to inhibit activity, but not to the point where the group was in danger of disintegrating. Phil took the trouble to find out exactly when the worker was leaving and then approached Mr Price and explained that the group had been a great help to him (Phil) and that it would be a pity if it died. It seemed unlikely, however, that Mr Price would be able to continue the same closeness in human relationships as the worker had succeeded in establishing. The worker felt that Mr Price seemed insufficiently alive to the needs or problems of individuals, and his training and background had not made him especially aware of much that went on in the group situation. On the other hand, he was particularly skilled and well-placed to provide projects and facilities for the group. As a result, the worker was fairly confident on leaving Midford that the Tuesday sessions would continue in some form, especially as both the group itself and Mr Price were anxious that they should.

6 The Detached Worker

Thus far in this book, consideration has been given to three broad topics, namely, what kind of people the unattached were, how they were contacted, and what the workers tried to accomplish with them within the local communities. The findings and experience of the workers in these three spheres give rise to many suggestions and implications for future services to the unattached. But before considering these, one further aspect of the project itself remains for discussion. This is the fundamental question of what kind of person the detached worker needs to be. Which skills, personal qualities, and specialized training – if any – does a job of this description seem particularly to demand?

In order to throw some light on these questions, it is proposed to look first at how the workers tried to help the unattached, and then at some of the more recurrent difficulties which arose during the course of the project. In so doing, the personal qualities and skills which were helpful or would conceivably have been helpful to the workers should become clarified.

In all of the cases quoted from Seagate, Northtown, and Midford the workers, whether dealing with individuals or groups, were not basically concerned with telling people what to do nor with trying to solve their problems for them. They could never take it for granted that they knew what was best for everyone. In any case, to have tried to dictate or deprive the unattached of the right to self-determination would have been of little value in helping them either to come to terms with themselves or to develop a sense of responsibility for their own affairs. Thus, when anyone consulted a worker with an individual problem such as his dissatisfaction with work, his leaving home, or difficult personal relationships, he made no attempt to provide ready-made solutions or to pass moral judgements on the rights and wrongs of the situation. Instead, both individuals and groups were encouraged to think out for themselves what was involved in any problem and in the consequences of any actions they might have taken or be contemplating.

The workers' relationship with their contacts was essentially a 'socratic' relationship, in which asking the right questions was more important than knowing the right answers and more useful than any lecturing and moralizing. In fact, some of the most effective communication was not with words at all but, for example, with a questioning silence, an approving glance, or a simple gesture. This happened not only with individuals but also with groups, and when decisions relating to group life and activity were needed they were taken as far as possible by the group itself, as, for instance, the selection of the cast for the Seagate drama group, the choice of activities for the Northtown school group, and of topics to be aired by the Midford discussion group. There are numerous examples to show how the workers encouraged groups to take on more responsibility for the organization of their own affairs.

Few of these young people had yet learned to accept much responsibility for their lives or actions. A passive approach whereby the workers sat around waiting for all the suggestions and decisions to come from the contacts would therefore have been futile. Much of the young people's acceptance of the workers was due to the fact that the workers provided 'something to catch on to' as one young person phrased it. Within realistic limits – realistic in the sense that it was not asking too much – workers were not afraid to make demands of the unattached. Thus some were variously encouraged to try out new activities or different standards of personal behaviour. At times, when they were undecided, the workers' task was to help them to sort out for themselves what they really wanted to do or be. At others the workers had to protect them from circumstances which would have made their development too difficult or too painful. Examples of such protective intervention were the Seagate worker's refusal to let Frank wreck the drama production, the success of which had become so crucial for the well-being of the other members (by bringing the matter to a head, the worker was also protecting Frank from the wrath of the group); the Northtown worker's intervention to prevent Marilyn from being ostracized by the others; and the Midford worker's constant watch to check members from making confessions in group discussions which would have embarrassed them later. In all this, the workers continually found themselves being forced to make decisions which demanded skill and insight. For example, how could the worker tell the difference between a situation which was too frustrating and one which would be a valuable learning experience because of the challenge it presented? At what point did the expression of criticism or hostility among the members cease being a valuable tool for change and become damaging instead because of the hurt which it inflicted? When should the workers try to encourage an idea or suggestion that had come from the group and when should they discourage – and how? These were just a few of the daily problems which confronted the workers. On the manner in which they were solved hung the success or the failure of the project.

Whether it was in the drama activity in Seagate, the school group in Northtown, the jazz club, camping project, or discussion group in Midford, the workers were most active in creating and maintaining situations in which people could become free to learn. The Seagate worker with his skill and enthusiasm for drama did much of his work by making use of the activity itself; the Northtown worker, who was a rather less flamboyant personality, did most of her work through the quieter club-like setting of the housecraft flat, while the Midford worker used a combination of both. The workers proved that effective help could be given both by working through an activity or by just sitting around and talking.

Just how effective such help really was must remain undetermined, especially in the absence of any follow-up after the project finished and in the absence also of any control groups or any qualitative techniques for measuring attitude change. It is reasonably certain that some of the changes which took place were the results of normal growth and maturation and the workers themselves were very conscious that the amount of influence they seemed to be having was limited, particularly with the more hardened cases. In part, this was attributed to the lack of contact with parents and the fact that nothing was being done to alleviate the poor home conditions from which many of the problems probably originated.

There can be no legitimate claims therefore to have brought about dramatic 'cures' or reforms in any individual's way of life. On the evidence of this project, it is doubtful if the detached worker could ever 'cure' young people, if only because of the tremendous amount of time and skill that such a task would demand. Where the more delinquent youth are concerned, a 'holding operation' to tide them over the more difficult years of middle and later adolescence when their problems seem particularly acute may well be the most that can realistically be expected of the detached worker. It may be still more realistic to think in terms of prevention rather than cure by trying to reach the unattached at an earlier age.

Thus the most that can be claimed is that a few people who were on the delinquent fringe may have been held back from more serious delinquency. Others who were 'purposeless' rather than delinquent seem to have found more satisfactory outlets for their frustrations by developing some of their latent abilities, and some were known to have derived support and encouragement simply by being able to talk with the worker. The presence of an understanding adult who had become a significant person in their lives and with whom these young people could feel free to talk about anything at any time was undoubtedly one of the best services that could have been offered to them. At its most effective, such a service demanded that the worker was always available to listen to a problem or to offer advice. Being permanently accessible or 'on call' was one of the most valuable, if demanding, features of the work and 'time-off' away from young people was a virtual impossibility without being particularly firm or actually going away.

One further point can be stated with certainty. The young people who were regular contacts of the workers experienced, some for the first time ever, the friendship of a sympathetic adult and his genuine concern for their condition. In view of the cynicism and despair which was so characteristic of many of them, such an experience was in itself valuable.

Much that has been written would seem to indicate that working with the unattached was often an exacting and very demanding task, yet one which by virtue of its unpredictable nature contained elements of excitement and whose rewards were considerable. Unfortunately, these were slow to appear, especially during the first eighteen months, when there were few tangible results to justify a sense of achievement. The workers were filled with doubt about their ability to gain the acceptance of the unattached on anything but a superficial level. The Central Committee constantly reassured them that rapid developments could not be expected and advised them not to be over-critical of themselves. While this advice was welcomed and to some extent accepted, the workers were inevitably left wondering whether the lack of clear-cut results was due to the nature of the job or to their own limitations. It became evident that workers engaged in a task of this kind needed a great deal of support and encouragement, and anyone who takes up or sponsors work with the unattached in anticipation of quick and easy results will soon suffer frustration and disappointment. It is essential to be able to work hard, for long periods, without necessarily seeing any direct return for one's efforts.

Another factor which at times could make the task seem almost unbearable was a feeling of isolation. By its very nature, the job was a lonely one, and the need for complete discretion made it still more so. Confidants had to be chosen with care and in this connexion the help given to workers by members of the local Advisory Committees was invaluable. It was in no way a reflection on either the generosity or the abilities of the Committee members when the workers began to feel that periodic committee meetings did not provide enough support. Two facts were inescapable. The advice which the workers sought was often of a specialized nature which few of the local advisers could be expected to provide – for instance how to cope with some particularly aggressive adolescent or at what pace to proceed in developing a relationship with a certain group or individual. Even where skilled social workers such as a probation officer or children's officer were serving on the local

Committees the problems of the workers and their need for consultation could seldom be timed to coincide with the date of a periodic committee meeting and the workers felt it unfair to make excessive demands on their time in between meetings.

Moreover there was little opportunity for the workers to discuss their work with each other or with people undergoing similar experiences during the first year of the project. Northtown, Midford, and Seagate were at least one hundred miles apart and there were no other detached workers within a closer radius. In Northtown, the worker was faced not only with isolation on the job but also with what might be termed a 'social isolation' from people of similar interests to herself. While she referred to her accommodation as a 'flat' it was in fact a single bed-sittingroom in one of the areas of dilapidated housing in Lymport. The other two workers were better housed, and they were also married, which lessened their sense of social isolation. But the need for complete discretion precluded talking frankly to potential friends about one's job and resulted in a personal isolation and an intense lack of company of one's own age and interests. In addition, feelings of being isolated in their work were acute for all the workers by the end of the first year.

Recognizing this, the Central Committee arranged for the workers to meet more frequently, and the author, a social group worker, was appointed as a part-time supervisor to discuss some of their difficulties with them. For these discussions, the workers prepared their own agenda and explored further those topics which were of immediate concern to them. It soon became clear that they wanted more direction in their aims as detached workers and what was expected of them. Much time was spent discussing the term 'unattached' and, going on from this, analysing the attitudes and behaviour of unattached young people which required the services of a detached worker. At this point the emphasis of the project was altered from observation and investigation to include direct work with one or two selected groups in each area; as a result, the workers now wished to discuss more specific problems, many about standards and values. To a disturbing degree, it was found that the unattached young people were often consciously or unconsciously attacking the worker's own standards and values. For example, when the Northtown girls brought to the worker gifts probably obtained by shop-lifting, should they be accepted as a welcome sign of affection from girls who had hitherto been unable to show much warmth towards an adult or should the worker refuse them and risk damaging the relationship? Or, what should the worker say or do when some of the Midford youths confided that they had stolen equipment worth two to three pounds from their employers and when both he and the youths knew that older men in the same firm stole fifty to one hundred pounds' worth of equipment each year and regarded it as a legitimate fringe benefit of the job? Or again, faced with all the discrepancies between traditional middle-class beliefs and middle-class behaviour, how was the Seagate worker to indicate to the drama group that middle-class values were preferable to the 'bum' philosophy? Even if there were no such discrepancies, by what right and according to which set of values was the worker to indicate that their philosophy was unsatisfactory?

These questions may seem remote or abstract. To the workers they were of real and practical significance, and found an expression and demanded an answer in every aspect of the work. It was important to their own peace of mind as well as to their effectiveness that they should know what their fundamental values were and feel confident in holding them. At the same time, it was necessary to accept and to understand why the values and standards of the unattached were different. Unless the detached worker is able or can be helped to think honestly about his own values, he will find the job bewildering, perhaps impossible. Some of the difficulties which arose demanded decisions which the worker felt it to be beyond his authority to make. Here is an extract from a letter which the Midford worker sent to the Central Committee requesting a decision of this kind :

In Midford I am at present dealing with a group of youths who plan to move and retail about £300 worth of stolen goods within the next few days. My contact with this group is only slight and I became involved in the affair rather by accident. I have been able to persuade one coffee-bar proprietor that he would be very foolish to act as a receiver and there is a chance that I might be able to frighten the prime mover into calling the whole thing off. . . . Naturally I have talked to the probation officer about the matter, but there seems little that can be done beyond what is already being attempted.

The point about this is that I am at present technically 'compounding a felony'. This does not worry me personally as I think the course of action that I am pursuing is a reasonable one.

However, I think there are moral issues here. . . . Obviously people like doctors and priests often 'compound felonies' in this sense, but am I, either legally or morally, in the same category? Officially, I am not acting in any professional capacity and even if I were, would it not be advisable to have some recognized code of conduct within the profession?

Further, is it fair of me to approach a local probation officer with a problem of this sort even though I do not disclose actual names? It would seem his duty to report any intended crime to the police.

In discussing this issue, it became clear that one of the most satisfactory solutions might have been to have gained the understanding of the police from the start of the project.

It came to be recognized that there is a degree of anti-social behaviour which the worker has a duty to report to the police. The New York City Youth Board, for example, has made a definite policy that in instances in which the community well-being and/or the well-being of the youths themselves is threatened, the detached worker must enlist the aid of the police or such other community agencies as are necessary to prevent it. In particular, workers must inform the police of such things as a threatened fight between gangs, a youth or gang known to be carrying firearms, and the sale of narcotics. This policy is fully explained to the youths so that, if the need to call in the police should arise, there is no question of having broken confidences.

The New York City Youth Board policy has clearly been evolved to suit local conditions and the three instances cited which require the workers to inform the police are fortunately encountered only infrequently at present in the United Kingdom. But the whole problem of the worker's relationship with the police is one which demands a clear policy since it will inevitably arise in working with those unattached young people who are also delinquent.

Other specific questions which the workers wanted to discuss are too numerous for detailed account but included: the similarities and differences between the attitudes and characteristics of the young people in the three areas and how far these differences were due to local social, cultural, and economic conditions; how to deal with the aggressive and destructive elements in a group; how to cope with the problem of rivalry for the worker's affection between different groups and individuals; how to limit the membership of a group and how to justify this to the young people themselves in a way they could understand (particularly acute for the Northtown worker in trying to discourage those in younger age groups from visiting her flat); how changes in attitudes are brought about; how to translate personal loyalty to a worker into loyalty to a club; the timing of the breaking of the news that a worker would be leaving his group; and, finally, the ethical implications of having contacted a group, allowed the members to become dependent upon the worker, and then for the worker to leave without necessarily being able to find an adult replacement.

Many of these questions will be seen to have strong emotional overtones. For example, on this last point concerning ethical implications, the workers sometimes felt that they may have been guilty of 'using' people for the purpose of an experimental project. Or again, on the question of the aggressive or destructive members of a group, the workers were often confronted by considerable hostility in the form of sarcasm, temper tantrums, or being ignored. It is never a pleasant experience to encounter hostility, but if the workers could discuss it and gain a better understanding of the reasons for it, there was less danger of their being hostile in return. Thus simply as an emotional outlet for their own feelings the meetings between the workers were valuable. Both the dangers of venting their feelings on the young people or of becoming over-involved emotionally in the situation could be lessened by talking with each other or objective outsiders and so resolving some of their own frustrations. The following extract from a report of the Seagate worker provides an example of a worker becoming irritated by a group, giving vent to such irritation and his subsequent assessment of what had happened:

Under the considerable pressure of the last drama production, I grew rather tired. My ability to control my feelings was not as strong as it ought to have been and I found myself increasingly affected emotionally by the whole activity. At one point, for example, I was very sharp and impatient with Andy for his constant destructive and cynical comments about the production. Later, after the performance had finished and it was decided to hold a party, I became very resentful at the selfishness of the cast in not making any attempt to finance or organize the party. The onus seemed once again to be left to me and, somewhat irrationally, I showed my annoyance.

I felt at the time that my reaction was irrational and that I was unreasonably protesting against the behaviour of the group. . . . Because of my tiredness, I had allowed myself to become rather involved in the situation. On reflection, it was a reaction that needed to be avoided in youth work yet one that is surely not uncommon at times among youth workers?

It is not surprising that sometimes all three workers were overtaken by tiredness, irritation, or even exasperation, and there was a need for someone to whom they could turn to be reassured that such feelings were natural and inevitable – someone who could act as a safety valve for their feelings of frustration.

To some extent this function was fulfilled by the supervisor. In retrospect, all the workers stressed the importance of the key position held by the supervisor and saw such a person fulfilling four major roles : firstly, as an adviser to whom they could turn for skilled help with the various problems which arose; secondly, as someone who could lead their discussions, act as a catalyst to their own thinking, offer some training while they were on the job, and provide a safeguard against overinvolvement; thirdly, as a link between the Central Committee and the workers, interpreting the aims and the problems of the one to the other; finally, as a coordinator, helping to maintain some consistency between the work in different areas through, for example, advising on the kind of records, case sheets, and other reports that should be kept. The workers felt that a supervisor acting in these capacities should be an intrinsic part of the administrative structure of any project of this kind. Given such an appointment, they considered that many of the other dangers, such as feeling isolated or of losing objectivity, could be reduced.

Two further difficulties which the workers experienced remain to be mentioned: first the need to be available to the unattached at all hours of the day. This made it awkward to find free time and the workers had sometimes to be pressed to take adequate time off. Even shopping, for example, could involve encounters with young people or their parents with the result that privacy was often impossible. The invasion of privacy occurred also at home, where young people dropped in at the most unexpected times and could create difficult situations such as having to write reports in a state of constant preparedness to hide everything at a moment's notice. The door bell rang constantly and, as it was not always convenient to spend off-duty hours out of the area, it was rare to have time at home uninterrupted.

The second difficulty was the recurrent question of identity. Without doubt this was one of the most serious problems in the eyes of the workers. It was such a persistent and involved one that it may be helpful to summarize the factors which have a bearing on it. There are three major reasons why the worker's identity should not be concealed: first, the worker's almost untenable position and consequent frustration when questioned by the unattached as to who he is and what he does. Such questioning is normal for the development of a relationship between the unattached and the worker. The latter develops relationships by sharing information about himself and by answering the suspicions of the unattached as they try to find out if this is the kind of adult with whom they want to associate. If an answer to the fundamental question of 'Who are you?' is avoided repeatedly suspicion is likely to grow. Moreover, if young people find out later who the worker is and what he has been trying to do, they may feel they have been deceived. Such a discovery may damage not only the worker's relationship with the particular group of unattached but also hinder future attempts by other adults to work with them.

Secondly, it became clear in the course of the project that the worker needs to be accepted not only by the unattached but also by the local community. An integral part of the job is to help the local community to a better understanding of the problems, to use local facilities to help the unattached, and to invoke the help of local social services. This can hardly be accomplished by a person of nebulous identity who tends to be distrusted. At least one worker experienced difficulties in establishing relationships with parents and other interested people in the town because of this.

Third, it is known that many of the unattached are suspicious and resentful of the authority of adults and that this is epitomized by their hostility towards the 'establishment'. In the last analysis, one of the aims of this project was to demonstrate to the unattached that not all adults are unsympathetic; that the 'establishment' is not necessarily against them, and that adulthood, of which many have a seeming abhorrence, is not necessarily synonymous with stagnation. It is sometimes thought that in order to convince the unattached of this the worker must either dissociate himself from the 'establishment' and all forms of public authority or must deny his adult status and pretend to be 'one of the boys'. This may gain a temporary acceptance, but is liable to defeat itself in the long run since the unattached may now attribute their warm relationship with the worker to the very fact that, like them, he dissociates himself from adults and adult status. Such an approach may therefore merely add to their conviction that it is impossible for people of the adult world or of the 'establishment' to understand or help them.

These are three good reasons for not concealing the worker's identity. On the other hand if the worker clearly identifies himself with authority, or social work, or the 'establishment' generally too rapidly, there is a very real danger that he will be immediately rejected. Not that this is invariably the outcome, as the success of the school teacher in Northtown has clearly shown. But because this danger is always present and because if it materializes it is rare that a second chance is given, it must clearly be reckoned with.

This conflict is at the core of the identity problem. There is no simple or universal solution to it, but certain guiding principles emerge. Whatever identity the worker assumes initially it must not be one which creates undue anxiety in the unattached. What creates anxiety for one group will not necessarily do so for another. For example, the Northtown coffee-bar youths suspected the worker of being a social scientist studying them. The indications were that even had she admitted to this they would not have been unduly alarmed and might even have enjoyed the situation. The need and importance of a period of unobtrusive observation to assess what type of approach is most likely to be acceptable is essential, since anxiety is provoked differently in different groups. It is necessary in any case simply in order to become acquainted with the social, cultural, and emotional backgrounds of the groups and individuals.

There is considerable evidence that no matter what kind of role the worker assumes, he must build, develop, and earn his identity in much the same way that he tries to earn his acceptance. This is a useful factor as it gives the worker time to develop a relationship gradually. Initially, for example, both the Northtown and Midford workers were only marginally involved with their contacts, and various individuals and groups were only vaguely aware of their presence. The initial reaction of many contacts seems to be determined not so much by what the worker claims or claims not to be, but by the way he relates to them – by what he says and by what he does. If his deeds and his words are acceptable, then to be a representative of authority or openly identified with the 'establishment' will not be a serious setback. The inevitable questions 'Who are you?', 'What do you do?', are bound to come, and they must be answered according to what the worker believes the questioners can accept. This may not be very much at first, but there is strong evidence from all three areas that later, when good relationships have been established, it is both desirable and possible to make a full and accurate reply and it is crucial at this stage that the worker is not prevented from telling the truth because of earlier claims to other identities. Thus it is important that whatever identity the worker assumes initially, it must not be one which he will have to deny later on in order to establish a deeper relationship. Much of the day-to-day work with the unattached consists of showing them realistically how and why ends cannot justify means. If the worker's very *raison d'être* is in any way a denial of this principle his work will have a very shaky foundation indeed.

Given these principles and that it is desirable that the worker be attached to some local youth or social welfare organization, he should neither unnecessarily conceal nor reveal his identity or motives initially. Stating that he is in some minor way attached to the sponsoring body, or that he is a research worker or a social scientist would all seem to be a practical proposition and lend themselves to further elaboration at a later stage when the youth have begun to acknowledge to themselves that no matter who or what the worker says he may be he has shown himself to be a friendly person. It is conceivable that a more accurate description of identity will be possible from the beginning once work of this kind has become more widespread and accepted. On the available evidence, the comforting probability is that the question of identity is one which worried the workers far more than it did the unattached. As anticipated, they started asking leading questions – but even when dissatisfied with the answers, as many obviously were, they continued to associate with the worker because he was already proving by his words, actions, and interests what kind of person he was. Even when she was a school teacher and thus using an identity which was clearly representative of authority the Northtown worker was able to gain acceptance.

A certain maturity of outlook is clearly required if one is to work effectively with the unattached. This maturity is needed not only to withstand the strain of a job of this kind but also in order to adopt the objective, non-judgemental attitude which is so fundamental to the success of the worker. In addition, those engaged on this project were convinced that some training was essential in the understanding of human behaviour, including 'normal' personality development and personality maladjustment, either before or whilst actually being employed as a detached worker. Also essential is a reasonable educational level, in order to grasp the more theoretical aspects of the job. It is difficult to define exactly what constitutes a reasonable educational level for these purposes, but a formal training in youth leadership is not the only, nor necessarily the most suitable, training. None of the three workers in this project had received such training, and the Seagate worker did not have any experience of working with a youth group prior to joining the staff. Of the other two, the Northtown worker had worked in a probation hostel and the Midford worker had been a school teacher.

Similarly, it is often asked if skill in any particular activity or activities is essential. While it is unwise to generalize about this from experiences of only three workers, they are worth a glance. The Seagate worker was skilled in drama and jazz. He attributed his acceptance by the 'nucleus' group in part to this, and it is interesting to speculate on the outcome of his time in Seagate if he had been without these skills. Conversely, the Northtown worker was not especially skilled in any activity, and this did not seem to detract from the effectiveness of her work. The Midford worker was skilled in both camping and mountaineering but found only a limited interest in his camping projects and none at all in mountaineering. At one stage, he found it helpful to acquire some knowledge of jazz, although the success of his work was never dependent upon his expertise in playing an instrument or in being able to teach the subject. His real contribution to the jazz activity in the Kon Tiki was his ability to help the members reorganize the club, a task which he might well have accomplished without being able to distinguish between one end of a trumpet and the other. These three different experiences suggest that although knowledge of a special activity can be helpful in itself, it is certainly not enough and may even go unutilized if the particular group of unattached either happen to be uninterested or cannot be stimulated into developing an interest. The most helpful qualities would seem to be wide interests and a capacity to adapt oneself to activities which either the unattached prefer or which strike a response in them. Skill in human relationships is the only specific expertise that can be advocated with certainty, especially if it is remembered that as much of the workers' time and effort may be spent in working with local adults as with unattached adolescents.

Indisputably the worker's personality is a vital factor contributing to success or failure in this kind of work. With a subject as complex as that of personality one is on extremely dangerous ground making any suggestions, but there is consistent evidence that the personal characteristics of warmth, ease with people, humour, imagination, and tolerance are all vital.

To summarize briefly, it would seem that three things are essential in order for most people to be effective as detached workers. First, a suitable personality; second, a basic knowledge and understanding of human growth and behaviour; and third, adequate support and guidance whilst on the job. This is not to suggest, however, that people who do not possess such qualifications or training cannot work with the unattached. Indeed, at the risk of labouring a point that has been stressed earlier, there is an urgent need that the unattached should be regarded as the concern of the whole community and not a domain sacred to some specialist youth worker or particular youth organization. One of the most thought-provoking ideas on the project was raised by a local adviser, who suggested that ways should be found of securing the cooperation of local residents such as coffee-bar proprietors, swimming bath attendants, or publicans, many of whom are sensible and understanding people and possibly capable of providing a valuable service if given some encouragement and 'know-how' in dealing with some of the situations in which they often find themselves. Unfortunately the idea came too late for this project but it is definitely worthy of active consideration.

7 Conclusions and Recommendations

The project upon which this report is based is concerned with a small number of people in only three areas of the country and only tentative conclusions or recommendations can be based on it. Further, it has deliberately been written to emphasize a method of developing and using a relationship with unattached young people and to examine the demands which such a task makes on a detached worker. While aware of the limitations arising both from the small numbers and from the selective focus of this report, the Central Advisory Committee felt that several major points emerged during the project bearing upon future services to the unattached.

That the unattached cannot be viewed in isolation is one of the most general but recurrent findings. The complexity of relationships which exist between the individual, his family, and the local community means that the problems of the unattached cannot be solved by any single procedure or agency. There is need for more coordination and cooperation between the various social agencies which deal with young people. Before considering this in more detail, however, let us look first at the unattached as an individual, then at his family, and finally at the local community.

THE INDIVIDUAL

Adolescent Counselling. It has been noted repeatedly that one of the most serious problems of the unattached, whether they recognized it or not, was the absence in their lives of sympathetic adults to whom they could turn for understanding and advice. For a variety of reasons customary sources of adult counsel – home, school, the church, or youth groups – were not being used by these young people.

Their own resentment blocked many from any adult help that may have been available. It looks as if only the personal approach of a detached worker or someone else who has the time and ability to reach out to them by methods like those described in this report will be able to help. While it has been difficult to assess the effectiveness of such help, there were notable changes in some attitudes and behaviour of young people during the project. It is not, we hope, unduly optimistic to say the findings were sufficiently encouraging to support the conclusion of Stott who maintains that:

so slight is the gradation between the spectacular breakdown of delinquency and the *malaise* of many 'normal' youths that the human contacts with adults and other adolescents . . . are bound in a very large number of instances to be a saving factor.[1]

The most important aspect of the service which the workers offered was that which aimed at providing human contact in a way which the unattached could accept and respond to, and this can be emulated by many existing social agencies if suitable personnel and adequate financial backing can be found. The greatest responsibility must lie with the Youth Service, but schools, churches, settlements, community and welfare associations, and the Youth Employment Service are each potential channels for work of this kind.

However, not all the young people were so resentful of adults or so inarticulate about their problems as the more extreme cases. There was every indication that the more articulate adolescents, often quite eager to talk about their problems, would have used an adolescent counselling service. The frequency with which the workers were used as 'neutral' adults with whom individuals could discuss personal problems might be taken as a measure of the extent to which some of the unattached sought adult opinion and advice. Problems of personal relationships with parents, amongst themselves, or with the opposite sex, dissatisfaction with work, and less definable feelings of discontentment and restlessness were recurrent topics of discussion. This finding strongly reinforces one of the suggestions of the Albemarle Report that the Youth Service should

1. Stott, D. H., *Delinquency and Human Nature*, Carnegie United Kingdom Trust, 1950.

provide more opportunities for adolescent counselling. It points out that even the 'best' parents are not always equipped to provide the advice their children require, especially if they are too shy to discuss with their parents the difficulties that worry them most. The Report therefore emphasizes that youth leaders should try to act as counsellors. Since counselling is such a time-consuming and demanding task, it further suggests that it may be necessary to recruit helpers such as priests, pastors, and social workers for this purpose.

If a counselling service to young people who already belong to a youth club is considered important, how much more urgent is the need for those outside any kind of youth organization? The experiences of this project showed conclusively that many of the unattached would perhaps have used advice or counselling facilities on their own initiative, but would certainly have done so with encouragement by the workers. It was also clear that, both within and outside the Youth Service, existing facilities are grossly inadequate or non-existent.

One notable exception has demonstrated during its short but successful history how some of the unattached will respond to the provision of a counselling service. This is the Young People's Consultation Centre in Hampstead, which was opened in 1961. During the first two years almost two hundred young people aged fifteen to twenty-three years visited the Centre. Half were referred by other agencies such as youth clubs, family welfare agencies, general practitioners, citizens' advice bureaux, and probation officers, but the others were young people who, it is claimed, would never have gone near a professional organization.[1] These had attended of their own initiative after learning about the Centre through friends or advertisements in the Underground, public libraries, or the personal columns of newspapers.

It is not being suggested either that all young people require an intensive counselling service or that they necessarily need any kind of organized counselling. But the findings of this project reinforce the growing evidence that in practice the need for adolescent counselling has gone unrecognized for too long.

1. Laufer, M., *A Psycho-Analytical Approach to Work with Adolescents* – A paper presented at a meeting of the British Psychological Society, September, 1963.

When the need has been recognized, it has been given too low a priority both by the Youth Service itself as well as by other agencies which claim to be serving young people.

THE HOME

Parent-Child Relationships. Without doubt, the finding to emerge most often was that while the social and economic background of the unattached varied considerably, a breakdown in family relationships was a common factor in all cases. Happy parent-child relationships were the exception rather than the rule. The adolescent and parental misery that stems both from a complete breakdown of family life as a result of separation, desertion, divorce, or death and from deep-seated matrimonial discord and less severe family misunderstandings amounts to a considerable total. The connexion between the anti-social behaviour of children and disturbed parent–child relationships has been shown too often to need to be laboured here. It is perhaps sufficient to say that the findings of this project add yet another piece of evidence of the overwhelming importance of a happy and stable family life.

Some tension between parents and children is inevitable as the latter grow up. One would not wish to exaggerate the problem of the unattached by overlooking this. But the strains which existed between the unattached and their parents were often far in excess of what might reasonably be thought of as 'normal'. This was particularly true of the relationships with the father; the breakdown in relationships there could be described as acute, while somewhat happier relationships were enjoyed with the mother. Was this a coincidence? It would be valuable to have more research to establish if in fact the breakdown of father–child relationships is more prevalent than that of mother–child relationships, and if it is, as a result, more significant in helping to create or intensify the difficulties which some of the unattached are experiencing.

Parental Counselling. It was encouraging to find that many parents were concerned about the way in which their sons and daughters were developing and about their unhappy family relationships. Some, as we saw in Seagate, were extremely anxious, but there was no one to whom they could turn in confidence for advice. This problem could be prevented, or at least mitigated, by the provision of more family counselling services: places where parents could obtain help about the handling of adolescents. For this reason, a valuable development in answer to a particularly urgent need would be the setting up of more Family Advice Centres as recommended under the Children and Young Persons Act 1963. There seems no reason why such centres could not provide some of the adolescent counselling services which have been advocated. For example, it has been suggested that if young people as well as parents could feel free to go to these centres, if there could be a greater understanding and cooperation between youth leaders and child care officers through more joint conferences and courses, then

the united efforts of the child care officers and the youth leader would make an important contribution, since much of the difficulty encountered by young people originates in the home and the relationship which exists there, while much relief for tension can be provided by the patient understanding of those outside.[1]

Whether such a scheme will ever materialize or not, it is certain that many parents are just as much in need as their children of the patient help and understanding of someone outside the family. It is possible that advice could be given them through some existing social or educational agencies as well as through Family Advice Centres. Many teachers and schools, for example, are in an excellent position to offer advice, provided they have sufficient understanding of the difficulties involved. A revitalization of Parent–Teacher Associations could make a useful contribution here. Some parents could also be helped by other adult educational organizations such as community centres or through an extension of the work of the Marriage Guidance Council.

It would be unrealistic to assume that all those parents in most need of these counselling services will make immediate use of them if they are provided. But even in the more extreme instances of inadequacy or apathy there are grounds for optim-

1. Fairclough, J., 'The Youth Service and Child Care', in *Youth Service*, vol. 4, No. 5, May 1964.

ism. There is, for example, the evidence provided by the Juvenile Liaison Officer scheme in Liverpool. J. B. Mays, writing of this scheme, suggests that

all too often it is assumed that because parents appear to fail in their task and their children show signs of indiscipline, they are *ipso facto* 'bad' parents. Experience has shown that where constructive efforts are made to help parents . . . a surprisingly large number will respond.[1]

The workers on this project met some of the parents of the unattached, often without intending to do so. They were convinced that more work with parents would have been possible if it had not been for the lack of a clear identity and the experimental nature of the project. Even thus hampered in the development of confidences, the workers were in a position to refer parents to other sources of skilled help.

The Place of Youth Leaders and Teachers. From this limited experience, it seems that parents unlikely to visit a welfare agency can be persuaded to do so if reached out to by a more personal approach than that afforded by the mere provision of a service. But whose responsibility should it be to attempt such work? It is certain that any social agency which is in regular and prolonged contact with a child ought also to be in a position to work with his parents. Youth leaders should make greater efforts to know the home backgrounds of their members: particularly unsettled behaviour of a member indicates a need for home visiting and regular contact with parents. This is not to suggest that a leader should or could be adequately equipped to cope with all the wide range of problems which may arise in family life. But if he has the confidence of parents, his advice or referral to a specialized source of help is more likely to be accepted than if he appears on the doorstep as a comparative stranger in a moment of crisis. It follows that some training in working with families which underlines the importance of understanding the home backgrounds of club members ought to be an essential part of professional youth leadership training.

Schools can also play a vital part. This was recently recog-

1. J. B. Mays, *Growing Up in the City*, Liverpool University Press, 1956, p. 159.

nized by the Newsom Report, with its findings that there is an urgent need to strengthen all existing links between home and school, and in difficult areas to create new ones by the appointment of members of staff with special liaison or home visiting responsibilities. This could scarcely be more strongly emphasized than by the experiences of the Northtown worker with the pupils in the secondary modern schools there.

Housing Needs. The unattached in Northtown were particularly affected by the overcrowded conditions in which they were living. This is not to suggest that bad housing was in itself a major cause of anti-social behaviour. The Seagate youths, who often lived in relatively large houses where they had a room of their own in which they could entertain friends, would immediately refute this. Nevertheless, in Northtown, the lack of privacy, the frictions and the irritations caused by overcrowding seem to have added tensions to families which already suffered more than enough, nor is it surprising that adolescents living under these conditions were only too eager to get out of the house and into the streets. It is hardly surprising either that parents were glad to see them go. What then are the housing needs of adolescents? Would it be unreasonable to suggest that an adolescent needs a bed-sittingroom of his own in which he can follow his pursuits and where he can invite one or two friends? In view of current housing costs, rents, and shortages, this may be unrealistic, but overcrowding in the statutory sense is not the only important consideration. The problem of overcrowding as it affects adolescents and their families would appear to warrant further research. In the meantime more community recreation facilities must be built to help offset the lack of adequate amenities at home. Both at the beginning and at the end of the project in Lymport the most attractive alternatives to overcrowded homes for many young people were still the streets and the pub. Far from new facilities being provided, a coffee bar and a cinema were closed down. The desperate inadequacy in some areas of social amenities, commercial as well as public, will be referred to again later.

Many of the findings have indicated a need for the improvement, coordination, and extension of existing welfare services in the community rather than the creation of new ones. In particular, it is believed that the following points regarding four aspects of community life are important and, if pursued, would help in alleviating some of the problems of the unattached. The four aspects relate to school, industry, the Youth Service and commercial facilities.

Schools. There has been frequent reference throughout this report to the difficulties which the unattached experienced during their school lives. This, together with the comments in the previous section about the home situations, endorses the findings of the Newsom Report, which has stressed the fundamental importance of the personal relationships existing between teacher and pupils. Linked to this is the recommendation in the Newsom Report that the training of teachers should include sociological and environmental studies with special reference to the problems of pupils in culturally deprived areas. It was seen in Chapter 4 that many teachers were correctly able to identify potential trouble-makers at the age of eleven. But very little use was made of this, because the teachers felt powerless to bring about change or prevention. This situation can only be described as tragic, especially since the Youth Service does not attempt to work with young people until they are aged fourteen.

No less disturbing were the Northtown workers' reports on some eight- to thirteen-year-old boys and girls, many of whom were already running wild and in trouble with the police. Some are clearly destined for serious delinquency unless they catch the eye of the law first or have parents who are sufficiently cruel and neglectful to bring themselves to the attention of some public or welfare officer. But those children with less spectacular evidence of their delinquency or of their parents' inadequacy may well have a history of five or six years of anti-social behaviour before the Youth Service begins offering them any opportunities. This policy of neglecting the under-fourteen-year-olds leads to unjustifiable wastage of human potential and is short-sighted. Without exception, all the workers felt that the younger age groups were more approachable and more amenable to adult influence than the older. In one area, the eight- to thirteen-year-olds so craved adult friendship that they were prepared to visit the worker in the face of both the worker's own discouragement and the open hostility of older girls. An obvious remedy for this is the provision of more recreation facilities of every description for these younger adolescents.

Another suggestion of the Newsom Report would bring about real progress if it could be implemented. This is that the teacher's understanding of the cultural and sociological background of his pupils and his skill in gaining their confidence and trust must be increased. This is very necessary before the considerable powers of the teacher to identify potential trouble-makers can be used to help the pupil instead of to apportion blame. But to place the burden of preventive work solely or even mainly on the teacher would be wholly unfair. Teachers must be given more support from outside. For example, they should be supported by more liaison between the school and other welfare organizations such as child guidance services, the Youth Service, and the Youth Employment Service, and by the appointment of members of staff with a special responsibility for liaison and home visiting which has already been mentioned.

More teacher–youth-tutors would also be valuable to help to bridge the wide gap which was seen to exist between school and out-of-school activities. The success of the Northtown worker in attracting and holding some of the most unstable girls in the school demonstrates what can be achieved through an appointment of this kind. But it is worth adding that all the workers who tried contacting the unattached through schools stressed the necessity of small classes or discussion groups and a sufficiently informal atmosphere to permit the development of warm personal relationships.

Industry and Problems of Work. Most of the unattached experience difficulty in negotiating the transition from school to work. Since many of them lacked stability, it was probably inevitable that adjustment to work would not be easy, but can anything be done to make the transition from school to work easier?

Schools, industry, and the Youth Employment Service are already doing a great deal, but much more could be done. Some of the suggestions made in the preceding paragraphs would obviously help. For example, periods spent by several workers in factories or workshops revealed some lamentable working conditions. In the smaller firms, welfare services were almost non-existent. A large firm with enlightened policies for further education of its apprentices was failing to secure the full benefit either to its apprentices or to its Board of following up the existing schemes. The Southtown worker in particular was struck by the vast disparity in the provision of opportunities for apprentices and for those workers of the same age group who were not apprenticed. These young shop-floor workers not only had fewer opportunities for further education but were afforded fewer social and recreational activities and encountered a less sympathetic attitude on the part of many of the older workers.[1] Training courses for operatives on how to deal with young workers joining the 'shop' would be as useful as introduction to industry courses for the school leaver; and senior executives and directors could profitably join in. It was interesting also that the young shop-floor workers who were not attracted by the firm's social and recreational facilities almost invariably failed equally to be attracted by what the Youth Service outside the firm could offer. This was to be expected, but it emphasizes the opportunity for management to play a greater role in youth services. Top management, however, must first be convinced of this opportunity itself. In the larger firms, trade unions along with management already concern themselves with physical conditions, but it would seem that the smaller firms do not give enough attention to such conditions. In addition to physical conditions, social and recreational facilities are of great importance. Is there not therefore a need for more trade union activity here, to call for and to help in much needed provision and improvement?

It was apparent that the Youth Employment Service also had largely failed as far as these young people were concerned. Most had been completely unaffected by the Service and had not gone to it for advice or guidance. Some seemed unaware of

1. See Appendix.

the existence of the Y.E.S. and others, especially in Seagate, were openly derisory of suggestions that Youth Employment Officers could help them. Since it has insufficient staff and inadequate finances, it would be unreasonable to criticize the Youth Employment Service for all these shortcomings. Genuine advice and guidance to any of the unattached will only be possible if a better trained, and more adequately staffed and financed Youth Employment Service is enabled to spend much more time on developing personal relationships and thus to gain the confidence and trust of the young people concerned. Youth Employment Officers ought to get to know young people earlier in their school lives than the final year. There is a valid argument that they should also be willing to meet young people in the informal settings where they are to be found. The links between schools and local industry could also be strengthened through a member of the school staff, who would need better qualifications than those of most of the existing careers masters. This ought to be somebody with knowledge of working conditions, especially in industry.

The Youth Service. The project produced ample evidence that the Youth Service as it is constituted today is inadequate to serve the unattached. Some of them had skirted various youth clubs, but attempts to draw them into the life of the club had failed. Some youth clubs, notably in Seagate, left them cold because they found them lacking sophistication. Even the best youth clubs failed to attract or hold many of them.

If the Youth Service is to attract more of the unattached, a reorientation in leadership and certain changes in facilities are required. It was precisely because the traditional approaches of the Youth Service had failed to attract them that this project was attempted. At the beginning it was impossible to see what the result would be. In retrospect, it is clear that the essence of the whole project was the establishment of a very special kind of relationship which has not been widely envisaged or achieved by youth leaders and others in the Youth Service. Initially, the workers had to offer the unattached an undemanding, uncritical, and tolerant attitude, as well as a willingness to like and to respect and a readiness to understand. From there it was possible to move on towards more demanding relationships and towards more positive values and goals. The ability to fulfil this kind of role was the common element amongst three workers who in other respects were exact opposites to each other. It is this element which detached workers must be trained to acquire and practise. The responsibility for recruiting and training people to work with the unattached rests mainly upon the Youth Service.

It is debatable whether the youth-club leader can attempt much direct work with the unattached of the kind who were contacted on this project. More detached workers could profitably be appointed to work from a youth club or a youth centre; the demands on the time of anyone working with the unattached are so great that if a club leader were to concentrate his efforts on them, he could do so only at the expense of his service to the general run of club members.

The problems and disruptions caused by even a handful of the more anti-social may ruin a club for the other members. Assuming that some of the unattached may want to join a youth club, it would be more fruitful for a detached worker to meet with them outside the club building or as a special group within it until such time as they are ready and able to accept the standards of behaviour which any youth club has a right to expect of its members. In some areas, there may be a need for special clubs for the unattached rather than for the 'normal' young person. Lymport was such an area and the worker, through the school housecraft flat, was in fact running such a special club. The Greenhouse Clubs which were started in London in 1958 and are still continuing are another example. They are based on the principle of restricted membership so that more intensive work is possible.

If some of the unattached are ever to find an answer to their problems this intensive work by skilled detached workers will be necessary. But there were others amongst them who were not anti-social or in need of much intensive work. They were not attracted to youth clubs because they were reluctant to commit themselves to regular attendance or to the obligations of formal membership. Many merely wanted a congenial place in which to meet. The popularity of the coffee bars was ascribed in part to the fact that they were undemanding and sophisticated meeting places. In some areas there are very few coffee bars and jazz clubs. The remedy for this lies in the hands of commercial enterprise, but it is also worth considering whether the Youth Service in its building programme might be well advised to provide more facilities of the coffee-bar type and so attract many young people.

Commercial Facilities. In Northtown, some of the girls expressed a preference for spending their leisure time in coffee bars, dance halls, and so on rather than in youth clubs, and they indicated that the kind of adult most acceptable to them was a businessman rather than a social worker, someone who would not attempt to 'guide' or 'help' or 'interfere' as long as they behaved reasonably well. Two points are worth making. Firstly, the Northtown worker was in effect a social worker but was not regarded by these young people as being interfering. Secondly, one wonders how long some of these young people are likely to 'behave reasonably well' even in commercial establishments and what their reaction is likely to be when the businessman does try to control them. But accepting the point that many young people may justifiably be averse to a youth-club atmosphere if it makes them feel they are being patronized, there is a genuine need, especially in areas such as Northtown or Midford, for many more commercial facilities such as well-run coffee bars, dance halls, and restaurants. It has been suggested that the Youth Service could do more in this field. In addition, it would seem that the commercial world could provide more facilities in order to meet social needs. Some firms, such as Mecca and Forte, have recognized this, but many others have failed to do so and to react to an opportunity which could benefit them as much as the young people.

CONCLUSION

Our detailed recommendations have covered the need for counselling, both of adolescents and parents; for the better equipment of teachers, youth leaders, and youth employment officers to enable them to understand and help the unattached; and for a greater realization by all sections of industry and commerce of the human needs of young workers, especially those who are not trainees or apprentices.

Improvement or extension of existing services, however, will not meet all the problems. A recent United Nations report showed that,

> even in countries where national and average family income, educational levels, housing conditions, welfare policies and services, health, medical facilities, and labour conditions have steadily been improving, juvenile delinquency is not necessarily decreasing; indeed, in more cases than expected, the opposite is taking place.[1]

We do not by any means infer from this that the extension of welfare services or improvements in material and social conditions are not needed. Rather, it seems that, while improved economic and social conditions may eradicate some forms of anti-social behaviour, new forms may arise to replace them. One of the latest outbursts of such anti-social behaviour is the series of disturbances between the mods and rockers; but in the course of this project, the most striking example was provided by the Seagate Drama Group. In comparison with Northtown and Midford, the parents of the Seagate youth were better off financially; the welfare services in Seagate were more numerous and there was plenty of commercial entertainment. But all this did not eradicate or solve the problems of people such as Howard, Andy, and Paul – those who, for varying reasons, felt themselves to be failures in an affluent but competitive society and in well-to-do but often affectionless homes.

It is not enough, therefore, to provide individual welfare and educational services: there must also be effective cooperation and coordination between them. Young people need above all to be seen and treated as whole persons. As R. M. Prideaux has so aptly phrased it:

> Young people want help in establishing their personal identity in the various social groups with which they have dealings. They do not wish to be dissected into such bureaucratic entities as 'client', 'patient', 'employee', 'consumer', 'citizen', and 'delinquent'.[2]

1. *Report of the Second United Nations Congress on the Prevention of Crime*, 1960.
2. Prideaux, R. M., Tenth Charles Russell Memorial Lecture, September 1962.

More effective liaison between the welfare services than often exists at present is therefore essential. It has been found during this project that the part which the detached worker was able to play in effecting such liaison was as important as his direct work with the unattached.

Again, the best welfare and educational services in the world may go unused by the people who need them most, unless such people are made aware of their existence, or, as is more likely in the case of the unattached and some of their parents, encouraged to use them in such a way as to overcome the social and emotional attitudes which often prevent them from participating. This the workers in our project were able to do. With the unattached, encouragement can only come, it seems, through personal contact on a level and in a manner which even antisocial young people will accept.

During the course of this project we have come to know and care for, at second-hand, the unattached boys and girls, the young men and young women who are described, under fictitious names, in the previous chapters and who have, without knowing it, contributed much to our own understanding of the problems which confront them and many like them in this country. We shall have failed in our responsibility to them if we have not brought out how great is the need for many more people to cultivate the qualities shown by the workers in our project.

If there were greater general understanding by the community of the unattached, there would undoubtedly be many fewer of them and the problems of helping those who remained would be less difficult. This is a matter of individual responsibility and every citizen should be concerned in it. Some members of the community may be especially well placed to help – fish-and-chip-shop managers, coffee-bar proprietors, and public-house landlords have unique opportunities. Yet, in this pressing contemporary problem, there is an urgent need for many more detached workers to offer friendship and help and to focus the attention of the educational and welfare services on the particular needs of the unattached. We ourselves are deeply convinced of these needs and of the possibilities of meeting them. We hope most sincerely that, as a result of this book, public opinion will be roused and action follow.

Appendix: The Unattached and Industry

The unattached and their conditions of employment were commented upon by all of the workers on the project. The Northtown worker's description of the girls in the soda-siphon factory has already been given (pp. 127–9). It would be appropriate at this point to report briefly the findings of the workers in Hilltown and Southtown. In both areas the workers took temporary jobs in factories.

The Hilltown worker was employed in 1961 in a small clothing firm. In the section where she worked were twenty other women and three teen-age girls. As in Northtown, no one seemed to enjoy working with the firm and criticisms against the lack of welfare services and the low rates of pay were frequent. Employees were paid on piece rates but there was no minimum wage. Consequently a girl might earn as little as £1 10s. a week when the factory was slack. Many people failed to earn three shillings an hour, and wages for a forty-two hour week varied from £3 19s. for a middle-aged married woman to £1 18s. for the young girls. Another source of complaint was the policy of the management to import foreign labour. Further, the management was not slow to stress that more immigrants could be employed should the need arise. Thus one girl, who legitimately asked that her money should be made up to a time rate of two shillings and sixpence an hour, was told that if she could not work any faster, the immigrants could, and she was promptly dismissed. There was no such thing as one week's notice. The immigrant workers were also unpopular because of their tendency to 'poach' work done by the English, booking it to their own account while the person who did the work received nothing. The worker herself lost eighteen shillings in one week as a result of this practice. All the young girls were seeking other work but in Hilltown at that time jobs were hard to find.

In Southtown, the male worker experienced a complete contrast when attached to the personnel department of a light engineering firm which employed over a thousand men. Two hundred of these were youths aged fifteen to twenty-one years, and of these a quarter were apprentices undergoing a four-year training scheme. In many respects, the conditions for the apprentices could be described as most enlightened. In addition to the training scheme, which allowed first block release and later day release to the local technical college, the apprentices enjoyed a very active social club with their own meeting room, sports teams, and newspaper. At the company's expense they were allowed to attend outside courses designed to broaden their general outlook and to make visits to other factories. On only one point did the worker find the apprentices critical. This was the lack of training they received after leaving the training school at the end of the first year of their apprenticeships. At this time, they were often put on a job in the factory without proper instruction or supervision, and if they made a hash of the job, they sometimes came in for much abuse. The men on the shop floor were not trained instructors and if they spent too much time helping the apprentices their own production rates dropped.

With this exception, the policy of the firm towards apprentices was good. Unfortunately, the same could not be said of the policy towards youths who were not apprenticed and who worked on the shop floor. It was amongst these young people that the unattached were most frequently to be found. The disparity between the treatment of apprentices and non-apprentices was probably more marked than in most firms exactly because the apprentices were being given such outstanding treatment. Nevertheless, certain practices towards the non-apprentices seemed undesirable. There was, for example, the inconsistent treatment with regard to further education. In some departments, a non-apprentice was allowed day release and the course was paid for by the company. In another department, the young person was refused day release and had to attend night school. He might also pay himself for the course.

There was no general company policy relating to the training of non-apprentices and everything seemed to depend on the departmental bosses.

In addition to facilities for block- or day-release courses, the workers noted that apprentices were allowed excursions to other firms, special work supervision and training, monthly meetings for lectures and discussions in the firm's time, and the possibility of attendance at youth courses. None of these opportunities were available to shop-floor workers.

The worker elaborated the disparity of treatment still further:

The apprentices were treated as if they were still capable of learning and allowed to establish their own youthful identity within the firm. The non-apprentices on the other hand, apart from not having so many amenities and concessions, were merged into the mass of the adult labour force and had little opportunity to establish a separate identity. Many of them, I fancy, would not give a shoe-string for further education, but nevertheless I think in the long run they would appreciate the care and attention that is given to the apprentices. When I asked an official to explain this difference of treatment between the two youth groups one answer was that it costs much money to train apprentices and the firm could not afford such training for all its adolescent workers. There is of course much truth in this and one would like to see much more aid given to firms which are prepared to help their young workers.

One final point worth recording was the attitude towards the Youth Employment Service. Many of the apprentices felt very strongly that their experience with this service had been a waste of time. The general pattern seemed to have been a brief interview with the Youth Employment Officer, with a Headmaster and parents present. The boys felt they had had no chance to say anything and that questions such as 'What do you want to do?' were often pointless because at school-leaving age they were not sufficiently aware of the possibilities. All stressed that a decision reached about employment with the Youth Employment Officer could shape their early adult life and even beyond, and that, for making such a responsible decision, an interview of two to three minutes was not enough. Few of the boys had used the Youth Employment Service in order to get their apprenticeships.

Suggestions for Further Reading

BOOKS

Braithwaite, E. R., *To Sir, With Love*, Bodley Head, 1959
Cohen, A. K., *Delinquent Boys*, Routledge and Kegan Paul, 1956
Feldmen, G., and Gartenberg, M. (eds.), *Protest: The Beat Generation and the Angry Young Men*, Souvenir Press, 1959
Fyvel, T. R., *The Insecure Offenders*, Chatto, 1961; Penguin, 1963
Hemming, James, *Problems of Adolescent Girls*, Heinemann, 1960
Jones, Howard, *Reluctant Rebels*, Tavistock, 1960
Kenrick, Bruce, *Come Out the Wilderness*, Collins, 1963
Konopka, Gisela, *Social Group Work*, Prentice-Hall, 1963
Kuenstler, P. H. K. (ed.), *Social Group Work in Great Britain*, Faber, 1955
MacInnes, Colin, *Absolute Beginners*, Penguin, 1964
Mays, J. B., *Growing Up in the City*, Liverpool University Press, 1955
Mays, J. B., *On the Threshold of Delinquency*, Liverpool University Press, 1959
New York City Youth Board, *Reaching the Fighting Gang*, New York, 1960
New York City Youth Board, *Reaching the Unreached*, New York, 1952
Spencer, J., *Stress and Release in an Urban Estate*, Tavistock, 1964
Sprott, W. J. H., *Human Groups*, Penguin, 1958
Sullivan, Dorothy F., *Readings in Group Work*, Association Press, New York, 1952
Turner, M. L., *Ship Without Sails*, University of London Press, 1953
Whyte, William F., *Street Corner Society*, University of Chicago Press, 1943
Wootton, Barbara, *Social Science and Social Pathology*, Allen & Unwin, 1959

REPORTS AND ARTICLES

Half our Future (Report of the Central Advisory Council for Education (England)), H.M.S.O., 1963

Halmos, P. (ed.), 'The Canford Families' (a study in social casework and group work, Keele, Staffordshire), *Sociological Review*, Monograph no. 6, 1962

Jahoda, G., and Chalmers, A., 'The Youth Employment Service – A Consumer Perspective', in *Occupational Psychology*, no. 37, January 1963

Kuenstler, P. H. K. (ed.), *Spontaneous Youth Groups*, University of London Press, 1955

Leighton, J. P., *Reaching the 'Unattached'* (Third M.A.Y.C. Memorial Lecture, 1963), Methodist Youth Department, 1963

Lowson, David, 'Delinquency in Industrial Areas', *British Journal of Criminology*, vol. 1, no. 1, July 1960

Mack, John, 'Juvenile Police Liaison Schemes', *British Journal of Criminology*, vol. 3, no. 4, April 1963

United Nations *Report on the Second Congress on the Prevention of Crime and the Treatment of Offenders* (London), New York, 1960

The Youth Service in England and Wales (Albemarle Report), H.M.S.O., 1960

More about Penguins and Pelicans

Penguin Book News, which appears every month, contains details of all the new books issued by Penguins as they are published. From time to time it is supplemented by *Penguins in Print*, which is a complete list of all books published by Penguins which are in print. (There are nearly three thousand of these.)

A specimen copy of *Penguin Book News* will be sent to you free on request, and you can become a subscriber for the price of the postage – 3s. for a year's issues (including the complete lists). Just write to Dept EP, Penguin Books Ltd, Harmondsworth, Middlesex, enclosing a cheque or postal order, and your name will be added to the mailing list.

Some other books published by Penguins are described on the following pages.

Note: *Penguin Book News* and *Penguins in Print* are not available in the U.S.A. or Canada

Contrary Imaginations

A Psychological Study of the English Schoolboy

Liam Hudson

Why does one boy become an arts specialist and his neighbour a scientist? Why do some pupils use their brains effectively and others not? Do we pay enough attention to personality in assessing ability?

In this controversial study Dr Liam Hudson, Director of the Research Unit on Intellectual Development at King's College, Cambridge, argues that personality counts for as much as ability in the student's choice of subject. He distinguishes between two types of personality, the scientific 'converger' and the artistic, imaginative 'diverger', and examines examples of each in depth. He then speculates on the nature of original thought, and the ways in which intellectual and personal qualities interact. His argument combines the disciplines of intelligence testing and psycho-analysis in a highly original way, and his clear and jargon-free presentation will appeal to all those interested in intelligent children, in psychology, or in both.

The Psychology of Childhood and Adolescence

C. I. Sandström

In this concise study of the processes of growing up Professor Sandström has produced a book which, although it is perfectly suited to the initial needs of university students and teachers in training, will appeal almost as much to parents and ordinary readers. His text covers the whole story of human physical and mental growth from conception to puberty.

Outlining the scope and history of developmental psychology, Professor Sandström goes on to detail the stages of growth in the womb, during the months after birth, and (year by year) up to the age of ten. There follow chapters on physical development, learning and perception motivation, language and thought, intelligence, the emotions, social adjustment, and personality. The special conditions of puberty and of schooling are handled in the final chapters.

Throughout this masterly study the author necessarily refers to 'norms of development': these neatly represent the average stages of growing up, but (as Professor Mace comments in his introduction) they must only be applied to individual children with caution.

The Psychology of Interpersonal Behaviour

Michael Argyle

Looks, gestures, and tones of voice may be powerful factors when people meet. Moreover these rapid and subtle messages are highly co-ordinated.

Experimental techniques have recently been developed for studying the minutiae of social behaviour scientifically: these are described here by a social psychologist. The study of social interaction demands a 'language' of its own, to which Michael Argyle supplies a clear key. But the reader will not be slow to grasp that 'the motivation of social interaction', 'the synchronization of styles of behaviour' between two or more people, and 'the presentation of a self-image' refer to things we encounter every day.

Certain specific skills, such as interviewing, group leadership, public speaking, and even child-rearing, are discussed in the light of the latest research, and the author devotes a good deal of space to mental health and to training in social skill. His outline of what amounts to a break-through in psychological analysis makes this a book which the student of psychology may well find indispensable; and the relevance of his material to every-day life offers irresistible reading to the plain man.

The Pelican History of Psychology

Robert Thomson

The Pelican History of Psychology is probably, both in span and latitude, the most comprehensive history of the subject in print.

Too often, other histories are anxiously concerned with philosophical concepts, confine themselves to the progress of basic experimental research, and stop short at the 1920s. Dr Thomson, on the other hand, extends his scope outside the main stream of theory, deals with ideas which are specifically psychological, and brings his history far enough forward to discuss the trends which have developed since 1945. His outline of the birth of psychology, in the early nineteenth century, of Darwin's impact, the achievements of the first generation of German, British, French, and American psychologists, and the major theories of Freud, Jung, and the Behaviourists, among others, is clear, logical, and authoritative: but this book extends beyond that.

The development of psychology in the years between 1918 and 1940 is traced by the author of *The Psychology of Thinking* in all its forms. Psychiatry, child psychology, industrial and social psychology, intelligence and personality testing are among the branches he discusses historically.

With its wide coverage and full bibliography this introductory history will appeal to students of psychology particularly: but it also provides the general reader with a sound and simple outline of the growth of a science which, in little over a century, has developed from a fringe activity to a central and potent study.

Childhood and Adolescence

J. A. Hadfield

Parents in these days are often caught between distaste for Victorian strictness and mistrust of the licence which sometimes seems to be encouraged by psychologists. They no longer know when to say 'Yes' and when to say 'No' to their children.

In this new book the author of *Dreams and Nightmares* draws on a long clinical experience to describe, in simple terms, a child's natural equipment, the theory of maturation, the phases of early development, the organization of personality, and the period of adolescence. There cannot be any easy rules for rearing children and only such knowledge, therefore, can help intelligent and sympathetic parents in their dilemma.

As the author shows here, in an atmosphere of love there need be no conflict between discipline and freedom. Moreover, parents who are prepared to promote a child's mental health – in other words, the full development of its whole personality – are setting it on the right path to be successful, moral in outlook, possessed of a strong will, and as intelligent as its nature allows.

Marital Breakdown

J. Dominian

A marriage collapses. Psychology, sociology, and medicine may say one thing: religion and law pronounce another. In this study, probably for the first time, a psychiatrist has made an unbiased attempt to bring together these different viewpoints.

How do men and women select their partners, asks Dr Dominian. And what are the factors that break a marriage up – sex, money, housing, parents and families, mental illness, or the inability to give and take emotionally? Do such influences as age or pre-marital pregnancy count?

The author makes no inspired guesses in answering these questions and is chary of ready-made solutions. Proceeding from the latest research he simply indicates the places where a deeper insight can help marriage counsellors and others to reconcile the parties and avoid breakdown. And he proposes ways in which the secular approach to divorce and the traditional Christian attitude might be harmonized.